Are You a Model?

On an Architectural Medium of Spatial Exploration

jovis

Anna-Maria Meister / Teresa Fankhänel / Lisa Beißwanger /
Chris Dähne / Christiane Fülscher / Anna Luise Schubert (eds.)

Table of Contents

Acknowledgments

A book like this is a truly collaborative project. From editors to authors, from graphic designer to student assistants, from supporters to sponsors to earlier conversations and events—this book has a family tree of roots and branches that we are grateful for. This book is based on the international conference "Are You a Model?", which was held at the Technical University of Darmstadt from November 2–4, 2022. The conference was organized by the Institute for Architecture, Theory and Science at the Technical University of Darmstadt, the Chair of Building History, Research and Preservation at Dortmund University of Applied Sciences and Arts, the LOEWE Research Cluster "Architectures of Order," the Platform for digital science and research FID BAUdigital, Deutsches Architekturmuseum DAM, and the Center for Critical Studies in Architecture. We thank the sponsors of the conference: Heinz-Stillger-Stiftung, Wüstenrot Stiftung, Jakob Wilhelm Mengler-Stiftung, Vereinigung von Freunden der Technischen Universität Darmstadt, and Graphisoft Rhein-Main. We are grateful to the student assistants at the Institute for Architecture, Theory and Science (led by Anna-Maria Meister), without whom this conference would not have been possible: Bea Engelmann, Sarah Knechtel, Valerie Kramer, and Lucia Martinovic. We would also like to extend our appreciation to session hosts Oliver Elser, Nadja Gaudillière-Jami, Christina Clausen, and Andreas Noback, who joined the editors in hosting the conference.

Additional parts of the book are based on the session "Invention and Inventory. Material Histories of Model-Making," held at the 76th annual meeting of the Society of Architectural Historians in Montreal, Canada, from April 12–16, 2023. This session was organized by Jia Yi Gu and Teresa Fankhänel and made possible by the support of the Eli and Edythe Broad Art Museum at Michigan State University.

This book is based on the collaborative work of six editors: Anna-Maria Meister, Teresa Fankhänel, Lisa Beißwanger, Chris Dähne, Christiane Fülscher, and Anna Luise Schubert, supported by Olivia Larsen. However, editing means nothing without contributions, and a great debt of thanks is owed to the numerous authors of the catalog for their commitment to publishing their research in this volume: Giulia Amoresano, Yana Boeva, Giulia Boller, Stefanie Brünenberg, Alberto Calderoni, Wonseok Chae, Diana Cristobal Olave, Carlotta Darò, Thomas Cyrillus Demand, Cansu Degirmencioglu, Kai Drewes, Ruth Ezra, Erik Herrmann, Carolin Höfler, Deniz Avci-Hosanli, Christian Janecke, Orkun Kasap, Evangelos Kotsioris, Silke Langenberg, Daniel Cardoso Llach, Sebastiaan Loosen, Eberhard Möller, Christina Moushoul, Andreas Noback, Ana Carolina Pellegrini, Eliza Pertigkiozoglou, Andreas Pilot, Stéphanie Quantin-Biancalani, Salome Schepers, Ecaterina Stefanescu, Mara Trübenbach, Simona Valeriani, Matthew Wells, Baris Wenzel, Roger Winkler, Maxime Zaugg, Holger Zaunstöck, and Tamar Zinguer. Our special gratitude goes to Annabel Jane Wharton and Thomas Demand for their conversation at the conference and their thoughtful consideration of the book's overarching questions through image and text.

We would like to take the opportunity to thank the designer of the book, Robin Weißenborn, who gave shape to the material form of our thoughts and concepts.

Lastly, we would like to thank JOVIS Verlag, especially Felix Torkar, Charlotte Blumenthal, and Susanne Rösler, for their dedication and care in the realization and supervision of the book.

This publication was made possible by the generous support of:

Professorship Architecture Theory, KIT
Fördergesellschaft Fachhochschule Dortmund e.V.
Heinz-Stillger-Stiftung
Department of Architecture, Dortmund University of Applied Sciences and Arts

Introduction: Are You a Model?

Anna-Maria Meister and Teresa Fankhänel

Models are epistemological objects. Through architectural models, spatial imagination becomes manifest at different scales, travels through myriad textures and materials in a cyclical series of translations, tests, and (partial) reproductions. In models, architecture is an expression of the possible and, in the broadest sense, also a substitute for the objectively intangible world, permanently being realized and made impossible simultaneously. By looking at these architectural models, model making, model seeing, and model being can be analyzed as epistemological processes: models both project and confirm, they speculate and simulate. Architectural models also play a precise role in societal negotiations of making and knowing: they are referents not merely of scale or form but of architectural knowledge – knowledge that is bound to systems of organization and order. Given the entanglements of organization and representation in histories of architecture, the model is a cultural and communication medium and a tool to *create* knowledge – not just to represent or conserve it. New knowledge is based on investigating the modes of production and reproduction of models through digital means, their aesthetic and functional intention and social reception, their physical attributes and sensorial effects, and their role in the historical and critical discourse of architecture.[1]

In architecture as a discipline that generally depends on substitute media and displaced working methods, the model has long been front and center in architectural thinking and doing. But models have undergone tremendous changes in recent decades. The introduction of born-digital tools and workflows has added a wholly new branch of three-dimensional modeling dependent on computational soft- and hardware; new simulation methods for economic, meteorological, medical purposes or investigative purposes have highlighted both the potential and limitations of modeling as a means of predicting or visualizing present and future; collections of big data points as one of the raw materials of digital modeling have led to entirely new challenges in their management, interpretation, and protection. Here, too, new models have generated key changes through the introduction of new modeling tools such as software programs like AutoCAD or SketchUp that allow the creation of drawn, extruded, or generated 3D models. Building Information Modeling (BIM) further connects the born-digital object to nodes of information about its performance (for instance as regards structural engineering, ventilation,

1 Much of the work in this volume was first presented at the conference "Are You a Model?", held at TU Darmstadt from November 2–4, 2022. Additional papers were presented in 2023 at the 76th SAH conference in the session "Invention and Inventory. Material Histories of Model Making," chaired by Teresa Fankhänel and Jia Yi Gu.

2 See Bernd Mahr, "Ein Modell des Modellseins. Ein Beitrag zur Aufklärung des Modellbegriffs," in *Modelle*, eds. Ulrich Dirks and Eberhard Knobloch (Frankfurt a.M.: Peter Lang, 2008), 187–218.

3 See Albert Smith, *Architectural Model as Machine. A New View of Models from Antiquity to the Present Day* (London: Routledge, 2004); Georg Vrachliotis et al., *Frei Otto. Thinking by Modeling* (Berlin: Spectorbooks, 2017).

4 Hans Reuther, "Wesen und Wandel des Architekturmodells in Deutschland," *Daidalos*, 1981, 98–110; Henry A. Millon, ed., *The Triumph of the Baroque. Architecture in Europe 1600–1750* (London: Thames & Hudson, 1999); Bernd Adam, "Barocke Architekturmodelle in Norddeutschland und ihre Stellung im Planungsprozeß," in *Architektur – Struktur – Symbol. Streifzüge durch die Architekturgeschichte von der Antike bis zur Gegenwart*, ed. Maike Kozok (Petersberg: Imhof, 1999), 381–396.

or the performance of other building components) both in the virtual realm and as a performance-based tool for evaluation and prediction of future uses in reality. While such technological shifts have an immediate effect on current architectural practices, they also raise compelling questions pertaining to future architectural repositories: A seemingly stable tool of architecture is called into question. What, then, does it mean to call something a model today?[2] What implications, projections, or desires are called to the table?

This collection investigates the role of models that transcend dividing lines of analog versus digital or representational versus conceptual. Shared by the editors is a desire to investigate together what an architectural model is, how it operates, and which kinds of knowledge it produces.

Asking More from Models and Their Makers

Far from being a mere rhetorical sleight of hand, to ask "Are You a Model?" is a tool – a step back to help reevaluate what might be regarded as fixed scholarly certainties. Each chapter poses a seemingly inconspicuous question to trigger a wide range of (sometimes opposing) responses: Does size matter? Who made me? What happened to me? What is my act? Am I the real thing? Do we look alike? What can you learn from me? And, occasionally, questions turn into demands: Give me access!

Often regarded as the first three-dimensional artifact of the architectural process in design theories, the model is both testing site and verification of what is usually called innovation – be it toward increasing digitalization of the building process, new structural concepts or materials, or the development of new form finding methods. However, beyond technological advancements, what is being tested through the model is architectural thinking as such: the transitions from and to a three-dimensional state of ideas.[3] And yet, art history has tended to approach models as either a source or an art object, which has led to models either helping to better understand projected, built, or lost architectures,[4] or to studying models for their own sake, as carefully crafted aesthetic objects, respectively.[5] In both cases, models are treated as discrete objects with limited agency.[6] Others have focused on technological and technical aspects of model production.[7] Recent insight into models as instruments as well as representational tools in the production and distribution of knowledge has been developed by cultural theorists and the historians of science.[8] As models simulating an existing reality, they are studied in their roles of staking claims, describing theories, and teaching scientific concepts. In architecture, one might posit that a model is not always descriptive of the world but a tool for world-making, hence often referring to something outside itself – something not yet imagined otherwise. And yet, architectural models serve multiple, even contrasting functions: representative for exhibitions or competitions, demonstrative as didactic or investigative tools, or generative as working models.[9] Sometimes, the reference does not exist yet, in other cases, not anymore. When models themselves become references (as in historical research), a complex play of indexicality unfolds.

By approaching architecture models from the vantage point of today's interconnected digital era and critically asking what models (can) do within a larger system or network, the research presented here opens up the discipline to new, relevant questions and methodological approaches. Models, in this regard, are no longer

5 Jutta Ströter-Bender, "Materialität und ästhetische Präsenz. Historische Architektur- und Landschaftsmodelle," in *Kulturen des Kleinen. Mikroformate in Literatur, Kunst und Medien*, eds. Sabine Autsch, Claudia Öhlschläger (Paderborn: Fink, 2014), 213–228; Sabine Autsch, "Große Künstler – kleine Räume. Das Atelier als Pappmodell," in ibid., 229–248.

6 Earlier scholarship often considered the model as a discrete category, both medially and in terms of its role. See: Carsten Ruhl, Chris Dähne, *Architektur ausstellen: Zur mobilen Anordnung des Immobilen* (Berlin: JOVIS, 2015); "Model Behavior," an exhibition from October 4–November 18, 2022, Cooper Union Foundation, New York; Cynthia Davidson and Anyone Corporation, eds., *Log 56: The Model Behavior Exhibition CataLog.* (New York: Anyone Corporation, 2022); Reinhard Wendler, *Das Modell zwischen Kunst und Wissenschaft* (Munich: Wilhelm Fink, 2013).

7 See "Das Architekturmodell in Zeiten der Digitalen Transformation" at Hochschule Bochum (August 2018).

8 See Emily Abruzzo et al., eds., *Models* (New York: 306090 Inc, 2007); Soraya de Chadarevian and Nick Hopwood, eds., *Models: The Third Dimension of Science. Writing Science* (Stanford, CA: Stanford University Press, 2004); Morgan and Morrison, eds., *Models as Mediators. Perspectives on Natural and Social Science* (New York: Cambridge University Press, 1999); Hans-Jörg Rheinberger, "Molekulare Modelle als epistemische Objekte, Ribosomen im Spiegel von 50 Jahren Forschung," in *Weltwissen. 300 Jahre Wissenschaft in Berlin,* eds. Jochen Hennig and Udo Andraschke (Munich: Hirmer Verlag, 2010), 76–81.

9 See Matthew Mindrup, *The Architectural Model. Histories of the Miniature and the Prototype, the Exemplar and the Muse* (Cambridge, MA: MIT Press, 2019).

understood as enshrining knowledge but as a means of knowledge production based on shifting constraints. Investigating models as objects of translations between materials, scales, and data helps to analyze concurrent projected ideologies, material procedures, or aesthetic strategies across seemingly clean-cut categories. If we treat the model as neither starting nor end point of architectural making (and thinking) but as exemplifying key moments of a processual praxis, we can come at them from a skewed angle, so to speak, enriching professional definitions and eschewing technological rhetoric.[10] Asking whether size matters foregrounds a deliberation of the (sometimes contentious) interdependency between models and their scalar relations;[11] the question about the 'making of' of models can expose marginalized actors and conditions of resource extraction, be it material or otherwise;[12] demanding access puts the model in the instrumental role of entering spaces that do not yet exist, or not anymore but also communicates a conventionally exclusive process to different stakeholders;[13] probing into the afterlife of materials that have been joined together as models points to a shifting (and temporal) validity of these fragile objects, their status in repositories and written accounts of architectural history, and their often surprising secondary uses;[14] looking at how models perform as actors or serve as stages foregrounds their theatrical dimensions and the quality of their relationship with architects and audiences;[15] following the myriad of copies and twins produced at a wide range of scales calls into question the difference between original and reproduction, and how materials and technologies used contribute to shifting systems of value;[16] understanding the use of data-driven stand-ins for simulations allows to evaluate new tools of optimization, manufacturing processes as well as behavioral study prior to physical construction as much as a complementary practice for studying historical specimens;[17] surveying pedagogical applications illuminates how objects can activate a sensorial approach between the assembly of entire models and their exploratory study, from subjective appreciation to targeted learning.[18]

As long as the architecture model was treated as a disciplinarily stable object lodged at certain moments in the creative and representational process, it was in focus but lost its fuzzy edges. It is those fuzzy edges the editors and contributors are interested in. They take the expertise of transitional procedures located in the model to critically reflect on categorical divisions and seemingly sequential steps in architecture production. By deliberately not discriminating between epistemological and technological concerns, they instead pose them as inseparable: digital models here are not the opposition of a cardboard study model; city models share traits and objectives with 1:1 mockups.

The political role that models played in the construction of architecture histories is one aspect across all sessions: city models were instrumental in territorial conquests or ideological reconstruction debates, and models of buildings convinced politicians to fund the impossible. By looking at transitions and medial translations of models across their own historical state (being made, being looked at, being used, being digitized, being archived, being destroyed etc.), the deliberately wide range of contributions connects historical evidence with current observations and vice versa, infusing precise detail with other angles of perception. Dealing with models in disciplinarily and materially different ways, this multi-perspectival approach probes models as agents precisely between fixed categories or

10 See Carolin Höfler, "Modelle in Prozessen," *MAP - Media | Archive | Performance. E-Journal für Medien, Kunst und Performance,* no. 10 (2019), special issue: Bewegliche Architekturen – Architektur in Bewegung, eds. Barbara Büscher, Annette Menting.

11 See chapter 1; also see Tom Holert, "Mikro-Ökonomie der Geschichte. Das Unausstellbare en miniature," *Texte zur Kunst*, March 2001, 57–68; Geoffrey Batchen, "Does Size Matter?", *Konsthistorisk Tidskrift*, no. 4 (2003): 251. Albena Yaneva, "Scaling Up and Down," *Social Studies of Science* 35, no. 6 (2005): 867–894; research project "Size Matters. Zur Massstäblichkeit von Modellen," at Zurich University of the Arts, directed by Reinhard Wendler (2013–2016).

12 See chapter 2; also see Ralf Liptau, *Architekturen bilden: Das Modell in Entwurfsprozessen der Nachkriegsmoderne* (Bielefeld: transcript, 2019); Teresa Fankhänel, *The Architectural Models of Theodore Conrad. The "Miniature Boom" of Mid-Century Modernism* (London: Bloomsbury, 2021); Matthew Wells, *Modelling the Metropolis. The Architectural Model in Victorian London* (Zurich: gta Verlag, 2023); David Lund, *A History of Architectural Model Making in Britain. The Unseen Masters of Scale and Vision* (London: Routledge, 2022).

13 See chapter 3; also see Kenny Cupers, ed., *Use Matters: An Alternative History of Architecture* (London: Routledge, 2013).

14 See chapter 4; also see Oliver Elser and Peter Cachola Schmal, eds., *The Architectural Model. Tool, Fetish, Small Utopia* (Zurich: Scheidegger und Spiess, 2012); Mari Lending and Mari Hvattum, eds., *Modelling Time. The Permanent Collection 1925–2014* (Oslo: Torpedo Press, 2014).

15 See chapter 5; also see Thea Brejzek and Lawrence Wallen, *The Model as Performance. Staging Space in Theatre and Architecture* (London: Bloomsbury, 2018); Annabel Jane Wharton, "Models as Ethical Agents," in *Log 56: The Model Behavior Exhibition CataLog*, eds. Cynthia Davidson and Anyone Corporation (New York: Anyone Corporation, 2022), 13–20.

clear boundaries, thereby not only synthesizing knowledge from several fields but producing new insights for the respective areas. In short, the collection acts as a refraction device to a formerly stable disciplinary obsession.

Expanding the Conversation

Investigating models for physical and societal spaces critically means to look at the history of implicit and explicit parameters – and those omitted – set by actors in charge; it also means shifting the focus to figures in the background, work done behind the scenes, or communities, materials, or processes not formerly included in architectural histories. Architecture, model making, and computer programming as practices were predominantly white and male-coded disciplines early on, and research, historically, has not questioned such accepted truths.[19] The approach of this project is therefore necessarily intersectional, in that it roots the question of modeling (past, current, alternative, or future) realities firmly in terms of diversity: Gender, race, class, cultural background, geographic origin, or academic trajectories all are material to model production, representation, and reception. In recent years, research in many disciplines has increasingly reflected the need for a large-scale, methodologically sound undoing of conventional entanglements to re-evaluate communities of interest in modeling and simulating processes and their receptions in order to understand and sustainably analyze them.[20] Hence, the focus of this collection lies not only thematically on *who* models the spaces for (past and future) societies, but also on how to expand and break canonical conventions through the inclusion of diverse perspectives, unexpected scales, or overheard voices. Asking "Are You a Model?" is not only an act of questioning, it is also a suggestive proposal.

16 See chapter 6; also see Helen Dorey, "Sir John Soane's Model Room," *Perspecta: Grand Tour*, vol. 41, 2008, 46, 26, 92–93, 170–171; Mari Lending, "Out of Place: Circulating Monuments," in *Exhibiting Architecture. A Paradox?*, eds. Eeva-Liisa Pelkonen et al., (New Haven: Yale School of Architecture, 2015), 25–33; Mari Lending, *Plaster Monuments: Architecture and the Power of Reproduction* (Princeton: Princeton University Press, 2017).

17 See chapter 7; also see *Simulation Shifts Design*, special issue, *Form*, no. 282 (March/April 2019). Andreas Noback et al., "Photogrammetric 3D digitisation of models from an architectural collection," in *Proceedings of the 26th International Conference on Cultural Heritage and New Technologies, ed.* CHNT-ICOMOS (editorial board) (Heidelberg: Propylaeum), 1–5.

18 See chapter 8; also see Ralf Liptau, "Kneten und Probieren. Architekturmodelle in Entwurfsprozessen der Nachkriegsmoderne," in *Architektur und Akteure. Praxis und Öffentlichkeit in der Nachkriegsgesellschaft,* ed. Regine Heß (Bielefeld: transcript, 2018), 119–130; Ariane Koller, "Puppenhaus. Das Interieur 'en miniature' als kultureller Denkraum in der Frühen Neuzeit," in *Reading Room*, eds. Christine Göttler et al. (Berlin, Boston: De Gruyter, 2019), 188–198; Beatriz Colomina et al., eds., *Radical Pedagogies* (Cambridge, MA: MIT Press, 2022).

19 New work highlights the role of women and gender-bias in man-made algorithms that structure machine learning and AI. See Mar Hicks, *Programmed Inequality: How Britain Discarded Women Technologists and Lost Its Edge in Computing (History of Computing)* (Cambridge, MA: MIT Press, 2018); Tanja Paulitz, *Mann und Maschine. Eine genealogische Wissenssoziologie des Ingenieurs und der modernen Technikwissenschaften, 1850-1930* (Bielefeld: transcript, 2012); Janet Abbate, *Recoding Gender. Women's Changing Participation in Computing (History of Computing)* (Cambridge, MA: MIT Press, 2012); Caroline Criado-Perez, *Invisible Women. Exposing Data Bias in a World Designed for Men* (London: Vintage, 2020).

20 Ruha Benjamin, *Race after Technology* (Newark, NJ: Polity Press, 2019); Aimi Hamraie, *Building Access. Universal Design and the Politics of Disability* (Minneapolis: University of Minnesota Press, 2017).

Does Size Matter?

On Models and Scale

Anna-Maria Meister

1 Think of Leonardo da Vinci's man-figure, Ernst Neufert's "man as measure of all things," or Le Corbusier's Modulor; in all of them, men, often white and male, defined the standard measures of man-made things and their environment. See Anna Maria Meister, "Ernst Neufert's Lebensgestaltungslehre: Formatting Life Beyond the Built," in *Learning by the Book: Manuals and Handbooks in the History of Knowledge*, eds. Angela Creager, Mathias Grote, and Elaine Leong, BJHS Themes (British Society for the History of Science, 2020), 167–185.

2 Dylan Mulvin, *Proxies: The Cultural Work of Standing In* (Cambridge, MA: MIT Press, 2021), 47.

3 Helmut Puff, "Ruins as Models," in *Ruins of Modernity*, eds. Julia Hell and Andreas Schönle (Durham, NC: Duke University Press, 2010), 255.

4 Ibid.

5 German text: "Eine kaum überschaubare Vielfalt [...] noch dazu in einem so kleinen Maßstab wie dem von uns gewählten 1:200. Hätten wir uns an den doppeltgroßen von 1:100 gehalten, wir hätten im Museum keinen Raum für dieses Modell gefunden. Die Besucher hätten es auch nicht überblicken können." See Fried Lübbecke in his book on the Treuners' model, quoting the Treuner brothers. Lübbecke, *Treuners Alt-Frankfurt*, 23–24.

6 Puff, 256–257.

7 Rudy Koshar, *Germany's Transient Pasts: Preservation and National Memory in the Twentieth Century* (Chapel Hill, NC: University of North Carolina Press, 1998), 213.

8 The original plaque on the model in the Frankfurt Historisches Museum did not label it "Trümmermodell" but "Plastische Skizze."

9 Albena Yaneva, "Scaling Up and Down," *Social Studies of Science* 35, no. 6 (2005): 867–894, 870.

10 Max Bill, *Die gute Form*, Exhibition catalog, Schweizerischer Werkbund, 1949.

11 Inge Aicher-Scholl used this expression in a letter to Theodor Heuss, where she explains the brochure with the school's concept. See Inge Scholl, letter to Theodor Heuss dated January 27, 1950; Archiv der Hochschule für Gestaltung Ulm.

12 German: "Die ganze Welt, vom Löffel bis zur Stadt, muß mit den sozialen Notwendigkeiten in Einklang gebracht werden." in *Die gute Form*, Exhibition catalog, Schweizerischer Werkbund, 1949; Claus Pias, interview 2011, 3sat.

The question of scale is built into the story of architecture models. The size, level of detail, or longevity of a model determines not only its appearance but its role in the process—what a model embodies is inherently linked to its scale. Long has the "right scale" as measure for building and their models been a question of appropriateness, of ethics, and—not least—of beauty. What then is at stake in a renegotiation of this relationship? When Western architecture, specifically scale, has been defined as a relationship to human bodies above all else,[1] how then is the model the material expression of its relation to its human maker—and their bodies? As the object-sized matter of architecture, models often act as discourse catalysts and proxies; they are, as the historian of science writes about the latter, "important materializations of a hypothesis about the world, forged into small, manageable, usable, workable, exchangeable, and reproducible chunks."[2] However, the already contentious relation between size and scale became especially fraught when model makers attempted to represent not architecture to be built but its destruction. When researching the reconstruction of West Germany after 1945, I came across the so called "rubble model" [Trümmermodell] of the Frankfurt city center, built in 1946 by the brothers Hermann and Robert Treuner. As historian Helmut Puff writes, the Treuners constructed a different meaning of the destroyed city precisely by turning rubble into ruins through operations of scaling.[3] Ruin here is not the equivalent of a destroyed building but the historical construction of a national symbol. The model was probably commissioned by those wanting to replace the old city of Frankfurt with modernist structures, turning it into a medium to further the political decision toward demolition and new construction.[4] The scale of the rubble model was not that of 1:200 but that of a synthesized ruin—a miniature monument.

The Treuner brothers had already built the famous "Altstadtmodell" [old town model] of the city since about 1926, a preservation of not only medieval city fabric about to be demolished, but of the idea of an "Altstadt" of Frankfurt altogether. This model—the city model—proved their ability to perfectly translate the city's destruction into a model of the same scale. The Treuners' choice of scale was pragmatic but presented several challenges, as the brothers faced a "barely graspable multitude [...] especially in such a small scale as the one we chose, 1:200. If we had kept to the double-size scale of 1:100, however, we would have had no space for this model in the museum. Viewers would not have been able to get an overview either."[5] The first challenge was the question of how to depict the level of detail of a lived-in neighborhood through small-sized flower bouquets or door handles. The second was how to reduce the human diversity present in the inner city to a model. To solve this, Puff explains, they created models entirely "devoid of human life," instead doing "away with the various impediments, technical or social, that limit access to actual, inhabited spaces."[6] In short, the model makers not only translated the built environment into a smaller size, but they shifted the scale from living subjects to constructed objects altogether.

The model of the bombed city was presented seemingly at scale, and yet, decisive qualities were exaggerated or distorted, while the model remained true to size. In fact, for the purpose of this reading, the rubble model demonstrates not one but three operations of scaling and scalar representation: first, the material scale of the rubble; second, the human scale of the missing inhabitants; and third, the societal scale of the ruin as monument to a destroyed city, which the model constructs. The actual rubble on the streets of Frankfurt became the medium to create the new scale for the city that historian Rudy Koshar describes.[7] The model of the destroyed Frankfurt materialized the architectural transformation from destruction to exhibit: the Treuners had taken the rubble from outside, ground it, and used it to represent rubble in the exhibition on a scale of 1:200. Urban destruction was scaled from the traumatic 1:1 to a "plastic sketch."[8] The act of emptying described above has much darker connotations in that second model—the rubble model. Choosing different granularities within the finished model afforded different relations between subject and object depending whether one looked at scaled rubble, scaled ruins, or scaled monuments. This manipulation depended upon the model being exhibited, hence, being viewed.

Scale is not merely an investigation of the relationships between size and semblance, but just as much between matter and temporality or narrative and formal expression. If one takes scale to be a verb instead of a noun, the seemingly fixed definitions of scale no longer hold. Where models perform as miniatures or stand-ins for architectural testing, scale becomes an operative rather than a static term: one of a defined relation that allows the probing of specific aspects of spatial configurations. As Albena Yaneva states, scale is indeed not a definition but a process, since any "static notion of scale understood as a proportional relationship between the world of models and the external real world, or a metric relationship, is insufficient to grasp architectural scaling."[9] Scaling, then, the motions and translations through which a design project develops, she continues, operates on several levels at once, materially (as sequence of produced models for different investigations) and socially (as collaborative practice of testing and assessing).

And yet, the fact that scale in a model is neither bound to a methodological definition became clear when I studied the processes of teaching and form-giving at the Hochschule für Gestaltung (HfG) in Ulm. Here, scale and size were differently connected: the method of the school to produce good design (inheriting the "good form" of Max Bill's earlier Werkbund exhibition) was independent of the scale of the designed object itself. Bill famously called for "the social reconciliation of the whole world [...] with social necessities" on all scales "from the spoon to the city."[10] And rather than offering design on a total scale (architecture's self-understanding at the turn of the century, aggrandized to total consequence during the Nazi regime), the HfG resumed to a scaleless approach, where spoon and building were developed following the same methods. According to the school's founders, this required a well-rounded humanist education, resulting in the much-copied *Ulm Model*, where design and theory are taught interdependently. One might argue that the scale of design at the HfG was not the object scale at all, but that of the human: what was designed were the good designers themselves. Raised to be a "democratic elite" they would, so the school founders hoped, re-democratize Germany after World War II through their own, equally good designs—modeling the good citizen through objects.[11]

The ethical and aesthetic charge of the model then rests firmly within these very negotiations of size with the model's scale, a relationship that is rekindled between the model as object and its environment or observers. In the contributions in this section, scale becomes an assessment of scale-appropriateness [*Maßstäblichkeit*]. Starting with the very concrete models of Heinz Isler, Giulia Boller looks at tools and methods that integrate form, material aspects, and flow of forces on a small scale. The move to the smaller scale becomes a quest for form, and the reduction of material by the small size of the model is the first step in the reduction of material for Isler's architecture at large. Ruth Ezra researches Muscovy glass, or more precisely, Siberian muscovite that was employed for window panes, lanterns, and ships' portals as well as "to glaze the windows in architectural models." By looking at how its incorporation into the early modern architectural imaginary created bridges between groups and methods, muscovite defined a new relation not just within the model but in reference to itself. Carlotta Darò looks at a (seemingly) non-material scale by investigating acoustic models on a scale of 1:10 or 1:20 as experimental objects that enable acoustic tests to be carried out. What was reduced here were not details of everyday life but the parameters that define the behavior of sound: the volume of the room, the absorption coefficient of the materials and the public, the frequency of the sound signal, through to the quality of the air. Delving into the gap between subjective perception and scientific measurement, models simulate not merely sound but certainty. Any such certainty, however, needed prior agreement. As Evangelos Kotsioris shows by detailing the negotations around the new building for the United Nations Headquarters in New York, models were used to materially construct consensus within them, precisely by offering themselves up to play due to their reduced size.

The question remains: what then *is* scale in relation to size? This section will probe the seemingly obvious connection between size and scale by assessing scaling as a process of negotiation not just on a material but on an affective, symbolic, or societal level. By eliminating scale as qualitative difference—as *Skalierungsproblem* (as media theorist Claus Pias calls it)—, the resulting objects could assume multiple interpretations.[12] Pias uses the term to describe processes for which linear shrinking or enlarging would not produce equivalent results, making an approach other than scaling understood as changing size necessary. Omitting scalar markers in the representation of architectural objects, stripping them of context and scale, is one way how models can become objects that transcend the *Skalierungsproblem*—but at the cost of shedding their fragile bond to the bodies of makers and viewers alike. Size, in the end, might not be the matter at question.

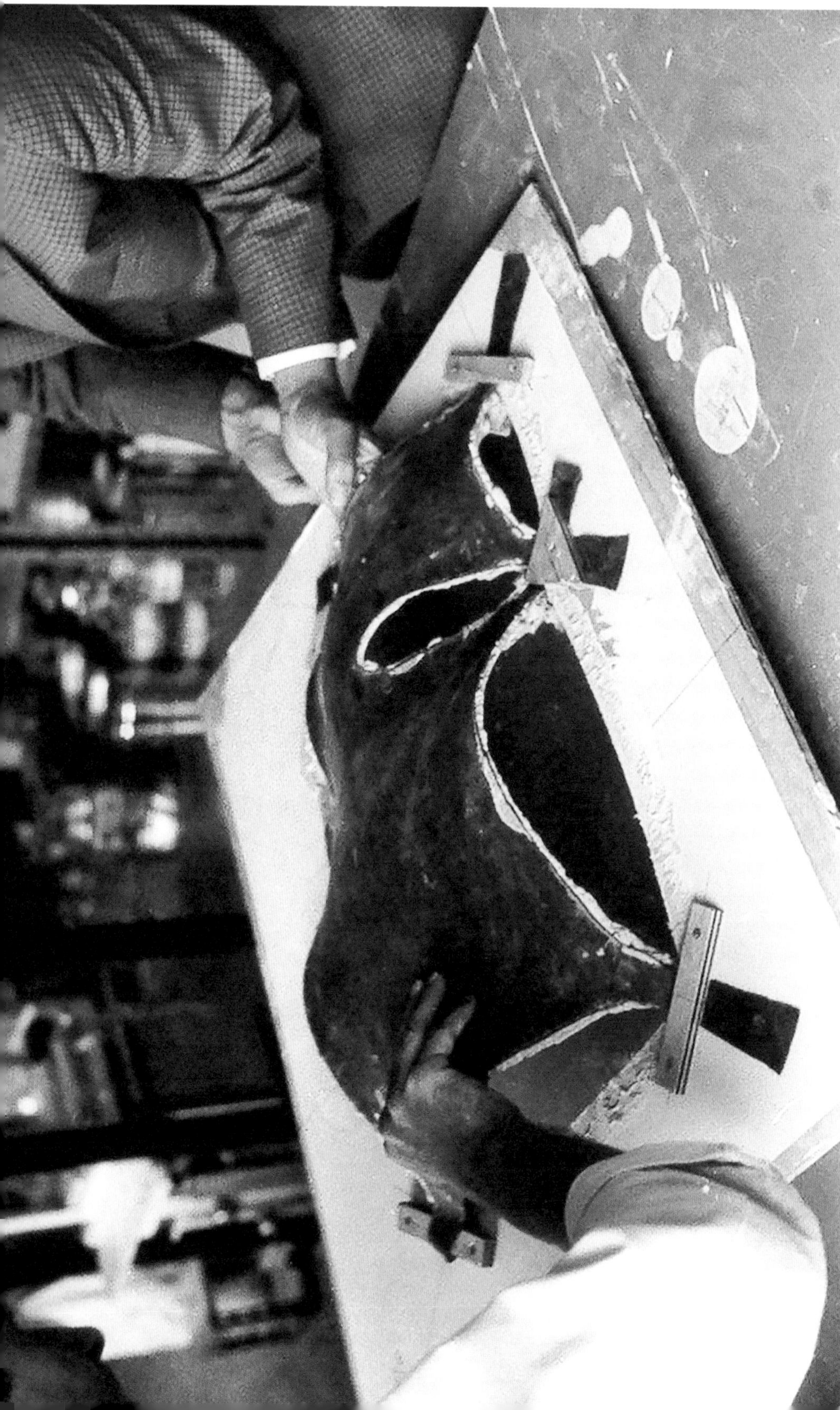

Form-finding model for the Sicli SA company building, 1968. [gta Archives / ETH Zurich]

Heinz Isler's Plaster Models

The Significance of Scale and Human Forces

Giulia Boller

At the end of the summer of 1968, a photograph caught a crucial moment: the act of flipping a physical model of a building into its final position. Two people stand on opposite sides of a work table. With calm and accuracy, their hands are simultaneously holding the timber board and the small-scale object. Behind them, a steel frame and a series of metal cans reveal the rear of a model workshop. The picture shows a central activity in the office of Swiss engineer Heinz Isler (1926–2009), taken in the basement of a single-story building on the river Emme, close to the town of Burgdorf (Switzerland). The model in the image is being turned upside down and right side up at the same time: the former reverses its spatial orientation as model to the opposite of its making; the latter describes the turn between the model's making and its demonstrative purpose. Two pairs of hands are behind this spatial and figurative movement. They transform a flexible membrane under gravity into an architectural model whose form is in static equilibrium.

Isler was acknowledged for his unconventional design approach based on the use of multiple physical models, with which he went beyond common engineering practice. His engineering office was far from the main academic institutions and professional networks, not only in geographic terms. At a time when computational methods were in their infancy, it was difficult to control free-form shapes that did not belong to any established structural typology. Spatial structures based on mathematical formulas were preferred since they could be calculated with simple analytical equations. Only a few structural designers made use of physical models to generate complex shapes with static meaning. The activities of the Institute for Lightweight Structures headed by German architect Frei Otto (1925–2015) are probably the best-known examples.[1] While Otto took advantage of his academic environment to hybridize his physical experiments with analytical calculations and digital models, Isler adhered to the physical model as the core of his working method throughout the different design phases.[2] His objects embodied geometric, structural, and aesthetic data that were continuously translated into different scales and materials by intensive human labor. The models were produced and elaborated in his office, where each room was dedicated to a specific activity: form-finding, model testing, drawing, verifying, and exhibiting.

1 The IL book series, edited by Otto's institute, published the research outcomes of investigations in multiple scientific disciplines. Regarding physical models, see Siegfried Gaß, ed., *Experimente=Experiments* (Stuttgart: Institut für leichte Flächentragwerke, IL, Universität Stuttgart, 1990).

2 Giulia Boller, "The Model as a Working Method. Heinz Isler's Experimental Approach to Shell Design" (PhD thesis, ETH Zurich, 2022).

Among Isler's multiple physical objects, the form-finding model depicted in the image was relevant for the early design phase. It materialized a shape in static equilibrium under a given system of external forces and boundary conditions. While Isler developed different form-finding approaches with physical models,[3] he considered the one with the hanging membrane as "the best method for design,"[4] leading to the most extreme free forms, such as the complex shell of the project for the company "Sicli SA" in Geneva (1967–1969), the scale model of which is visible in the photograph. Its principle was rather simple: by hanging a membrane between supports, gravity load, expressed by a liquid mixture of gypsum and water, defined a double-curved tensile surface. When conducting the experiment, Isler preferred an isotropic rubber material to a fabric, as it guaranteed a funicular shape under pure tensile forces, without any interference in the shape due to the textile's threads.[5] In reference to Robert Hooke's inverted catenary, the method expresses an inverse formulation of equilibrium, as the inverted object represents a shape under pure compression, which is appropriate for materials with low tensional resistance, such as Isler's concrete shells.

The hands of Isler's collaborators show the model being reversed from its hanging membrane configuration to its final position in space, and they express a relevant aspect in conducting the physical experiment. The movement encapsulates an engineering practice that would have been lost in a few decades in favor of computational models: the act of touching the physical structural object and working around it. The principle of the hanging membrane works at any scale, because the static structural behavior of the resulting form in equilibrium can be scaled linearly to the size of the structure.[6] However, its use as a design tool is related to finding the appropriate size of the object. The model needed to be small enough for two people to have both enough space to work on it and sufficient weight to turn it, but it also had to be large enough to reduce incorrect outcomes. Isler's extensive experience with form-finding models determined that a longitudinal length of approximately 60 centimeters was typically appropriate. Consequently, the scale of the object was defined based on the plan dimensions of the initial design. For the Sicli study visible in the photograph, the model's size was created at a scale of 1:100 (which corresponded to 57.50×30.00 centimeters).[7]

The same two pairs of hands in the photograph highlight the dialog between Isler's collaborators and the physical object during a dirty experimental procedure, as reflected by the white spots on the working table. The materials constituting the form-finding apparatus (wooden board, drawing paper, rubber membrane, plaster mixture) show the artisanal character of Isler's explorations, despite a procedure that required extreme precision in the execution of the experimental steps. While the white paper drawing with the scaled plan of the Sicli project was glued onto the wooden board to define the hole from which the rubber membrane was to be suspended, the elastic material was cut following the proportions in the plan and fixed to the wooden board. During the hanging experiment, a plaster mixture was poured onto the membrane and, once hardened, the three-dimensional object was flipped over by Isler's collaborators. The form-finding apparatus needed a few refinements after the initial tests, and the experiment was iterated until the most appropriate shape met aesthetic, functional, and structural requirements.[8] In a limited timeframe, eleven plaster models were produced for the Sicli project.[9]

3 Heinz Isler, "New Shapes for Shells – Twenty Years After," *Journal of the IASS* 20 (1979): 9–26.

4 Ibid., 2.

5 Heinz Isler, *Modell Sicli, 2. Gypsversuch* (unpublished document, 1968), 217-0153, 4/9, gta Archives / ETH Zurich.

6 Bill Addis, "Physical Modelling and Form Finding," in *Shell Structures for Architecture*, eds. Sigrid Adriaenssens et al. (New York: Routledge, 2014), 33–43.

7 Heinz Isler, *Protocol Sheets About the Form-Finding Studies for the Sicli Project* (unpublished document, 1968), 217-0153, 4/9, gta Archives / ETH Zurich.

8 Heinz Isler, *Niveau Unterschied* (unpublished document, 1968), 217-0153, 4/9, gta Archives / ETH Zurich.

9 A more detailed explanation of the different design studies can be found in John Chilton & Chu-Chun Chuang, "Rooted in Nature: Aesthetics, Geometry, and Structure in the Shells of Heinz Isler," *Nexus Network Journal* 19, no. 3 (2017): 763–785; Yvan Delemontey, "Un patrimoine d'exception: genèse et devenir d'une 'forme libre' en beton. L'usine SICLI à Genève, C. Hilberer architecte, H. Isler ingénieur, 1966–2017," in *Le béton armé. Histoire d'une technique et sauvegarde du patrimoine du 20e siècle*, ed. Matteo Porrino (Gollion: inFOLIO, 2019), 149–175.

While the photograph's frame cuts off the full figure of Isler's collaborators in favor of the small-scale physical model, the sleeves of their clothing provide further insight into the engineering practice and allow for precise identification. They illustrate the differences in procedures, tools, and media adopted during the different design stages. On the left, a model maker wears his lab coat. His rolled-up sleeves bear witness to his pivotal role in the model workshop. Reading the protocol sheets recording the results of the physical experiment, it is even possible to find his name: Anton Friedli. He was in charge of experiment preparation, the choice of apparatuses, and the gypsum pouring technique. Earlier pictures show one of his younger colleagues, Hans Glanzmann, helping him lift the timber plate onto temporary supports to let the membrane find its shape under gravity load. As can be seen from the handwritten annotations, two people were necessary to do the hanging operation to ensure precise and clean execution while the material was still liquid.[10] After the experiment was completed, another professional came into play to help turn the model upside down and evaluate the found shape. His role is recognizable by looking at the sleeves to the right of the picture: a collaborator in a plaid jacket and white shirt—most likely an engineer. His clothes, almost touching the physical model, demonstrate that he was not involved in the experimental procedure. Nevertheless, his presence provides a link between the model workshop in the basement of Isler's office and the office rooms upstairs, where the engineers verified the experimental outcomes and prepared the documents for the construction site together with the draftsmen. The model maker studied the geometric features of each gypsum model in the form of paper tables based on the three coordinates, while the structural implications were understood by the engineer. As a result, several consequent multiple physical models were produced and worked on, and each time their size was scaled up, until the size of the building was reached. Measurement models helped understand structural behavior at an appropriate scale to provide reliable results by placing a sufficient number of electrical resistance strain gauges and evenly distributing weights on their Plexiglas surface. Prototypes were built to test specific construction techniques at a scale closer to the one of the full-scale building. Even the built shell was considered as a full-scale physical model, as happened in the Sicli project, where the drop-shaped area with two supports converging at different heights was continuously monitored on site.[11]

If the equilibrium shape found through the form-finding model could be scaled up to the size of the building, structural, functional, constructional, and aesthetic requirements asked for multiple translations between scales, people, office rooms, and media. As a consequence, the object depicted in the photograph represents "only the first link in a whole chain of investigations."[12] The success of the experiment was due to specific protocols set over multiple tests. It relied on the experience of Isler's staff, who were able to spontaneously reply/react to the answers that the physical model was giving them from time to time. While the history of form-finding models often underlines their ingenuity, the new shapes eventually obtained depended just as much on the hands that fabricated and elaborated these small-scale physical objects. As the photograph of the small-scale Sicli physical model exemplified, "laboratory work also exists amid practical constraints [...]. Unravelling these factors is essentially a historical enterprise."[13]

10 Heinz Isler, "Generating Shell Shapes by Physical Experiments," in *Bulletin of the IASS* 34, no. 1 (1993).

11 Heinz Isler, *Protocol Sheets About the Monitoring Studies On-site* (unpublished document, 1969), 217-0153, 4/9, gta Archives / ETH Zurich.

12 Isler, "New Shapes for Shells," 10.

13 Peter Galison, *How Experiments End* (Chicago: Chicago University Press, 1987), 277.

Wilhelm Lasse Jordan entering one of the acoustic models of the Sydney Opera House, 1982. [Sydney Opera House collection, photographer unknown]

The Acoustic Scale

Immersive Reduced Spectacles

Carlotta Darò

The selected image pictures the Danish acoustician Wilhelm Lassen Jordan stepping into an acoustic model of the Sydney Opera House. Entering from a spectacular organ door, the engineer has an amused expression while immersing himself in the articulated shape of the hall. Beyond the altered proportions between the man and the architecture, the mimetic relationship to the 1:1 project is clearly selective, since one can observe how the public in neoprene and cardboard heads, the wooden shape, and material of the interior are deliberately simplified. Conversely, some elements are realistically miniaturized like the organ pipes and the acoustic floating acrylic panels (also called donuts due to their circular shape); the 1:1 version of these being removed during the last renovation in 2020. Like in a doll's house, these features convey the impression of a tiny spectacle room where one can play the ritual of a concert.

In the context of acoustic modeling, scalar physical reproductions serve as epistemological tools producing information and anticipating a wide range of conditions of a built project. This epistemological function is connected with traditions of technical and scientific modeling, where mathematical models are used as agents of mediation between the existing world and its theoretical representation.[1] Addressing the difference between painting and sculpture during the 15th century *paragone*, Leonardo da Vinci stated that the former, based on perspectival rules, excelled for its scientific precision (converting infinite distances in points on a flat surface) as opposed to sculpture, distinguished for its realism and the capacity of imitating nature as it is. If prospective views add an array of intellectual information to artificially reproduce the phenomenal world on a planar surface, sculptures conversely transpose this very nature into a three-dimensional mimicry object.[2] One could easily apply these considerations to models, the three-dimensional representation of architecture as opposed to drawings (plans and sections). Architectural models, nevertheless, despite their three-dimensionality and mimetic properties, usually distinguish themselves from sculptures because, as the corresponding 1:1 object, they are envelopes instead of full volumes, they are generally built by addition instead of being shaped by subtraction. Models are mainly empty, they allow the observer to see the inside, to get details of the interior, to sense atmospheric features, and—if the scale makes it possible—to enter

1 Mary B. Hesse, *Models and Analogies in Science* (Notre Dame: University of Notre Dame Press, 1966).

2 Mario Carpo, "The End of the Projected Image," in *The Second Digital Turn: Design Beyond Intelligence*, ed. Mario Carpo (Cambridge, MA: MIT Press, 2017), 99–130.

them. Furthermore, architectural models are what in science one calls material models (as opposed to mathematical ones) in the sense that they have physical aspects of resemblance with the object they reproduce.[3] Technical architectural models can also have a material quality in the sense that they may include physical, albeit impalpable, properties of architecture, making the *explicandum* of a phenomenon observable (visible or physically perceptible).

Physical models for acoustic tests began to be already explored during the 1930s; at the same time the field of room acoustics was making significant attempts in visualizing the behavior of sound in enclosed volumes. Experimentations using three-dimensional models were initiated by the German acoustician Friedrich Spändoch, who compared the behavior of sound of a 1:1 existing room to its 1:5 replica.[4] By adapting the speed of the signal to its reduced scale and converting it again to the human proportion, he obtained valuable results similar to the 1:1 acoustics. However, Jordan was among the pioneers in using these tools to predict acoustics during the design process for concert halls and philharmonics.[5] Based on the principle that, as any material model, the object itself is analog to the project in reality, acoustic models display elements and features of resemblance with their 1:1 version (still to be built). Testing acoustic through this particular mode, indeed, is the result of a process of equation resulting from the comparison between acoustic measurements of 1:1 architecture and scaled versions of it.[6] More than the resemblance to the physical object, acoustic models are made to simulate the behavior of sound within a scaled atmosphere. Once several parameters (such as the composition of air, the signal frequencies, and the absorption coefficient) are adjusted to observe similar acoustic responses to similar impulses, models may serve as predictive tools for projects not yet materialized. In this sense, acoustic models are effective instruments working by analogy in its very etymological sense (which in ancient Greek means quantitative "proportion").[7] Rather than aiming at visual semblance, they are meant to perform similarly and allow to extend the architectural representation vocabulary beyond the pure texture of shapes and the materiality of volumes.

However, it is worth noting that acoustic physical models do not provide a direct perceptive sonic experience inside the physical body, since the acoustic result is usually recorded, by miniaturized microphones inserted in miniaturized humans, sometimes adjusted to the bigger-scale parameters, and played back afterwards through mono- or binaural listening. Yet, despite the scalar inadequacy with humans, entering physical models is a long-standing practice as demonstrated by several examples from the Renaissance up to Jordan's telling picture.[8] Other psychological and physical effects seem to play an important role in the immersive experience, even if there is no possible proportional analogy between the presence of the observer and the architectural envelope. One can conclude that the egocentric perspective, rather than looking at reproduced miniaturized puppets of humans, is what makes the immersive experience a striking anticipation of a project to come, even though there is no scientific coherent relationship of scale between the object and the experience it provides. This is something that, despite the advent of virtual acoustic modeling, still seems valuable and sought after by many acousticians specializing in musical architectural programs.[9]

What seemed to be at the core of the physical acoustic model method (illustrated by Jordan entering the model) was precisely the merger of scientific measurements with sensational experiences—

3 Mary B. Hesse, "Material Analogy," in *Models and Analogies in Science* (Notre Dame: University of Notre Dame Press, 1966), 57–64.

4 Friedrich Spandöck, "Akustische Modellversuche," *Annalen der Physik* 20, no. 4 (1934): 345–360.

5 In 1941, Jordan defended his doctoral thesis in electrical engineering at the Royal Technical University Copenhagen on electroacoustic materials and models. See: Wilhelm Lassen Jordan, "Elektroakustiske undersøgelser af materialer og modeler" (Dissertation, Royal Technical University Copenhagen, 1941).

6 Richard I. G. Hughes, "Models and Representation," *Philosophy of Science* 64 (1997): 325–336.

7 Jonathan Sterne, "Analog," in *Digital Keywords, a Vocabulary of Information Society and Culture*, ed. Benjamin Peters, (Princeton and Oxford: Princeton University Press, 2016), 31–44.

8 Henry A. Millon, "Models in Renaissance architecture," in *The Renaissance from Brunelleschi to Michelangelo: The Representation of Architecture*, eds. Henry A. Millon and Vittorio Magnago Lampugnani, (London: Thames and Hudson, 1994), 19–75.

9 Carlotta Darò, "Acoustics at 1:10: Miniaturizing Atmosphere," in *The Sound of Architecture: Acoustic Atmospheres in Place*, eds. Angeliki Sioli and Elisavet Kiourtsoglou, (Leuven: Leuven University Press, 2022), 117–129.

despite the contextual disconnect between the two. Beyond any scientific analogical process, the playful dimension inherent to the way human beings interact with miniaturized reproduced scenes of the world is also part of the way science and other disciplines such as architecture address the practice of modeling. In his introduction to the book titled *Physical Models*, Bill Addis argues that since the mid-19th century the use of technical models has a lot to do with men playing with toys. He underlines how popular science journals, for instance, used this contrasting idea for explaining 1920 experiences with the Boulder Dam, featuring titles such as "Toys that save millions" and "Toy dams to save lives".[10] Quoting 1930 engineering criticisms, the same argument was conversely used for discrediting models: "a vet would hardly be entrusted to operate on an elephant if he had gained his knowledge of anatomy from a mouse."[11] Far from being explicitly used as toys, acoustic models are rather conveyed as gathering objects, providing a perceptual experience that can be shared, assessed, and manipulated by the multiple interlocutors of a project. A certain 'operative amusement' provides empirical knowledge and communication that can be shared. This clearly relates to the public, performative, and participative dimension of urban scale models, as discussed by Maxime Zaugg during the conference.[12] It goes back to the emptiness of models, as opposed to the fullness of mimic sculptures, and to the capacity of these objects to host performative and atmospheric phenomena, possibly intertwined with the presence of the public.

10 Bill Addis, ed., *Physical Models, Their Historical Current Use in Civil and Building Engineering Design* (Berlin: Wilhelm Ernst & Sohn, 2021), xii.

11 Addis, *Physical Models*, xii.

12 Maxime Zaugg, "In the Eye of the Beholder: New Representation Techniques for Public Urban Scale Models" at the conference "Are You a Model?" (Darmstadt, November 2–4, 2022).

Embroidered raised work casket, wood, tortoiseshell, metallic purl, linen, silks, white metal, brass, pearls, and mica, England, signed "A.B., 1674." [Colonial Williamsburg Foundation, Museum Purchase, 1956-300]

Mica as Model

Ruth Ezra

In *On Longing*, poet Susan Stewart writes, "The toy world presents a projection of the world of everyday life; this real world is miniaturized or giganticized in such a way as to test the relation between materiality and meaning."[1] Stewart understands toy here not in the modern sense of a partner for child's play but rather in the historical sense of a scalable device capable of entertaining the imagination of grown-ups, whether that be an automaton or a model railway.

One such device, produced by and for women in mid-seventeenth-century England, was the raised work cabinet, a lidded box whose embroidered sides featured mythical or biblical narratives set in fictive environments full of castles, grottos, and gardens.[2] For teenage girls, the task of adorning these containers with narrative programs amounted to a "masterwork"—the culmination of a rigorous, if at times tedious, drawing room education.[3] Mastering the art of embroidery meant not only the process of selecting, tracing, and stitching design elements sourced from printed pattern books, but also that of elaborating the resultant raised images still further through the addition of precious materials (metal, coral, seed pearls, even feathers) sure to attract both the eye and the hand of a box's user.[4]

In the case of a cabinet now in the collection of Colonial Williamsburg, it is small slices of glittery white mica—a potassium aluminum silicate hydroxide—that, so attached to the building's façade, function to convey the protective transparency of a fictive window. The embroiderer or else her supplier would have cut laminae of the thinly dressed mineral to the size of small spangles before securing each of the tiny rectangular "panes" to the stitched architecture with metallic thread, a process that often required piercing small holes in the flexible but robust laminae. Diminution does not come without estrangement, as Stewart teaches. Yet what makes the mica windows of raised work cabinets such as the Williamsburg example so suggestive as scaled-down architecture is their capacity to engender exactly the opposite effect: mica demonstrates a remarkable capacity to sustain an essential congruency between model and referent on the material level.

To understand how an exact equivalency could pertain between the miniaturized fenestration of an anonymous teenage embroiderer's masterwork and what was known to be possible at the time for the execution of protective, transparent glazing at full scale, it is

1 Susan Stewart, *On Longing: Narratives of the Miniature, the Gigantic, the Souvenir, the Collection* (Durham: Duke University Press, 1993), 57.

2 For representative examples, see especially Kathleen Epstein, *British Embroidery: Curious Works from the Seventeenth Century* (Williamsburg, VA.: Colonial Williamsburg Foundation, 1998); and Andrew Morrall and Melinda Watt, eds., *English Embroidery from the Metropolitan Museum of Art, 1580–1700: Twixt Art and Nature* (New York: The Bard Graduate Center for Studies in the Decorative Arts, Design, and Culture; New York: The Metropolitan Museum of Art; New Haven: Yale University Press, 2008).

3 On embroidery and education see: Morrall and Watt, eds., *English Embroidery from the Metropolitan Museum of Art, 1580–1700*, 145–166. See also Rozsika Parker, *The Subversive Stitch: Embroidery and the Making of the Feminine* (London: Women's Press, 1996), and Sarah Randles, "'The Pattern of All Patience:' Gender, Agency, and Emotions in Embroidery and Pattern Books in Early Modern England," in *Authority, Gender, and Emotions in Late Medieval and Early Modern England*, ed. Susan Broomhall (London: Palgrave Macmillan, 2015), 150–167.

4 For an overview of techniques see Cristina Balloffet Carr, "The Materials and Techniques of English Embroidery of the Late Tudor and Stuart Eras," in *Heilbrunn Timeline of Art History* (New York: The Metropolitan Museum of Art, 2000–). http://www.metmuseum.org/toah/hd/mtee/hd_mtee.htm (June 2010).

useful to go back a century to trace the supply chain that brought mica to the British Isles. Though the mineral would later be extracted from seams in the Scottish Highlands during the Second World War, in the early modern period, it was only with the chartering of the Muscovy Company in 1555 that it entered circulation in England. In 1568, the English poet George Turberville wrote home from Russia with news of the "Manners of the Country and People." Among his observations were the following lines:

> "They have no English glass; of slices of a rock
> Called Sluda, they their windows make, that English glass doth mock;
> They cut it very thin, and sow it with a thread,
> In pretty order like to panes, to serve their present need;
> No other glass, good faith! doth give a better light,
> And sure the rock is nothing rich, the cost is very slight."[5]

Turberville's letter describes a sight—windows composed of variously sized mineral laminae sewn and set into tinned iron grills—he clearly judged to be a rudimentary form of fenestration. Yet at the time of his observations, English furnaces were still a century away from manufacturing colorless lead crystal (called "flint glass") of reliable transparency.[6] That English glass, despite its defects, might nonetheless have made a mockery of the vernacular fenestration Turberville witnessed suggests just how undeveloped the state of the glass industry was around Moscow.

Indeed, the Muscovites had few options save for stone. No glass was manufactured in Russia until the late 1630s, and it was only in the 1660s that multiple small furnaces sprang up south of Moscow.[7] Slude, cut thin and sold by weight, was, however, sufficiently transparent so as to let some light into houses while also being tough and elastic enough to withstand an onslaught of hail, rain, sleet, or even squalls of water, for the substance proved its efficacy as a glazing material not just on land but at sea as well. Merchant ships loyal to Elizabeth I carried the light, glimmering cargo up from Moscow along the Northern Dvina River delta and onwards across the Barents Sea.[8] What was at best a curiosity to Turberville would soon emerge, in the 17th century, as an export commodity particularly important for England's maritime economy and navy: resilient in the face of atmospheric shifts in humidity and more heat-resistant than glass, thinly cleaved mica laminae sealed portholes while also keeping compasses dry and lanterns aflame.[9]

Back in London, what the poet Turberville once mocked in his letters as inferior to glass became, at a century's remove, a prized object worthy of scrutiny and experiment at the Royal Society precisely because it was so distinct. Robert Hooke in his 1665 *Micrographia* singles out the substance as a body that "seems to have as many curiosities in its fabrick as any common mineral I have met with: it is transparent to a great thickness; it is compounded of an infinite number of thin flakes joyned or generated one upon another so close and smooth."[10] Thus, to return to the Williamsburg cabinet, at the very same time that Muscovy glass was being passed around Gresham College, it was being circulated in less august drawing rooms, where travelers' tales like Turberville's, of thinly sliced rocks sewn with thread, can be understood as having been rather ingeniously instantiated—and one can say domesticated—in the hands of teenage girls who, back home in England, reached for the mineral's diminutive leaves when glazing the fictive architectures in which they set their biblical needlework narratives.

5 George Turberville, "Certaine letters in verse...out of Moscovia, 1568," as printed in Richard Hakluyt, *The Principall Navigations, Voiages and Discoveries of the English Nation, Made by Sea or Over Land...* (London, 1589), 408–413, and F. R. Grahame, *The Archer and the Steppe, or The Empires of Scythia: A History of Russia and Tartary* (London: James Blackwood, 1860), 473. For Turberville's language see H. Leeming, "Russian Words in Sixteenth-Century English Sources," *The Slavonic and East European Review* 46, no. 106 (1968): 4.

6 See discussion of George Ravenscroft and the impetus for "crystalline glass resembling rock-crystal" in Ruth Ezra, "Deconstructing Glass and Building Up Shards at the Early Royal Society," *Renaissance Quarterly* 75, no. 1 (2022): 96. For the earlier moment when colored glass was instead the ne plus ultra of fenestration, with English donors seeking "Glasse beyond the Seas," rather than domestic products, see Daniel Jütte, *Transparency: The Material History of an Idea* (New Haven: Yale University Press, 2023), 174.

7 For mica as a construction material see Richard Hellie, *The Economy and Material Culture of Russia, 1600–1725* (Chicago: University of Chicago Press, 1999), 127, 133, 140. See the examples on view in the recent exhibition, "Muscovite Windows: The Art of Mica Craftsmanship," at the Kolomenskoye Museum (August 31–November 28, 2021), accessed September 29, 2021, https://magazineart.art/exhibition/cljudjanyh-del-mastera-gid-po-vystavke-moskovitskoe-steklo-v-kolomenskom/.

8 For the trajectory and arena of trade see J.W. Veluwenkamp, "The Murman Coast and the Northern Dvina Delta as English and Dutch Commercial Destinations in the 16th and 17th Centuries," *Arctic* 48, no. 3 (1995): 259. Giles Fletcher, *Of the Russe Commonwealth* (London, 1591), 10v.

9 For examples of mica as a glazing medium in model portholes see *Warship, 50-gun fourth rate small two-decker*, English, ca. 1691, 265 × 940 × 210 mm (scale 1:48), National Maritime Museum, Greenwich, Caird Collection.

10 Robert Hooke, *Micrographia, or Some physiological descriptions of minute bodies made by magnifying glasses* (London: Jo. Martyn, 1665).

Not only do these fantasy cityscapes model in microcosm the real-life, slude-paned buildings of far-away Muscovy—right down to the sewn construction of the many-paned windows—, but they attest to the way that a peculiar mineral commodity, sourced via the Barents Sea, delivered into the workshops and drawing rooms of English craftsmen a "ready-made" solution to a perpetual artistic problem: that of representing transparent materials and their attendant, fleeting light effects. This was a problem that had previously tested the limits of even the most accomplished painters working with oil, glaze, and varnish—and a problem that would persist well into the 20th century. In the case of architectural models, one need only think of Mies van der Rohe's use of celluloid to represent glass, celluloid being attractive for its flexibility, ease of cutting, and mimicry of vitreous reflection, qualities that mica shares and, in its deliberate use as diminutive fenestration in early modern embroideries, arguably anticipates.[11]

These embroidered windows "test the relation between materiality and meaning" by asking their viewers to consider what it means for a modeling material to stand not for something else—as the laminae do elsewhere in the same cabinet, resembling the surface of water pooling at a grotto—but in one-to-one relation to its referent. When studied in tandem with Turberville's text, the threaded, diminutive fenestration of this decorative cabinet obtains an uncanny degree of material verisimilitude wherein mica stands for itself. Such a strong verisimilitude or correspondence is taken by scholars to have been the exception in early modern architectural modeling practices—practices that favored the use of a single material (wood or clay or even a turnip) to convey form and volume rather than the actual, phenomenological effects (by which I mean mica's peculiar glimmer and transparency) of a soon-to-be-built physical structure.

To follow Simona Valeriani, the laminae glazes on these fantasy castles are "building artefacts" that collect facts about material qualities, production techniques, design principles, and strategies indigenous to Russia, that their makers and manipulators never experienced firsthand but realized at a remove using a material and written accounts that had and could travel.[12] What is particularly striking is that women embroiderers found in their own needlepoint technique a method of construction homologous to that of the sewn windows of Turberville's poetic if slightly disparaging description.[13]

While these fantasy structures and their fenestration could perhaps more nearly be categorized, following Alina Payne's typology, as *Kleinarchitektur* rather than models in their truth-to-material if not in their scale—the important point here being that even if the structures are make-believe, the choice of glaze is not, indeed, it is the real material of Muscovite windows[14]—, they might nonetheless encourage historians to cast a wider net for "evidence" of the use of models in England during the late 16th and 17th centuries. Such a net, in its capaciousness, would also take seriously the resourceful ingenuity of the embroiderer-architect.

11 Matthew Mindrup, *The Architectural Model: Histories of the Miniature and the Prototype, the Exemplar and the Muse* (Cambridge, MA: MIT Press, 2019), 169; Ludwig Mies van der Rohe, "Hochhäuser," *Frühlicht* 1, no. 4 (Summer 1922): 122–124.

12 Simona Valeriani, "Facts and Building Artefacts: What Travels in Material Objects?", in *How Well Do Facts Travel? The Dissemination of Reliable Knowledge*, eds. Peter Howlett and Mary S. Morgan (Cambridge, MA: Cambridge University Press, 2010), 43–71.

13 Lisa M. Klein, "Early Modern English Embroideries: Contexts and Techniques," *Bulletin of the Detroit Institute of Arts* 75, no. 2 (2001): 38–41.

14 Alina Payne, "Materiality, Crafting, and Scale in Renaissance Architecture," *Oxford Art Journal* 32, no. 3 (2009): 373–374.

Planners of a world capitol—From left, Charles Le Corbusier (France), Nikolai D. Bassov (Russia), Howard Robertson (Britain) and Wallace K. Harrison (United States).

What Kind of Capitol for the U. N.?

The architects say they will emphasize the functions of the buildings, not symbolism.

By GERTRUDE SAMUELS

ON the twenty-seventh floor of the RKO building of Rockefeller Center is the workroom of a group of men of many nationalities. Their surroundings are commonplace and incomplete, but the men are oblivious of them. They are working hard—and in haste.

It is an immense oblong room. Pushed together in the foreground are three tables with green blotters, white pads and neat stacks of yellow pencils; at the windows are several drawing tables. In between are raised tables bearing clay buildings which can be pushed about at will, and a heliodon, a device for showing the sun's apparent motion.

Walls are covered with detailed studies of zoning, blueprints of housing, building conceptions, aerial photographs of a six-block site near the East River, Manhattan. Finally, there are studies of floor space, footage and staff requirements of the unique organization which has drawn on the planners' skills—the United Nations.

These men are the architects and consultants of the Big Five powers and five smaller countries, and this is their "planning and conference room" where they meet daily for two-hour conferences. For the past few weeks they have been pitting their ideas, experience and philosophies against the greatest building challenge of their careers—the U. N. headquarters.

THE emphasis is on early agreement. They will submit their finished plans to the General Assembly as soon as possible. Once the plans are approved, work can begin on the site—an $8,500,000 gift of John D. Rockefeller Jr.—which covers about eighteen acres of land bounded by East River (Franklin D. Roosevelt) Drive, Forty-second Street, First Avenue and Forty-eighth Street.

Tentatively, the design calls for three to four groups of buildings, probably eight buildings in all. The aim is to have a building for the Secretariat ready for occupancy by next March, the General Assembly's home by about August, 1948.

From what is known of the plans, it is possible to forecast what a visitor to U. N. headquarters in 1949 will see: three thirty-five to forty-five-story skyscrapers—one at the south or Forty-second Street end of the site for the staff of the Secretariat, two at the north or Forty-eighth Street end for specialized agencies. He will walk around a newly created park dotted with fountains. He may pause for a critical appraisal before the straight, clean, vertical lines of the Secretariat building, "which will have a conspicuous lack of modernistic scribbling"; wander through the three low chambers of the Councils which flank this structure, or continue to the General Assembly building in the central plaza.

SOMEWHERE along the way he may want to examine the paintings, sculpture, murals and interior decoration or he may head directly for the conference chambers with their glassed-in booths for translators and their radio, press and movie sections. He may want to look over the offices of foreign delegations, the International Labor Organization and World Health Organization in the twin skyscrapers at the north end of the site. He may drop in at the U. N. library or visit the arcade of shops.

BUT all this is in the future. What keenly interests architects and laymen today is how—or whether—the monumental hopes of the United Nations, pledged to world unity, peace and the worth of the human person, can be reflected in the headquarters.

Of the League of Nations building in Geneva it was written that "to sustain the lasting homage to peace, three qualities were required—the strength of a fortress, the lyric grace of a temple and the stateliness of a palace." Should this new center of international affairs be a symbol of the world's post-war hopes? Can the idea best be reflected in classical architecture, or by combining classical, or "traditional," with modern architecture? Should it, on the contrary, be Cartesian—throwing imitations and tradition overboard and following the modern idiom to reflect confidence in the here-and-now? Or should it be detached from man's high aspirations, and simply be a functional mass drawn to requirements like any new factory or commercial building?

In the popular mind, because of the limitations of the site and because modernists were called in (Continued on Page 55)

GERTRUDE SAMUELS is a staff member of the Sunday Department of The Times. Her article is based on interviews with architects of the United Nations Headquarters Planning Board and talks with many other leading architects.

MAGAZINE, APRIL 20, 1947. 9

Clipping from *The New York Times Magazine* showing architects Le Corbusier, Nikolai D. Bassov, Howard Robertson, and Wallace K. Harrison in front of a plasticine site model used to test design iterations for the United Nations Headquarters Complex in New York, 1947. [Gertrude Samuels, "What Kind of Capitol for the U.N.?" *The New York Times Magazine*, April 20, 1947. Archives and Library, The Museum of Modern Art, New York]

A Soft Model of Architectural "Consensus"

Evangelos Kotsioris

> "For four months, ten of the world's most honored architects had stood together in a Rockefeller Center drafting room, playing with blocks."[1]

This rather infantilizing image of grown-ups toying around with building parts was chosen for a June 1947 *Time* magazine article to summarize the arduous process that had led to the preliminary design of the United Nations Headquarters (hereafter UN HQ) complex in New York. Conceived as the permanent base of the United Nations after the end of World War II, the project was meant to be an architectural manifestation of a new era of alliances across borderlines to protect world peace. Thus, the reported story went, the concept scheme of the complex was the outcome of a frictionless partnership among the members of an international Board of Design, which included ten of the world's best modern (and unsurprisingly male) architects. In the weeks and months prior, the mythology of this purportedly harmonious collaboration had been meticulously constructed in both mainstream newspapers and architectural magazines. The repeated imagery depicted the architects of the Board working together in concert.[2] Napkin sketches, big rolls of drafting paper, or expressive chalk strokes on blackboards were nowhere to be seen, however. Instead, the main protagonist of these images was a rather uncommon design medium: plasticine.

The UN Board of Design had been assembled in New York during the first half of 1947 by its assigned leader, American architect Wallace K. Harrison, who had already gained notoriety in the United States and abroad thanks to his key role in the design of the Rockefeller Center. For Harrison, plasticine was the medium of choice, after having used it extensively while testing different permutations of the Rockefeller Center only a few years earlier.[3] Typically a mixture of calcium salts, petroleum jelly, and aliphatic acids, plasticine was characterized by the perpetual malleability of a non-hardening clay. Contrary to the much harder and fragile plaster, or hard-to-cut and assemble cardboard, plasticine was especially easy to use, and—above all—quick to sculpt and re-sculpt by hand. Impossible to harden by firing, plasticine models simultaneously signified two seemingly opposing architectural traits: the allure of possibility and the anxiety of impermanence.

1 "Workshop for the World," *Time*, June 2, 1947.

2 See, for instance: "The U.N. Plans for Its New Headquarters in Manhattan," *New York Herald Tribune*, February 26, 1947; "United Nations: Men at Work," *Architectural Forum* 86, no. 3 (March 1947): 11; "Planning for Peace: Plans for United Nations Headquarters Proceed on Wartime Speed Schedules," *Architectural Record* 101, no. 4 (April 1947): 72–81; Gertrude Samuels, "What Kind of Capitol for the U.N.?," *The New York Times Magazine*, April 20, 1947.

3 Teresa Fankhänel, *The Architectural Models of Theodore Conrad: The 'Miniature Boom' of Mid-Century Modernism* (London: Bloomsbury, 2021), 62–64, 128.

Not least, it was a material ideally suited for a group design process—after all, the UN Board of Design was anything but homogeneous. It included such disparate figures as Oscar Niemeyer from Brazil, Le Corbusier from France, Howard Robertson from Britain, Ssu-Ch'eng Liang [Liang Sicheng] from China, and Nikolai D. Bassov from the Soviet Union—to name only half of them. Instead of hosting an international competition, that would single out a sole winner, Harrison suggested to a series of collective design charrettes that in the aftermath of the war would symbolically communicate a cooperative effort across nations.

In response to Harrison's suggestion, an ad-hoc workshop for the Board to convene in person was established in February 1947. The space was located on the 27th floor of the Radio-Keith-Orpheum (RKO) Building, conveniently situated right above the Radio City Music Hall at the Rockefeller Center. There, a(nother all-male) group of draftsmen was tasked with developing each architect's proposed ideas into fully dimensioned schemes overnight. Drawings, however, were only considered as a secondary tool of design collaboration. The heart of the workshop was a fully equipped model-shop, which would produce a parade of plasticine models to collectively discuss and debate the various iterations proposed by the architects.[4]

Ahead of the arrival of the global invitees, Harrison had ordered that the main room of the workshop would be furnished with a six-by-twelve-foot model table representing the project site in the East edge of Manhattan's Midtown, the surrounding streets and buildings, and the East River, and even a plasticine miniature of the RKO Building itself for scale comparison (seen in front of Le Corbusier in the accompanying image). In an adjacent room, Harrison's trusted model maker René Paul Chambellan (with whom he had previously worked on the Rockefeller Center), along with junior members Joe Giordano and Anthony Zie, were tasked with producing massing models of each scheme proposed at a 1:500 scale, so that they could be collectively evaluated on the site model.[5] As Harrison rushed to pacify the alarmed architects during his introductory remarks on the day of the first design meeting, the site model and the plasticine blocks on it were not meant to replace the masterful minds and hands of the architects; rather, they were placed there just for "starting to play around with the masses."[6]

Harrison understood early on that working primarily with plasticine models—a largely unknown tool for his international guests who worked outside New York's mass zoning code of 1916—would function as a kind of equalizer for the heterogeneous mix of the Board members. Instead of relying on virtuosic gestures on paper or on walls, the architects would have to literally gather around the model table and be forced to work, if not play, with one another. Consequently, between February 17 and June 9, 1947, the RKO Building workshop produced literally dozens of plasticine models that demonstrated all kinds of possible configurations of the UN HQ complex. Each scheme combined the three main programmatic components of the brief that was agreed upon early: a slab tower for the Secretariat, a sculptural volume for the General Assembly, and a block of auxiliary chambers and meeting rooms. In the name of a supposedly selfless and impartial co-creation, schemes did not bear the name of the architect responsible for them; instead, they were anonymized and simply labeled with a serial number, as if the proud craft projects of young schoolchildren that shouldn't be favored over each other.[7]

4 Herbert Warren Wind, "Profiles: Architect, III: A Taxi to the U.N.," *The New Yorker*, December 4, 1954, 71.

5 Victoria Newhouse, *Wallace K. Harrison, Architect* (New York: Rizzoli, 1989), 117; George A. Dudley, *A Workshop for Peace: Designing the United Nations Headquarters* (New York and Cambridge, MA: Architectural History Foundation and MIT Press, 1994), 64.

6 Dudley, *A Workshop for Peace*, 74.

7 For a day-to-day chronicle of these meetings, see Dudley, *A Workshop for Peace*.

For a savvy professional like Harrison, the primary role of plasticine was that of a defusing tool; a soft medium of diplomacy that gave the illusion of being able to reconcile opposing design ideologies, let alone male fragility. Often presiding above debates in meetings, Harrison would selectively pick certain design elements from one architect's proposal and cunningly suggest to merge them with the desirable traits of another. Even though this idiosyncratic process of design-by-committee was widely publicized as a harmonious and collaborative effort to deliver "A Workshop for Peace" for the UN, behind closed doors the entire endeavor quickly unraveled into a tumultuous battle between architectural dogmas.[8] As a report in *Life* magazine from May 1947 chronicles put it: "The difficulty of getting 10 top architects to agree to anything became apparent... When powerful egos collided, tempers grew short."[9]

Predictably enough, the most "dissenting" voice among the group was Le Corbusier. While repeatedly arguing *in camera* that the Board of Design should simply accept his ingenious proposal, in publicity photographs staged around the model table, Le Corbusier always made sure to appear as if he was indeed immersed in a symphonious spirit of collegiality. Eventually, due to group fatigue, and much to the outrage of the Swiss-French *maître*, at the end of May 1947 the UN Board of Design settled on a hybrid scheme—a "chimera" of the two surviving models put forth by Le Corbusier (Scheme 23) and Oscar Niemeyer (Scheme 32), fused together in plasticine to form Scheme 42.[10]

After an uphill marathon of 45 design meetings, and endless plasticine models cobbled together from individual proposals, the Board seemed to finally reach unanimity through exhaustion. As Harrison's young assistant, George A. Dudley, later retold the story of the last major design meeting dated May 20, 1947: "There was no final point at which Harrison, or anyone else, said 'This is it.'"[11] Rather, a performative conclusion seems to have been reached through the lack of disagreeing comments, effectively granting Harrison permission to present a "final design" scheme to the Headquarters Advisory Committee. Throughout this deceivingly participatory process, plasticine was deployed as a seemingly neutral negotiation agent that was capable of reconciling divergent intentions and resolving conflict among strong-minded individuals. And by introducing an unfamiliar modeling material at the center of the UN HQ design endeavor, Harrison paradoxically enacted perhaps the grandest of his designs: a soft model of architectural "consensus."

8 The widely circulated description of the UN HQ complex as a "workshop for peace" was coined by Harrison during his presentation to the Headquarters Advisory Committee on May 21, 1947. George Barrett, "U.N. Capital Plans Stress Function," *The New York Times*, May 22, 1947.

9 "Famed Architects Unveil U.N. Home," *Life*, May 26, 1947, 31.

10 Dudley, *A Workshop for Peace*, 73–75.

11 Ibid., 313.

Who Made Me?

On the Material Production of Models

Anna Luise Schubert

1 Several contemporary architecture firms are known for their extensive use of models in their design process and excessive in-house production, including OMA (Office for Metropolitan Architecture), Foster + Partners, and BIG (Bjarke Ingels Group). Herzog & de Meuron even provide access to the collection of their models in an archive/exhibition space in Basel, where they are displayed alongside plans, sketches, diagrams, films, and other objects. See the firm's website, accessed February 25, 2024, https://www.herzogdemeuron.com/kabinett/.

2 See Teresa Fankhänel, *The Architectural Models of Theodore Conrad. The "Miniature Boom" of Mid-Century Modernism* (London: Bloomsbury, 2021); David Lund, *A History of Architectural Model Making in Britain. The Unseen Masters of Scale and Vision* (London: Routledge, 2022); Matthew Wells, *Modelling the Metropolis. The Architectural Model in Victorian London* (Zurich: gta Verlag, 2023).

For those studying architecture, model making can be a dangerous endeavor that sometimes demands personal sacrifice. During the long days leading up to final critiques, the crowded studios and workshops of architecture schools have seen it all: blood dripping onto cardboard from deep cuts in hastily working hands; noxious fumes rising from styrofoam split by a red-hot metal string; materials worth a month's rent piling up in corners; disc sanders erasing the imprints of fingertips; glue, dust, and splinters covering exposed clothes, skin, and tools. The anxiety of using a circular saw for the first time, or the stress of the one-and-only attempt at a plaster cast are all part of the collective folklore surrounding architecture education.

Despite these risks, physical models have been a prevalent tool in architectural education and production, stubbornly persisting even in the light of digital modeling. And just as some had (preemptively) declared the death of the physical model upon the advent of 3D modeling software, the utility of architectural models had been equally debated throughout history, with architects and their clients assessing their benefits compared to perspective drawings both as design tool and medium of communication and display. The increasing popularity of architectural models from the end of the 19th century led to the emergence of the distinct profession of the "model maker," which externalized the act of their making from the architectural design process within the architecture office. Conversely, some offices have chosen to keep their model making in-house and continue to produce physical models as part of everyday office life.[1] In recent years, historical case studies of the work of professional model makers have increasingly produced research interest,[2] in line with the broader turn to investigate the means of architectural production, its working conditions, material extractions, institutions, and networks. This research provides initial insights into the impact and methods of model makers, as well as the agency of their works, and argues for an understanding of the building design process as collaborative. The case studies demonstrate that professional model workshops not only illustrate the work of architects but, in practice, also influence the design process and the reception of the project itself through choices related to execution, materials, and more during the model making process. Further research from geographies beyond Europe and the USA is crucial to gain additional perspectives on this profession.

Outside of professional workshops, models can be created under extremely different conditions, by laypeople or highly skilled makers, with huge budgets or out of scraps, quickly and with low effort or with much time and care. This section investigates diverse processes of model making, their tools and actors, their material histories, and assesses the conditions under which models are produced. Whether working models hastily glued by architecture students, elaborated competition models crafted by specialized workshops, complex digital models collaboratively enhanced with BIM software, study models excessively produced by underpaid office interns, public city models immortalized in bronze metal, or a presumably "automated" model of parametric design—the stories of their making reveal networks of people, power structures, invisible labor, economic imbalances, resource extractions, as well as highlight debates and trends of the architectural profession and community.

Marking a turn of architectural practice to self-model-making as a tactile tool for the design process at the end of the 19th century, Matthew Wells describes the debate around a clay model by Edward Schroeder Prior presented at the Royal Academy exhibition in London. A tangible and intimate relationship between a model and its maker is illustrated by Erik Hermann's case study of the so-called Reliefmeter of Croatian artist and architect Vjenceslav Richter as a proto-digital example of dynamic modeling. In comparison, Eliza Pertigkiozoglou analyzes the database structure of 1970s software for hospital constructions as a "model of practice" that was informed by an existing building system and planning organization, and re-structured them vice versa. While the first two contributions present individual architects as model makers, and the other features a governmental organization in collaboration with a contracted commercial enterprise, all highlight the reciprocal influences between the models and their makers' practice. How does the modeling process impact the design process? What agency does a model maker have over the design process? When is this intentional and by whom? How can a model be an interface to the design practice? How have the methods and significance of architectural model making been affected by evolving techniques and technologies? What cultural and local specificities can be found in approaches to model making in architectural education and practice?

Following the traces of an almost forgotten maker of the model for a low-cost housing project as part of the Nordic countries' development aid in post-colonial Tanganyika, Sebastiaan Loosen questions the attribution of expertise and knowledge in relation to power imbalances, while providing an example of how to read the gaps in sources. The model maker in this case study had many more responsibilities in the housing project, but his work and contributions were almost not documented. The model here becomes an epistemological entry point for a history that includes marginalized people and tacit knowledge. The investigation of the physical shaping, undoing, and remaking of objects from matter helps to examine the process of how architecture models and the spaces they help imagine come into being—even if the hands involved in their making disappeared from the official records. Following the material scraps and the techniques required in their composition can thus lead to the forgotten, the unknown, and the underlying in such future spaces, and can open up the politics of current ones that might slowly come undone.

Model of a Cottage by Edward Schroeder Prior, 1895. [“Our Illustrations,” *The British Architect*, vol. 43 (May 17, 1895): 348–349]

A Step Nearer Their Work

Perception and Authorship in a Model at the Royal Academy

Matthew Wells

> "The Architecture Room this year contains two models of buildings, in addition to the usual drawings. What may be hoped from such an innovation?"[1]

Displayed in the corner of the Architecture Room at the 1895 Royal Academy Summer Exhibition in London was a model of a house by Edward Schroeder Prior. It showed only the external form of the building, with the interior represented only by small plan drawings neatly pinned to the corners of a baseboard. Despite the house's innovative butterfly plan, the true innovation that attracted the above comment from the *Builder* was not simply the design of the house but the presence of the model in the exhibition combined with its material expression. Although "comparatively rough in appearance," the editorial—likely written by the journal's editor Henry Heathcote Statham—noted that it was "revolutionary in its tendencies."[2]

This radical potential was found to reside not only in its form or character but in its authorship. As the journal explained: "We strongly suspect Mr. Prior of having made the model with his own hands. He is quite capable of it."[3] Fixed to a base and roughly occupying a diamond-shaped outline, the model featured rubble walls, a pan-tile roof, leaded casements, tall chimneys, surrounded by lawns and paths. This depiction of materiality is both descriptive and naturalistic: the rubble stone walls are coarse and irregular, the weather-boarded gable ends are rough and uneven. The cumulative effect was to offer a more naturalistic image of a building than any previous model maker had been able to achieve in cardboard, plaster, or timber. As a tactile way of developing formal ideas and intellectual concepts simultaneously, architects began to see the potential of model making through their own hands, with Prior's model signifying an emerging shift in architectural practice at the end of the 19th century.

The model of the house was seen by approximately 300,000 exhibition visitors over the summer of 1895. That July, some fifty individuals had written to various British magazines with opinions about how the architectural profession should display their designs at the Summer Exhibition.[4] Almost everyone was dissatisfied with the Royal Academy and discussed topics including the purpose of architectural exhibitions, how the exhibition should be curated, the employment of external artists, and questions of authorship around the attribution

1 "Architecture at the Royal Academy," *Builder* 68 (May 4, 1895): 323.

2 Ibid.

3 Ibid.

4 "The Representation of Architecture at the Royal Academy," *Builder* 69 (July 6, 1895): 1–3; "The Representation of Architecture at the Royal Academy: Concluded," *Builder* 69 (July 13, 1895): 21–28.

of work to assistants, model makers, and draftsmen. Many architects called for more architectural models to be displayed. Others welcomed the exhibition of "models of all sorts—of whole buildings or portions of them."[5] Prior himself wrote to the *Builder*'s editor and proposed that the Royal Academy should only admit submissions from architects "which are modelled and can stand on the same basis as the sculptor's models, as the work of the artist himself."[6]

Model Making Is a Creative Act

Prior subsequently clarified his views on model making as a creative act in an essay titled "Architectural Modelling," which addressed subjects such as the purposes of model making for architects, the practical use and representational qualities of materials, and the conceptual role of the medium in comparison to other artistic disciplines. From the first line, "The architectural model is not recommended to the profession as a new device for client-getting," Prior aimed to establish a clear purpose for models in contemporary architectural practice: they were for architects, not clients, who he believed were unable to understand drawings and could, at most, be shown sketches of initial designs.[7] According to Prior, it was risky to show clients a model for two reasons. First, a model was too revealing of the architect's intentions: "It is dangerous to show what is so near the truth." Second, a model was an experimental tool for the architect, but because of its legibility, "it may provoke criticism." When used in the office, however, in the context of furthering a design, models were vital for architects as they enabled an opportunity to review work "before the imprimatur of the builder is set upon it."

Prior also had extensive thoughts on how models were made, and his essay suggests a wide variety of materials. For sketch models cardboard or French putty, a type of impure soap, could readily take the form of architectural surfaces. For more elaborate models, wax was indispensable due to its ability to represent both the color and texture of real materials. Powdered pigments could suggest colors, and any required texture could be achieved by adding sand or powders to a combination of paraffin and turpentine. Wax could be applied to pasteboard and worked with modeling tools to replicate the material texture of a wall. In turn, these models could be used to discuss aspects of construction with craftsmen—aspects which otherwise resisted representation in drawings, such as "the desired texture and arrangement" of a wall. And while the specification and contract ought to dictate how a building should be assembled, a "serious practitioner" should always produce a model in order for the contractor and craftsman to "see" what the contract states: the architect "will be loath to trust the success of the operation to drawings, plans, and specifications."[8] This attitude was closely aligned with the Arts and Crafts idea that architects should not only understand the principles of construction but also be trained in artisanal building techniques—an attempt to reform design against the perceived decline in standards of quality caused by wholesale industrial production. Prior's contribution to these debates was that architects could explore their own subjectivity towards the texture and materiality of a building through the production of models.

5 "Representation of Architecture at the Royal Academy," 3.

6 "Representation of Architecture at the Royal Academy: Concluded," 27.

7 Edward Schroeder Prior, "Architectural Modelling," *Builder* 69 (June 29, 1895): 482.

8 Ibid., 483.

Another central case for model making was the three-dimensional nature of models. Similar to his earlier letter, Prior's essay argued: "It is continually forgotten that an architectural design is a sculpture in the round." The "present habits" of architectural practice, he continued, caused a separation between the architect and his work. In order to bridge this gulf, "[t]he model brings the architect a step nearer his work than the drawing did."[9] The expressive nature of model making meant that the medium was a representation suited for an emotive purpose rather than a purely imitative one. In part, this was related to the choices and types of materials used. Wax models, for example, could convey "feeling to oneself rather than facts to another ... the use of wax is but a door to experiment."[10]

Prior proposed that the way that architects made drawings was largely to blame. The standardized use of technical drawing instruments such as T-squares encouraged parallel composition in plan and elevation, while drawing plans and elevations on separate pieces of paper had the effect of separating the design into abstract categories. Instead, Prior proposed, "if modelled first, the design would have had unity of plan and elevation impressed on it from the first."

And yet despite these prominent calls for model making, the benefits of perspective drawing over an architectural model (and vice versa) was a recurring issue in debates over architecture throughout the 19th century. One attempt to institute a systematic approach to architectural media came in the form of an investigative committee on public competitions. In a report written by the Royal Institute of British Architects, it was proposed that in the process of selecting an architect by competition, a "correctly made" perspective drawing from pre-determined viewpoints, rather than a model, could depict the effects of proposed designs and therefore held primacy in the judgement of an architectural scheme.[11] In practice, however, much of the contemporary discourse in the popular press praised the potential of an architectural model to be understood by a lay audience who was not conversant in orthographic drawings or might be swayed by the exaggerated beauty of a colored perspective. These debates continued after Prior exhibited his work at the Royal Academy, when the artist Dugald Sutherland MacColl proposed that in future any model on display should be covered in part by a screen, "pierced with eyeholes at a height corresponding to the height of the spectator's eye on the scale of the model."[12] Fixing the viewpoint of an observer would render the model into a perspective, separating the subject from the object, and flattening its three-dimensional character—ironically turning a model into a form of drawing, an act that sat in complete opposition to Prior's conception of architecture as a three-dimensional art form—a lodestar for 20th century architects across central Europe including Hans Poelzig, Hans and Wassili Luckhardt, Hermann Finsterlin, and Bernhard Hoetger.

9 Ibid.

10 Ibid.

11 "Extract from a Report of the Committee appointed to consider the subject of Public Competitions for Architectural Designs. Laid before the Special General Meeting, held 24th January 1839," *Civil Engineer and Architect's Journal* 2 (May 1839): 183.

12 "Architecture and the Royal Academy: A Discussion V," *Architectural Review* 13 (1903): 47.

Vjenceslav Richter posing with his reliefmeter, ca. 1980s. [Reprint from the newspaper *Vjesnik*]

Vjenceslav Richter and the Reliefmeter

Proto-Digital Modeling for a Future in Flux

Erik Herrmann

This model story begins with a confrontation. In the first frame, a man stares intensely at an enormous panel. Entranced, he scrutinizes the dimpled and pitted canvas before him like an athlete sizing up their opponent. The next frame, taken moments later, reveals the aftermath of the confrontation. The man now turns to face an audience out of frame. He is animated and excited, his hands gesticulating. The flat surface of the canvas is now distorted—pushed and pulled into waves of rippling extrusions, revealing a previously concealed system of sliding metallic pixels. The photographs are from a 1980s edition of *Vjesnik*, the state-owned newspaper of Croatia under the Socialist Federal Republic of Yugoslavia, and the man in the photos is Vjenceslav Richter, a Croatian sculptor and architect whose rebellious and visionary nature shaped Yugoslavia's radical interwar arts scene. In 1963, Richter launched an ambitious program of visual research he termed "Systemic Plastics." Executed in graphics and sculptures, this genre of work explored the continuous mutability of spatial structures, with Richter manipulating mathematical matrixes to produce complex patterns and effects.[1] Lacking technical and financial resources, Richter developed "hand" computing methods to visualize the aesthetic and formal outcome of algorithmic systems, simulated through rote calculation or dice rolling. The architect's purpose-built implement for this research was the reliefmeter, an enormous grid of hundreds of interlocked aluminum extrusions that slid forward or backward to create pixelated reliefs. For the contemporary reader, Richter's device resembles pin art or pinscreen art toys made for the executive's desk. The reliefmeter is an intricate kinetic sculpture and perhaps plausibly a useful compositional machete, but how precisely does it function as a model? No mere novelty, Richter used his device to advocate for a synthesis of art and architecture with an ambitious program of research experiments ranging from systems-based graphics to radical utopian urbanism. While his contemporaries focused on novel forms of digital expression, Richter sought to understand future digital systems' social and emancipatory potential.

Although not electronic, Richter's reliefmeter model is mutable, quantifiable, and addressable through mechanized pixels. An elegant and expedient protocol of visual encoding and transmission, the pixel is the smallest addressable element of an image. The pixel is a

1 Božo Bek, ed., *Juraj Dobrović, Julije Knifer, Vjenceslav Richter. Yugoslavia. XII Bienial de Sao Paulo* (Interrepublic Coordinative Committee for Cultural Relations with Foreign Countries of R.S.F. Yugoslavia, 1973).

ubiquitous cultural touchstone today, but the term was first introduced in technical circles in the mid-1960s—as a portmanteau of the terms "picture" and "element." This etymology is misleading, however, as pictures and images have very little in common on a technical level. In his 2017 essay "Everything Is Already an Image," architect John May offers concise definitions differentiating images from drawings or photographs—unlike their analog and chemical counterparts, they are produced by discrete signals. May notes: "Images are inherently dynamic, and our tendency to think of them as static or fixed is a result of the psycho-historical residue of drawings and photographs."[2] The prescience of Richter's pseudo-orthographic/pseudo-signaling model positions it precisely between two epistemologies of tools and time. His work reconciles the continuous performance of analog sculpting with the discrete probabilistic regime of machine signalization.

The same year he developed his first reliefmeter prototype, Richter participated in the second edition of New Tendencies, an international art movement with explicit aims to shatter the illusion of creative genius and to replace the cultural concept of the artist with visual researchers—researchers expected to employ computers toward new aesthetic possibilities.[3] Emerging in the late 1950s/early 1960s, shaped primarily by the proto-cybernetic philosophy of Max Bense, Information Aesthetics broadly explored the consequences of Claude Shannon's information theory on artistic production and consumption. In their visual research, computer art pioneers like Bense's student, Georg Nees, sought verifiable evidence towards an objective, mathematical basis for aesthetic beauty.[4] While most computer artists of the period emerged from engineering backgrounds, Richter's unique approach as a sculptor and architect focused on the social dimension of new relationships between people and machines. Richter was deeply versed in artistic mediums, raw materials, and techniques for manipulating them in his training as a sculptor. Whereas traditional materials were static and predictable, pliant and malleable to the artist's whims, Richter anticipated the computer would be capricious, spontaneous, and volatile.[5] Many of his contemporaries (including Nees, as mentioned earlier, Frieder Nake, Kurd Alsleben, Herbert W. Franke, and others) were translating their design intent into symbolic code in laboratory settings. Richter instead pursued a far more embodied and humanistic approach, beginning with the conception of the computer as an active collaborator rather than a passive instrument. The reliefmeter is not a discrete assemblage but an abstract membrane proposing one possible method for direct dialog between artists and machines. It is an embodied interface for reaching out and touching the digital ether of discrete signals. While the inevitable delay of early digital processors and ponderous interfaces slowed the work of his peers, Richter's interface allowed him to work in real time.

The reliefmeter supported dynamic real-time creative acts of continuous plasticity, informing Richter's work not only in graphics but also in the fields of urban planning and architecture. In his speculative techno-utopia *Sinturbanizam* [synthetic urbanism] project, Richter sought to develop emancipatory civic models and ideal urban forms based on social self-management: the social and economic model of Cold War-era Yugoslavia. The reliefmeter was a stalwart center of this twenty-year project, a proto-digital interface for maintaining simultaneous focus on the individual and collective in designs of new political and technological dimensions. In his work with the reliefmeter, Richter posited architecture not as a static organization of space

2 John May, "Everything Is Already an Image," *Log* 40 (Spring/Summer 2017): 12.

3 For more on New Tendencies, see Margit Rosen, Peter Weibel, Darko Fritz, Marija Gattin, *Landesbildergalerie* (Steiermärkisches Landesmuseum Joanneum, and Zentrum für Kunst und Medientechnologie Karlsruhe, 2011). *A Little-Known Story about a Movement, a Magazine and the Computer's Arrival in Art. New Tendencies and Bit International, 1961–1973* (Karlsruhe: ZKM/Center for Art and Media, 2011).

4 Frieder Nake, "The Semiotic Engine: Notes on the History of Algorithmic Images in Europe," *Art Journal* 68, (April 2014): 80.

5 Vjenceslav Richter, "Dilemma" *bit international* 3 (1968): 27.

but as a mutable substrate adapting its performance to unknowable outcomes. The reciprocal relationship between Richter's work with the reliefmeter and his urban visions is most overt in a 1968 version of *Sinturbanizam*, which includes sliding residential units to liberate inhabitants spatially. Richter's extensive drawings and writings for the project include unique simultaneous perspectives and writings speculating on the space-time of his future utopia.[6] Examining Richter's mobile structures and his visionary architecture, it is impossible not to conclude that the dynamic reliefmeter evinced Richter's understanding that the future of architecture was not in static objects but within a digitized ether in perpetual flux.

Unfortunately, the daring and prolific Richter never enjoyed institutional, economic, or technical support from large tech corporations of the time, like Siemens or Bell Labs, limiting his engagement with the digital future he foresaw. Instead, he spent his career waiting on the computer. Despite these challenges, Richter's work with Systemic Graphics and *Sinturbanizam* in the 1960s demonstrates the promise of technology in absentia—Richter never conformed his project to the strictures and whims of tech conglomerates, instead remaining independent, restless, and focused on the socio-political dimensions of his work. Today, tech conglomerates still dominate the digital landscape, employing graphical user interfaces or GUIs to construct our relationship with digital systems. GUIs are the membrane between users and machines, allowing a selective flow of inputs and outputs. Graphical user interfaces are also, as new media pioneer American Artist offers, "an abstracted representation of a person's relationship to a machine."[7] In this sense, software engineers dictate a user's relationship to machines through GUIs. Interfaces inevitably obscure much more than they ever reveal, often producing passivity in digital consumers. While his contemporaries developed their work as proofs of concept for an emerging computer industry, Richter uniquely designed and constructed his interface and—by extension—his relationship to a future of machines. His real-time visual research with the sliding pixels of the reliefmeter instilled his architectural work with sensitivity to organizational flexibility, dynamic performance, and constructed temporality. Richter modeled a digital future that embraced intuition, happenstance, and participation. Most significant for the audience of this collection, Richter pursued his singular and uncompromising work by modeling not only novel forms but his relationship to the machine.

6 "Institute of the Present: Vjenceslav Richter's Sinturbanizam." Institutul Prezentului, accessed October 4, 2023, https://institutulprezentului.ro/en/2020/02/28/vjenceslav-richters-sinturbanizam/.

7 American Artist, "Black Gooey Universe," in *Unbag* 2, accessed June 23, 2023, https://static1.squarespace.com/static/59238d36d2b8575d127794a4/t/5a60bdecf9619a7f881b02a0/1516289526013/UNBAG_2_AmericanArtist.pdf.

Bertil Melin, the Swedish director of the Nordic Tanganyika Project in Kibaha, showing a model of low-cost housing to President Julius Nyerere and on the far left is carpenter and model maker Mr. Dennis, ca. 1963–1964. [Torvald Åkesson, *Education - In Marble Halls or Under Trees. Low-Cost Houses in East Africa, Especially Ethiopia and Tanzania*, compiled self-published report, Stockholm, ca. 1965, formerly library collection Royal Institute of Technology, Stockholm]

Mr. Dennis' Model

Organizing Knowledge in the Postcolonial Era

Sebastiaan Loosen

The Photograph

Mr. Dennis—full name unknown—was a Tanzanian professional in the building sector. His biography, the nature and extent of his expertise, and his contribution to the built environment in Tanzania are unknown; maybe even impossible to reconstruct and assess. My only clue is this photograph, where he figures in the margins, and which depicts a white man pointing to an architectural model in front of another man wearing a colorful shirt, surrounded by other men with a wide range of facial expressions, on what appears to have been a bright and sunny day. This image has stuck with me ever since I encountered it in a remarkable, self-compiled, and most likely unsolicited report of a confessional nature by a Swedish architect/aid worker, Torvald Åkesson.[1] The man explaining the model of a low-cost housing unit is Bertil Melin, director of the Nordic Tanganyika Project: a Nordic aid project initiated shortly after Tanganyika's independence in the early 1960s. The man closely following his exposé is President Julius Nyerere, and the men peeking over his shoulders and showing various degrees of interest in the model are most likely part of his entourage.

The man on the far left, with a calm and resigned posture, is Mr. Dennis: the carpenter who not only made the models, but also shared his expertise with the Swedish site architect on the planning, construction, and detailing of these newly built houses. Together with his family, he even "test-lived" in one of the houses. The few lines in Åkesson's report that point to these multiple roles that Mr. Dennis occupied, suggest that the label "carpenter" does not do full justice to the multi-faceted know-how he brought to the housing project in question.

While the model rests peacefully on the table, by gathering a wide range of actors around itself, it acts as a central node that organizes and facilitates a certain distribution of knowledge. By drawing on this agency of the architectural model, in this essay I intend to flesh out the model's role in this postcolonial context as an object enmeshed in networks of power and knowledge and, through the model's maker, Mr. Dennis, to reflect on the archives on which we rely to write architectural history.

1 Torvald Åkesson, *Education: In Marble Halls or Under Trees. Low-Cost Houses in East Africa, Especially Ethiopia and Tanzania*, compiled, self-published report (Stockholm, ca. 1965).

The Director & the President

The photograph takes us to a time, halfway through the 20th century, when the international political landscape was being substantially restructured. Anti-colonial struggles successfully led to independence, colonial empires crumbled, and former colonial relationships gave way to new ties between the Global South and North, in many ways still marked by a profound inequality. In this reconfigured landscape, "development" emerged as a key concept that structured the political and economic imperatives, and "aid" and "cooperation" became the keywords to describe the supposedly more benevolent interventions of the North in the South. The Nordic countries quickly became key actors in the development scene and its burgeoning markets.

In 1963, Sweden, Norway, Finland, and Denmark signed an agreement with the Tanganyikan government for a substantial education-oriented aid project, consisting primarily of a farmers' training center, health center, secondary school, and community center. Nordic architects were mobilized to build the required infrastructure and, in parallel, to develop pilot housing schemes that translated Nyerere's socialist Ujamaa policies into rural planning schemes based on small cooperative village communities.

Following this logic, one might see in the image Melin, the director, explaining to President Nyerere how the model in front of him represents a technologically and typologically improved version of the so-called Swahili house typology—a local typology that the young country's newly-established National Housing Corporation adopted, in a rationalized form, as its key typology of low-cost housing provision for the rest of the decade, constructing them mainly with cheap imported materials such as cement blocks and corrugated metal sheets.[2] Thus, as much as the historically grown Swahili house form embodied the material culture of the trade-dominated Swahili city states along the East African coast, its "modernized" version embodied the material and immaterial flows of an emerging global market. In this context, foreign aid expertise and post-independence diplomacy brokered Swedish steel, Swiss cement, or British petroleum—to name a few examples—to newly independent countries.

Built to communicate Nordic-driven research on the "best" way to build and live in Tanganyika, the model in this image became an avatar of development aid expertise. It took part in a particular knowledge economy, where directors and presidents played important roles, but where the model was also inevitably mediating between what was considered valuable expertise and what was regarded as mere unlicensed know-how.

2 Dick Urban Vestbro, *Social Life and Dwelling Space: An Analysis of Three House Types in Dar Es Salaam*, Report (Lund: Department of Building Function Analysis, College of Architecture, University of Lund, 1975).

The Architect

In this context, "expertise" was a commodity with political and economic value that was traded in the framework of aid diplomacy. Thus "Tropical Architecture" was the technoscientific guise under which architectural expertise bridged the late colonial and the postcolonial eras, serving as a noteworthy force that prolonged Europe's hegemonic position in the Global South. It suggested climatic considerations of thermal comfort to be the key concern for architects when responding to the myriad challenges of the Global South.[3] Modeling climatic conditions was central to acting out this hegemonic expertise: when, in the 1950s and 60s, the first manuals started to appear to guide architects in their work overseas, they were full of climatic charts, prediction models, sun shading tools, and so on.[4]

3 Hannah le Roux, "The Networks of Tropical Architecture," *The Journal of Architecture* 8, no. 3 (Autumn 2003): 337–354; Jiat-Hwee Chang, *A Genealogy of Tropical Architecture. Colonial Networks, Nature and Technoscience* (London: Routledge, 2016).

Torvald Åkesson was one such architect, whose expertise opened the door to positions overseas, although his background had more of an agricultural than climatic flavor. Having served since 1961 as Director of the Building Research Department at the Ethio-Swedish Building Institute of Technology in Addis Ababa, he was particularly well-suited to lending his expertise to Nyerere's agriculturally-oriented view on development as site architect for the Nordic Tanganyika Project from 1963 to 1965. Åkesson's aforementioned unusual self-compiled report is one of the rare entry points at our disposal to understand "architectural expertise" as it played out on the ground. When describing his activities, he emphasized both how isolated he was as an expert, and how dependent he was on social workers, health inspectors, and nursing sisters to come up with a housing strategy tailored to East Africa's needs. He seriously questioned the relevance of his own expertise, writing: "I am an architect. I look at a very well-constructed native hut, a product of long tradition, and of ages of experience, the house formed out of local material, fitting the landscape and surroundings perfectly. ... I feel a harmony and maturity in the rooms. But do I really understand where I am? ... Now, I am supposed to immediately import sheets, cement, fittings, building methods, equipment and advice and replace this work of art for a human life I never lived."[5] Coming from a man who, before his job as site architect at the Nordic Tanganyika Project, served as Director of the Building Research Department in Addis Ababa, these reflections have considerable weight and aptly capture the difficult position in which architectural expertise found itself.

As site architect, Åkesson was very likely present when this photograph was taken, yet he is not pictured in the photograph. It is not unlikely that he might have been the one taking the photo—perhaps even consciously including Mr. Dennis in the picture frame?

4 Maxwell Fry and Jane Drew, *Tropical Architecture in the Humid Zone* (London: Batsford, 1956); Otto Koenigsberger et al., *Manual of Tropical Housing and Building. Part 1: Climatic Design* (London: Longman, 1974).

5 Åkesson, "Education."

The Model Maker

Torvald Åkesson, Björn Christoffersen, Jan Ola Nilsson, Tapani Kapala, Oddvar Bjærum, Gunnar Lysholm... While we know all the names of the Nordic aid workers involved in the Nordic Tanganyika Project, I cannot give you Mr. Dennis' full name. If it were not for Åkesson's unusual report and his informal crediting of Mr. Dennis' role in the caption to this photograph, we would not even have known his first or last name—Mr. Dennis belongs to the disenfranchised who all too easily get lost in the folds of history.

In the foreign aid-funded knowledge economy, those named "experts" tended to be westerners, while locals were often considered to be "craftsmen" at best. Åkesson's caveats about his own "expertise," and his recognition of Mr. Dennis' role as exceeding that of a carpenter is an invitation to at least put this categorization of knowledge under suspicion. This suspicion is empirically supported by scholars who, by relying innovatively on non-institutionalized archives in other geographic regions, have started to unearth documents that prove that many of these "carpenters" and "craftsmen" were, in fact, highly professional actors in the building trade, despite the many statements to be found in the hegemonic archives of the North suggesting a professional *terrain vague* in their overseas territories.[6] Indeed, theoretically and historically, political theorists and historians have critically addressed this unfair attribution of knowledge by pointing to the epistemological dimension of colonization and its long-lasting effects that still shape our current world order.[7]

6 Michelle Joan Wilkinson, "Shadow Work: Architecting While Black in British Guiana," *ABE Journal: Architecture beyond Europe*, no. 21: Architectural Expertise in the Foreign Aid-funded Knowledge Economy.

7 Boaventura De Sousa Santos, *The End of the Cognitive Empire. The Coming of Age of Epistemologies of the South* (Durham, NC: Duke University Press, 2018); Sabelo J. Ndlovu-Gatsheni, *Decolonization, Development and Knowledge in Africa. Turning Over a New Leaf* (London: Routledge, 2020).

There is not much we know of Mr. Dennis, or of how far his expertise stretched, except that his own demonstration house in which he lived—as documented in a few photographs in Åkesson's report—was considerably different from the model presented to Nyerere in the photograph.[8] While it has a similar spatial arrangement, the walls were made using advanced mud techniques instead of cement blocks, and the thatched roof required a different timber structure than the light asbestos roofs eventually used in the project. Undoubtedly, Åkesson had something like Mr. Dennis' house in mind when marveling at the local building culture and questioning his own "expertise" based on imported products and techniques.

The Model & Our Archives

At face value, this photograph represents an engineered product of Nordic aid expertise, presented to the people of Tanganyika to "further their development." Instead of adopting this narrative, critically or otherwise, in this essay, I have tried to read the model as a contested site of knowledge by pointing to its makers. The photographic framing—presumably by the self-critical aid expert Torvald Åkesson—captures the architectural model right between Director Melin's pointing finger, President Nyerere's restrained and observing gaze, and Mr. Dennis' silent, resigned posture. As such, it can be seen as taking part in organizing and facilitating a certain distribution of knowledge, showcasing foreign aid "expertise" as politically valuable, whilst rendering local know-how unworthy of mention.

Moreover, the struggle to name the model's maker is indicative of our unbalanced archives, which tend to reproduce the narrative of the African continent being merely on the receiving end of aid. In reality, however, aid expertise was heavily reliant on collaborations with many unnamed local "craftsmen" such as Mr. Dennis. While most archives in the North document in detail the ins-and-outs of their own experts sent abroad, they rarely portray this dependency on local resources; were it not for Åkesson's unusual report, the knowledge that Mr. Dennis invested in this low-cost housing project would have gone uncredited. More generally—next to family archives, oral history, personal notebooks, and letters—photographs of models such as these are amongst the very few material traces at hand to articulate the interdependency of two worlds meeting in the context of "aid": an interdependency which historians urgently need to unearth further.

8 Åkesson, "Education."

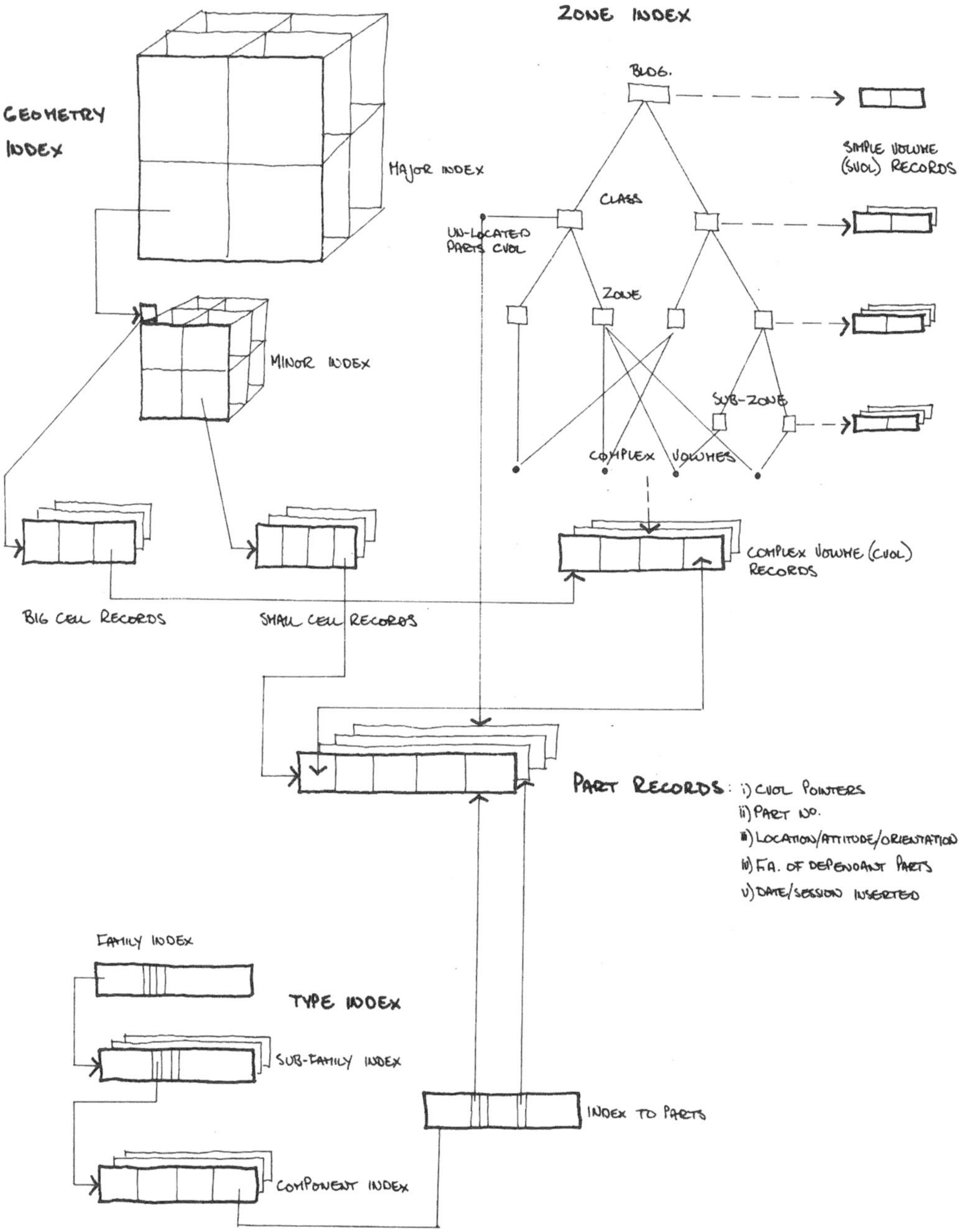

Figure 3.6: OXSYS BUILDING FILE STRUCTURE

Diagram of OXSYS database structure, drawn by researchers at the University of Edinburgh who were analyzing the system as a case study, 1979. [Bijl, Aart, David Stone, and David Rosenthal, *Integrated CAAD Systems*, final report of the research project DGR 470/12 funded by the Department of Environment (DoE), Edinburgh: EdCAAD (Edinburgh Computer Aided Architectural Design) Studies, March 1979. Figure 3.6: "OXSYS Building File Structure"]

Building Models of Practice

The OXSYS Software for Hospital Design, 1970–1980

Eliza Pertigkiozoglou

Diagrams of peculiar architectural models illustrated the final report of a study on computer-aided building design funded by the UK Department of the Environment and published in 1979.[1] They were peculiar as they were not the usual architectural representations of buildings in scale; rather, they illustrated how buildings were stored and accessed *as data* in computer memory. To grasp the inner workings of emerging computer applications for the building industry, a group of state-funded researchers at the University of Edinburgh constructed these schematic depictions of digital data relations to illustrate how software organized building elements and user operations. The diagram featured here depicts the database structure of a software named OXSYS, developed throughout the 1970s for the design of hospitals in the administrative region of Oxford. Although it was initially developed for specific purposes—for hospital design based on a prefabricated construction system—, by the end of the decade, OXSYS was hailed within the British architectural computing circles as the most comprehensive, potentially generalizable, and marketable system available.[2] Its success urged the Edinburgh researchers to examine the system closely as a case study (a model?) to learn from. Ultimately, OXSYS performed as a model in a threefold manner: it was a model for hospital building, for organizing building information, and a software model.

Unlike other models in this volume, the makers of this unconventional building model were not individual architects, craftspeople, or artists but a government agency and a contracted commercial enterprise. The Oxford Regional Health Authority (ORHA)—delegate of the Department of Health and Social Security in the Oxford region—commissioned the development of OXSYS to Applied Research of Cambridge Ltd. (ARC)—a consultancy that spun off from Cambridge University's School of Architecture to undertake applied work for government and industry.[3] ORHA envisioned a computer system that would streamline the design and construction of hospitals in its administrative region by encoding building standards and automating their application in future projects. In this regard, the software was similar to Mr. Dennis' model discussed by Sebastiaan Loosen: it was embedded within specific networks of power and put in place to govern the design and construction of buildings by administering expertise.[4]

1 Aart Bijl, David Stone, and David Rosenthal, *Integrated CAAD Systems* (EdCAAD – Edinburg Computer Aided Architectural Design, 1979), 3-29–3-39.

2 Ibid., 14.

3 See A. L. Arschavir, "Introduction to Health Building Seminar," in *Handbook*, 1976, GB 160 H5/37/A1/1, Oxford Regional Health Authority Collection, Oxfordshire History Centre Archives; and Mary Louise Lobsinger, "Two Cambridges: Models, Methods, Systems, and Expertise" in *A Second Modernism: MIT, Architecture, and the "Techno-Social" Moment*, ed. Arindam Dutta (Cambridge, MA: MIT Press, 2013), 662–663.

4 Sebastiaan Loosen, "Mr. Dennis' Model. Organizing Knowledge in the Postcolonial Era," in this volume, 44–49.

"The fundamental concept of OXSYS [was] to replace the image of a building on paper with a readily accessible, easily manipulated image in a computer memory that can be analyzed, evaluated, and modified," summarized an ORHA brochure.[5] Curiously, while the computer system was for building design, it did not design anything per se. As OXSYS developer Paul Richens clarified, "its function [was] to collect design information from the design team."[6] This collection of information embodied what the ORHA brochure referred to as the image of a building in a computer, and it took material form as the software's database. However, the database did not describe just buildings. By structuring building data *and* ways to access and manipulate them, it described ways of working. This essay reads the database structure vis-à-vis its context of production to argue that OXSYS modeled the regional authority's practices more than its buildings. In doing so, the essay proposes a novel approach to studying historical software as *models of practices*. Such an approach invites attention to how computational systems produce operative representations of existing practices, embedding their directives and assumptions.[7]

5 Brochure "The Oxford Method" by the Oxford Regional Health Authority, 1975, Ed Hoskins' personal collection.

6 Paul Richens, "The OXSYS System for the Design of Buildings," in *CAD 78: Third International Conference and Exhibition on Computers in Engineering and Building Design, Brighton Metropole, Sussex, UK, March 1978* (Guildford: IPC Science and Technology Press, 1978), 633.

A Model of Building

When ORHA commissioned ARC to develop software for hospital design in 1970, it had already a method of prefabricated construction in place known as the Oxford Method. Since 1963, ORHA's architects had been formulating this construction system, outlining dimensional rules, a set of industrial building components, and standard construction details in numerous technical drawings on tracing paper.[8] Over a period of almost two decades, until the late 1970s, the regional authority had deployed the Oxford Method on more than fifty hospital designs.[9] Only a handful of those were created using OXSYS.[10] That is to say, the application of the Oxford Method did not rely on a computer system; the Method was already in use and financially beneficial for the authority. Yet, the vision of computerizing design and automating the production of voluminous construction documentation, promoted by the central government at the time as a way to modernize the bureaucratic state, was promising and aligned with the regional authority's already streamlined approach to design.[11] In this context, ARC took up the task of translating the Oxford Method into a computational system.

ARC's developers organized the software around two interconnected databases: the Codex and the Building File.[12] The Codex was a database of prefabricated components and their properties, such as dimensions, materials, and costs. The Building File combined the entire building description by associating three indices: the Codex with the geometry and the zone indices.[13] In this file structure, zones and components related to each other indirectly through the geometry index that resembled a three-dimensional framework consisting of cell records or, as the regional architects put it, "boxes of space."[14]

OXSYS' database structure was inventive for its time but not arbitrary. A closer look reveals that it was a careful and elaborate inscription of the three basic principles of the Oxford Method— rules of geometric coordination, a set of industrial components with predetailed assemblies, and predefined functional zones—into computer files. Much like the framework of OXSYS' geometry index, the Oxford Method was governed by an orthogonal tartan grid that provided "a strict dimensional discipline" describing at once room dimensions and building structure through spatial subdivisions.[15] In both building and

7 For the notion of "operative representation" see Michael S. Mahoney, "What Makes the History of Software Hard," *IEEE Annals of the History of Computing* 30 no. 3 (July 2008): 8–18. For a discussion about directives embedded in models see Matthew Hunter "Modeling: A Secret History of Following" in *Design Technics: Archaeologies of Architectural Practice*, eds. Zeynep Çelik Alexander and John May (Minneapolis: University of Minnesota Press, 2020), 45–70.

8 Arschavir, "Introduction to Health Building Seminar."

9 Ibid.

10 Printed pamphlet "Oxford Method / OXSYS questions," 1981, GB 160 H5/37/A2/11, Oxford Regional Health Authority Collection, Oxfordshire History Centre Archives.

11 For more on the computerization of government functions in the UK see, for example, Mar Hicks, *Programmed Inequality: How Britain Discarded Women Technologists and Lost Its Edge in Computing* (Cambridge, MA: MIT Press, 2017), and for hospital standardization efforts see Alistair Fair, "'Modernization of Our Hospital System:' The National Health Service, the Hospital Plan, and the 'Harness' Programme, 1962–77," *Twentieth Century British History* 29, no. 4 (December 1, 2018): 547–575.

computer systems, the grid framework held together hospital zones and building components. As for the prefabricated components and their assemblies, ORHA's handbook compared them to the kit of the construction toy Meccano, in which "there are a minimum number of pieces which can be assembled in a large variety of ways without having to detail these junctions each time."[16] The handbook further explained that the Codex was a "computerized catalogue" of the Oxford Method's construction kit. OXSYS's database was a digital model of the building method.

A Model of Practice

Beyond describing buildings in the computer memory, the database suggested possible ways to access and modify that description. The file structure allowed "two main routes [...] to describe the whole complex of the building," explained ARC's managing director, Ed Hoskins.[17] The "relational route" enabled the layout of the various functional zones such as hospital departments and rooms, while the "geometric route" allowed for the placement and retrieval of components within the three-dimensional grid framework. The "relational route" was handy at the stage of hospital planning when the building had no physical properties yet. The "geometric route" was pertinent for the dimensional coordination of all engineering systems and construction details. Together, these two operative routes construed building design as a planning and coordination exercise. More than design activities, planning and coordination are activities of managerial nature—ways of administering design and construction work.

Of course, the adoption of computer-aided design methods with OXSYS surfaced questions of work organization within ORHA. OXSYS development was a costly investment for the regional authority with uncertain outcomes. Questions of how the authority's architecture department would use and potentially benefit from it had to be addressed early on. To endorse the software's feasibility, ORHA's architects started framing its development as an opportunity to "re-structure the design process, and re-constitute the design team."[18] For the regional architects, the process of hospital design was a "merely complex" problem—it did not require any innovation, just the investigation of the best possible configuration to meet numerous technical requirements and the coordination of an immense amount of information.[19] By automating parts of the process, OXSYS would streamline planning and coordination and help the office strategically relocate their personnel resources around these two activities. As the software would assist the coordination of a multitude of data and parameters, a smaller team with diverse expertise to evaluate design options in early design stages would suffice.[20] If the Oxford Method had previously helped regulate construction, OXSYS would regulate design work.

The authority's discourse on OXSYS highlights the assumption underlying the database structure: for the software, hospital design *was* planning and coordination. However, this assumption predated its digital architecture; it was already entrenched in the systematic approach of the Oxford Method. By standardizing building components and construction details but allowing for variation in height and plan, the Method afforded a variety of hospital configurations within the discipline of the grid. This configurational flexibility corresponded to ORHA's administrative requirements. As a regional authority responsible for a relatively small region, ORHA needed

12 Ed Hoskins, "The OXSYS System," in *Computer Applications in Architecture*, ed. John S. Gero (London: Applied Science Publishers, Architectural Science Series, 1977), 357–363.

13 Bijl, Stone, and Rosenthal, *Integrated CAAD Systems*, 3-36–3-37.

14 D. J. Carter, "The Oxford Method Engineering Services System," in *Handbook*, 1976, GB 160 H5/37/A1/1, Oxford Regional Health Authority Collection, Oxfordshire History Centre Archives.

15 Ibid., GB 160 H4/13/A1/1.

16 Jon Gibbons, "Oxford Method Concepts," in *Handbook*, 1976, GB 160 H5/37/A1/1, Oxford Regional Health Authority Collection, Oxfordshire History Centre Archives.

17 Hoskins, "The OXSYS System," 360–361.

18 Jon Gibbons, "Designing Hospitals with Computers: The Effect of CAD on Design Management and Office Organization" in *CAD '80: 4th International Conference and Exhibition on Computers in Design Engineering, Brighton Metropole, Sussex, UK, March, 1980* (Guildford: IPC Science and Technology, 1980), 305.

19 Gibbons, "Oxford Method Concepts."

20 Gibbons, "Designing Hospitals with Computers," 302–303.

a limited number of healthcare facilities but with a wide variety of functional requirements and building scales.[21] The modular system of the Oxford Method was not just a construction strategy but a way to manage hospital building through a controlled variety. The translation of the Oxford Method to OXSYS database structure encoded the design and administrative practices of the regional authority *together* with the construction system. And while the building method already contained assumptions about work organization, its translation into computational terms made them explicit and operable. By structuring both data and operations, the software's database built (in) a model of practice.

21 Arschavir, "Introduction to Health Building Seminar."

Give Me Access!

On Models in Participatory Processes

Oliver Elser

1 Myriam Pflugmann, "Norman Foster: National Indoor Athletics Stadium, Waldstadion, Frankfurt am Main (unbuilt), 1981," in: *The Architectural Model. Tool, Fetish, Small Utopia*, Catalog Deutsches Architekturmuseum, eds. Oliver Elser, Peter Cachola Schmal (Zurich: Scheidegger & Spiess, 2012), 120–121.

Access can mean two things: Access to an otherwise closed area. Or, in a less spatial sense, access means the lowering of barriers to understanding.

An architectural model is considered more comprehensible than an architectural drawing. Lay people can imagine a building better from a model than from plans. Curators of architectural exhibitions love models because they know that their audience will respond to them with gratitude.

So the model per se is a "tool for access." But then why is there a need for a session called "Give me access!"? Isn't that an invocation of a self-evident fact?

In the movie "Zoolander" (USA, 2001), Ben Stiller stands in front of an architectural model. He doesn't understand it and shouts, "What is this? A center for ants?" Then he sweeps the model off the table, ponders for a moment, and then says that it must be at least three times as big so that children can be taught in it. The joke works so well because no one can imagine that someone could be so stupid as not to get the basic idea of an architectural model.

But it is precisely this self-evident fact that needs to be questioned. In the exhibition "The Architectural Model – Tool, Fetish, Small Utopia," which took place in 2012 at the Deutsches Architekturmuseum (DAM), the first chapter was therefore titled "Convincing and Deceiving." Every model, so the thesis goes, is supposed to provide a persuasive performance and must lie to do so. To put it a little more kindly: Certain aspects are hidden and others are emphasized.

Among other examples, a model of an Olympic stadium planned for Frankfurt from Norman Foster's workshop served as an example of a deliberate lie. In order to be able to show the delicate supporting structure of the roof, its covering of steel panels had been omitted.[1]

The session "Give Me Access!" aimed at the political dimension of a special category of architectural models whose goal is to communicate with non-experts. Maxime Zaugg describes how it took two attempts to convince the critical population of Paris by means of models of the new development of the former Les Halles (market halls) quarter in the 1960s and 1970s. The second decision-making process involved the use of endoscopes, an optical technique that allows people to immerse themselves in models and take the perspective of pedestrians. Detailed models of Romanian grocery stores were made by Ecaterina Stefanescu, who also recreated the homes of the store owners in a second step. In both cases, the objects serve to make the everyday lives of Eastern European migrants accessible—although anyone could also visit the original stores at any time. Deniz Avci-Hosanli and Cansu Degirmencioglu have devoted themselves to the extensive use of models in the transformation of Istanbul under Kemal Atatürk in the 1920s and 1930s. None survived in the original, but the contemporary media contain quite a few illustrated accounts of exhibitions where these compelling—or even overwhelming—models were on display. Tamar Zinguer showed the history of sandbox models in a parallel narrative: On the one hand, these served therapeutic purposes and were used in child psychology as early as the 19th century. At the same time, however, the military also used sandboxes to train officers, since battlefield planning based on maps alone did not offer enough clarity.

The model stories from Paris and Istanbul clearly show that accessibility is controlled by massive forces. In both cases, models serve a propaganda purpose. Participation is only feigned here. The Romanian grocery stores are not a work of manipulation, but rather a tricky experimental arrangement to make something private public by way of reproduction. A model of an apartment seems something less voyeuristic or intimate than would be the case if a photograph of the same situation were displayed in an exhibition space.

Asking for the conditions in whose interest the accessibility should actually be produced thus aims at politicizing the architectural model. It is not an innocent tool. And its use in planning processes is not to be understood a priori as participatory, that is, as good and right.

So, if you appreciate the architectural model for being a participatory tool, take a look at a picture by photographer Anja Niedringhaus. It is titled "Fallujah, Iraq, November 2004. Before starting their patrol in the early morning hours, American Marines of the 1st Division, 3/5, study the model of a neighborhood composed of bricks." The photo is held in the collection of the Museum für Moderne Kunst in Frankfurt am Main (MMK), among many other images of the photojournalist, who was murdered in 2014, at the age of 49, in Bhanda Khel, Afghanistan. The model here is a medium of attack and defense. It is about human lives in a war that at this point, in 2004, is already no longer based on retaliation for the terrorist attacks of September 11. At the time of the shot, the soldiers are highly concentrated on writing something down, each one individually. Are they making drawings of the model? Because this one is instructive but cannot be taken along on the upcoming patrol.

The question of the accessibility of models has another component besides the political dimension. In the field of architecture, there is a tendency to treat models as static objects and often to present them in exhibitions like sculptures. However, if models are to grant access, they must be taken down from their pedestals. They demand their context back! Many models were not intended to be showpieces, although they are now presented as such. To name just one of many examples: The 1975 model of the Multihalle by Carlfried Mutschler and Frei Otto is now one of the most valuable works in the DAM collection. Its value is conditioned by its rarity, as there is nothing comparable on this mayor work even in the Frei Otto collection at the saai in Karlsruhe. A considerable increase in value results from its fragility. The fine mesh of the hanging model is so fragile that the object may neither be lent nor moved at all. So it now stands in the display area of the depot. Yet it only shows half the truth. Gone, for example, are the many large-format cameras that were necessary to map the irregular roof geometry of what was probably the very first "blob" built, and thus to be able to build it at all.

Accessibility in this case would mean reconstructing the original "performance" of the model or at least proving through photos and drawings what it was once used for—so that it does not stand around in the depot, bereft of all traces of its history.

A view of the *Sergideki Istanbul* [Istanbul on Display] exhibition with models of the Eminönü area in the foreground, 1939. [V. Birson, "Sergideki Istanbul" [Istanbul on Display], *Istanbul Belediye Mecmuası* 15, no. 176–177 (July–August 1939)]

The Politics of Cutting and Gluing

Architectural Models as Propaganda in Early Republican Turkey

Cansu Degirmencioglu and Deniz Avci-Hosanli

Models as a Tool of Nation-Building

The state-initiated modernization of Turkey, which began in 1923, was driven by a sense of urgency to "catch up with the West." As Sibel Bozdoğan remarks, this led to a strong reliance on "the power of representation," especially through "visual and material culture to express modern ideas, institutional reform, national identity, and social progress."[1] New buildings with modernist tendencies and their visual representations—visibly differing from the bygone aesthetics of the late Ottoman period—became part of the visual repertoire of the new regime. One popular way to announce and promote changes in the built environment was to publicize architectural models of the new buildings. Accordingly, architectural models became politically charged media and conveyed the new state's messages to citizens via newspapers, magazines, as well as public exhibitions, which became interfaces of these encounters. The photographs of miniature models proudly illustrating "the things to come" became a go-to visualization tool for the early Republican press.

In addition to its political context, the widespread dissemination of model photographs was closely linked with the emerging parallelism between interwar architecture and mass media culture in Western modernity. The increasing popularity of architectural models as a means of visually representing new spatial concepts coincided with the emergence of architectural photography and its expanding circulation in print media. According to Davide Deriu, this form of visualization, resulting from the convergence of architecture and photography during this era, played a pivotal role in shaping the "image-repertoire of modernism."[2] Consequently, in the early Turkish Republic, photographs of architectural models acquired iconographic significance, serving not only as conveyors of new ideas but also as elements of modern visual culture.

1 Sibel Bozdoğan, "Introduction: Modernization, National Identity, and Visual Culture in Turkey," *The Journal of Decorative and Propaganda Arts*, no. 28, Turkey Theme Issue (2016): 7.

2 Davide Deriu, "The Architectural Model in the Age of Its Mechanical Reproducibility," in *Proceedings of the Second International Conference of the European Architectural History Network*, ed. Hilde Heynen and Janina Gosseye (Brussels: Koninklijke Vlaamse Academie van Belgie voor Wetenschappen en Kunsten, 2012), 166.

Exhibiting Models

In June 1939, the governor and mayor of Istanbul, Lütfi Kırdar, inaugurated "an exhibition to fully demonstrate the decadal development of the nation in the industrial field."[3] It was the 11th *Yerli Mallar Sergisi* (the domestic products exhibition), highlighted by the exhibit *Sergideki Istanbul* (Istanbul on Display), which showcased the contemporary renovations of Istanbul in architectural models. A prominent tool for national propaganda, such exhibitions had become spatial embodiments of Turkish modernization during the 1930s, and as Bozdoğan puts it, "showcases for modern architecture and republican public space" of the period.[4] They had various themes including industry, art, and public health, which held not only "cultural, pedagogical, and recreational significance"[5] but also displayed "a national pride to show the progress of the new nation."[6] The most iconic exhibitions of the early Republican period included Istanbul's domestic products exhibitions, the Izmir International Fair, and other exhibitions that were held at the Sergi Evi (Exhibition House) in Ankara. Architectural models were popular media in these events as they vividly displayed the upcoming changes, planned and executed by the state.

Based on the renovation plans of Istanbul prepared by urbanist Henri Prost, the models in "Istanbul on Display" were built by Hakkı Sait Tez, who was instructing model making courses at the Yüksek Mühendis Mektebi (School of Higher Engineering).[7] These models, some of which are visible in the image, represented the basic principles of the Prost plan, such as the opening of wide boulevards, the demolition of sheds around historical buildings, and the construction of modern units such as entertainment venues. In line with contemporary efforts to modernize the city's appearance, these models visualized not only the creation of the new Republican Istanbul but also the eradication of the so-called "outdated" Ottoman Istanbul. Moreover, the miniature models of the projected buildings such as Taksim Gazinosu (Municipality Club) and Kadıköy Halkevi (People's House), which belonged to the ruling party, symbolized the upcoming westernization of not only the building fabric but also the lifestyle of Istanbulites. The models and their public representations shared a sense of problematizing the old, either by ignoring the existing built fabric or by making visible the contrasts between the old and the new.

The exhibition was thus a tool to persuade the public to adapt to the new lifestyle and its new built environment. Because of a culture steeped in hundreds of years of history, such adaptation required systematic propaganda to familiarize the public with the interventions and changes in the existing built environment of their city. In a way, this was a demonstration of the state officials' "belief in the capacity of form to remake content."[8] This part of the exhibition attracted so much attention that as soon as the exhibition was closed, the models were transferred to the Izmir Fair welcoming both local and international audiences.

Reaching beyond the domain of architectural professionals, models engaged with the public through newspapers, popular publications, and thematic exhibitions held for the masses. The exhibitions were, in a sense, stages to enable the interactive participation of the audience—the public—, and the architectural models acted as political icons to consolidate the building power of the state in public opinion. When a model is not displayed to the public and only featured in a newspaper through a certain image and perspective, it projects the view of employers (state) and producers. The public only sees it from a designated angle, in line with the general function of

3 V. Birson, "Sergideki Istanbul" [Istanbul on Display], *Istanbul Belediye Mecmuası* 15, no. 176–177 (July–August 1939): 131.

4 Sibel Bozdoğan, *Modernism and Nation Building: Turkish Architectural Culture in the Early Republic* (Seattle: University of Washington Press, 2001), 137.

5 Ibid.

6 Ibid.

7 "Eminönünün Imar Projesi Maketi" [The Model of the Eminönü Development Project], *Akşam*, April 23, 1939; "Süleymaniye Camii Ile Civarının Alacağı Şekil" [The Future Shape of the Suleymaniye Mosque and Its Surroundings], *Cumhuriyet*, May 13, 1941.

8 Bozdoğan, "Introduction: Modernization, National Identity, and Visual Culture in Turkey," 7.

newspapers. Although it is also a pre-established setting, the model in the exhibition creates a more democratic and participatory environment, the layperson is invited to see and inspect the models as the ruling class does. As argued by architectural historian T. Elvan Altan, architectural models, when viewed and inspected from all angles, are effective in convincing the actors outside the architectural profession, such as employers and potential users, and in strengthening the public support for the state.[9] Hence, as a representation tool, the architectural model became an agent of "persuasion" through its utilization in various popular media that echoed the official voice of the time.

Photographing Models

After the inauguration of the exhibition in Istanbul, Kırdar's full opening speech was published in the municipality's journal, featuring many photographs of the models displayed, taken by "Foto Sabah."[10] Later, these photographs received further coverage in newspapers, which demonstrated that architectural models were mainstream in the popular culture of the young nation and part of the reformist iconography. Once a photograph of an architectural model was reproduced by thousands of newspapers and entered households, it was turned into an image that people were frequently exposed to in their daily lives. Even though it was reduced to two-dimensionality in photographs, the propagandistic potential of the model was invaluable for the reformist regime that invested in the power of the visual realm.

While popular periodicals reproduced and amplified the political power of architecture by putting the spotlight on architectural models, the exhibitions functioned as interactive spaces of encounter between the modernization ideology of the state and the citizens, playing their designated parts in the construction of the nation.

9 See T. Elvan Altan, "Mimarlık Tarihi Bağlamında Maket," in *Düşünme ve Görselleştirme Aracı Olarak Türkiye'de Mimari Maket | 20. Yüzyıldan Bir Kesit* (Istanbul: Pelin Derviş Yayın Projesi, 2020), 70–91.

10 Birson, "Sergideki Istanbul."

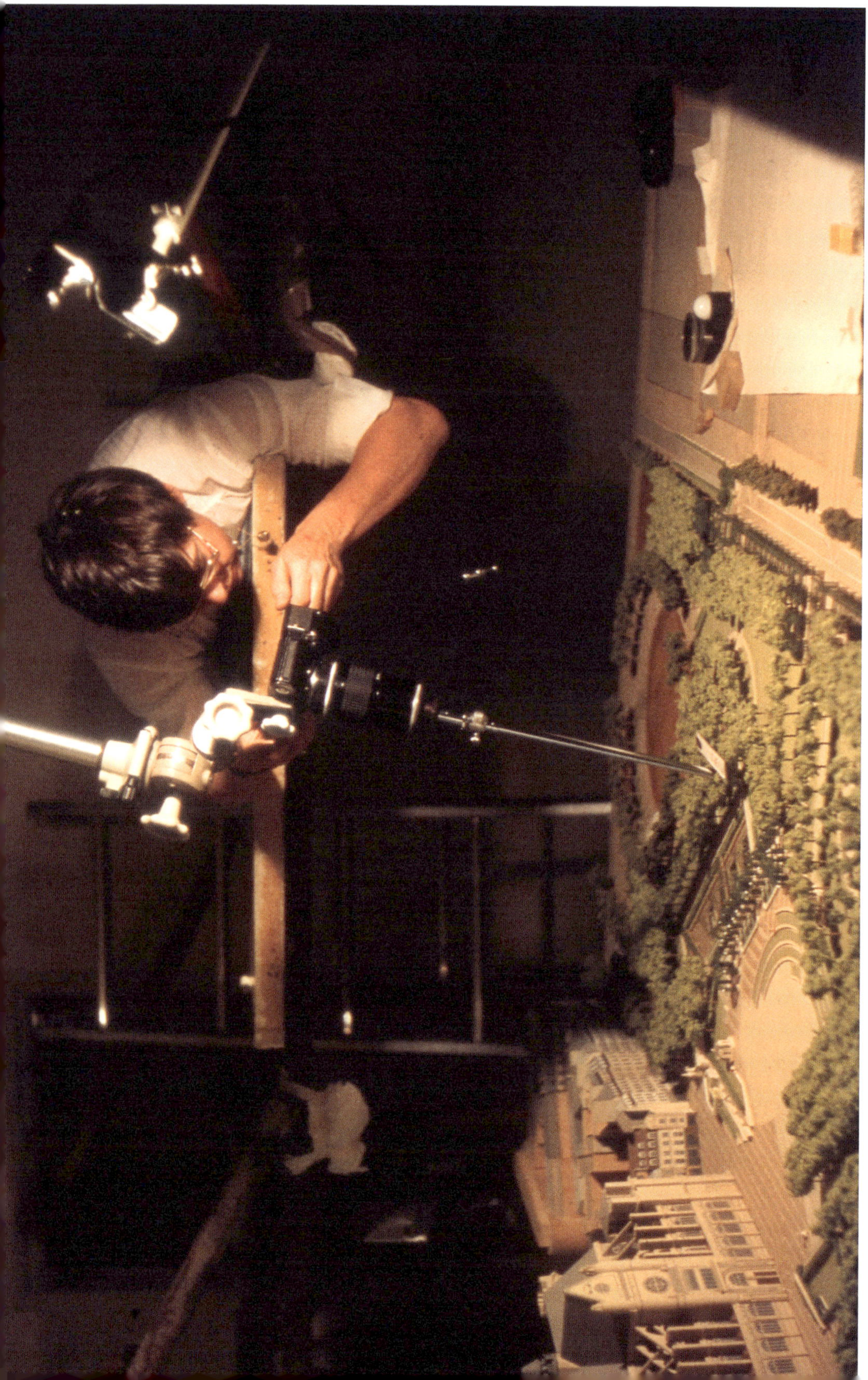

Jardin des Halles, Paris: view of the model being photographed with a Relatoscope by Françoise Masson, 1981. [Fonds Louis Arretche (1905–1991). Académie d'architecture/Cité de l'architecture et du patrimoine/Archives d'architecture contemporaine, file: 258 AA 244/1 (doc. SV-21-06-22-05)]

In the Eye of the Beholder

New Techniques of Representation for Public Urban Scale Models

Maxime Zaugg

Public Urban Models and Their Prosthetic Devices: Exploring the Example of Les Halles in Paris, 1968–1984

In late 1960s France, the urban scale model took on an important role as a mediating tool between experts, such as architects or urban planners, and the public. In 1968, in anticipation of the urban renewal of Les Halles, an exhibition was mounted to show the potential redevelopment options that had emerged from a competition, a competition that had not been presented to the public until then. Within the spectacular premises of the *Hôtel de Ville,* in the center of a high-ceilinged room, an intricate 1:500 scale model of the urban fabric of the first and second *arrondissement* of Paris was presented. The site of Les Halles was cut out of this larger "contextual" model, measuring approximately 4.50m by 3.00m—it was (quite literally) a hole, or *trou* in French—to enable the display of each competition proposal within its prospective urban surroundings. The citizens of Paris could stand close to the model, separated only by a thin railing, and look at the six designs as they were inserted successively into the larger model from below, using a specially designed lift. This lift heightened the cinematographic quality of the viewing experience, highlighting the differences between the individual proposals. The intense reaction that this display elicited from the Parisian public took the politicians and architects (who were not used to such pronounced user participation) by surprise. Following major public backlash and criticism of the participatory approach, as can be read in the local newspaper *Le Monde* of the time, the redevelopment of Les Halles was negotiated, and then renegotiated, over several years, involving new designs, ideas, and proposals that sought to address the public's demands.[1] Models remained key actors in this long, drawn-out process. In 1974, an important new phase began, when a second competition was launched for the redevelopment of the Les Halles project. Once again, models were used as part of the participatory process. However, having learned from the 1968 experience, the compositional and technological characteristics of the urban models were adapted to enhance their legibility to the untrained eye. This led to a change in the materiality of the models and the use of warm colors, with prominently pronounced greenery. Accessories such as small cars and humans enlivened the static model. However, it's worth considering whether the earlier exhibition's models from 1968 were misunderstood by

1 See: E. M. "'Il faut que les Parisiens nous disent ce qu'ils veulent' déclare M. Doublet," *Le Monde*, April 27, 1968. E. M. "Des associations d'habitants demandent que le Conseil de Paris révise ses méthodes de travail," *Le Monde*, May 30, 1969.

visitors, or whether they simply disagreed with the architects' radical proposals. If it's the latter, one could argue that the visual tweaks in the newer urban scale models were designed to subtly sway visitors to the side of the organizers and architects based on the visual presentation of the models.

The Relatoscopy: A New Technique for Urban Planning

With the rise of public participation in urban design in Europe from the 1960s onwards, the physical urban scale model became an essential mediator between professionals and the public in urban renewal projects and urban design competitions. However, the extent to which scale models communicate future or planned schemes and engage the public in urban discourses depends on a variety of factors. While technical properties such as scale, abstraction, composition, and materiality are important for the legibility of the urban scale model, the way in which the model is publicly displayed also influences its interaction with and accessibility to its audience, as seen in the public exhibitions in Paris. Furthermore, the agency of the urban scale model is also strongly influenced by various mediation techniques, including its photographic and cinematic representation in popular media, both print and television. Equally, the scenography in which an object is presented and the camera with which it is filmed have a significant impact. The ability of urban scale models to engage the public is influenced by the development and refinement of mediation techniques. In the case of Les Halles, scenographic methods were combined with photographic techniques, with the technique of "relatoscopy," to present these urban scale models more effectively to the public.

The introduction of relatoscopic techniques through the endoscope—a visual prosthetic device—allowed architects, photographers, and most likely technicians to take photographs at eye level, showing the project from the user's perspective. Derived from the medical technology of endoscopy, relatoscopy was first employed in architecture and urban design by architect Martin Schulz van Treeck in collaboration with photographer Françoise Masson.[2] The use of relatoscopy for model photography required considerable set-up around the model to get the right angles with the relatoscope. This meant that the scale models were often made specifically for the intended shots. For example, as can be seen in the image, part of the urban scale model on the right is missing because it wouldn't be in the shot, showing that the models were made and aligned specifically for the purposes of the relatoscope. Through this new technology, the ability of urban scale models to speak to a public, non-professional audience changed radically.[3] It eliminated the bird's-eye view, which showed the project in its wider urban environment, and instead restricted the audience's perspective to a single, partial viewpoint. In his text, *Les Nouvelles Techniques de Représentation en Architecture,* Van Treeck explicitly reflects on the relationship between relatoscopy and the public, arguing that it is the best tool to target, construct, and portray the "real" experiential moments of an architecture's future inhabitants.

The model images of the new proposed Les Halles projects shown to the public between 1974 and 1982 were often photographed with the relatoscope, also known as the "maquettoscope." They showed wide open public spaces and broad boulevards that connected the city to the gardens, allowing for Paris' signature monuments to

2 Martin Schulz van Treeck, *La relatoscopie, Les nouvelles techniques de représentation en architecture*, (Institut de l'environnement: CERA, 1974), 23–43. Martin Schulz van Treeck, "Möglichkeiten der Darstellung und Abklärung architektonischer Projekte," *DETAIL* no. 4 (July–August 1974): 636–642.

3 For more on the relationship between relatoscopy and the public, see: Martin Schulz van Treeck et al., *Die Relatoskopie* (Arras: Exhibition catalog, 1974), 19. For more on relatoscopy, see: Schulz van Treeck, *La relatoscopie, Les nouvelles techniques de représentation en architecture*, 23–43. Schulz van Treeck, "Möglichkeiten der Darstellung," 636–642. Martin Schulz van Treeck et al., *Die Relatoskopie*.

seamlessly blend into the new project. Concentrating mainly on the model's lush greenery, these images (and the project itself) were well-received, presenting a sharp contrast with the official Les Halles project that had repeatedly been criticized for its lack of human scale.

While this approximation of the experience of the citizens themselves increased the legibility of the model (and thereby the project) for a non-expert audience, it simultaneously made public opinion more vulnerable to manipulation, giving greater control to the architect in its representation. The exclusion of certain urban perspectives in favor of others is, of course, carefully orchestrated through rigorous scripting that prevents the audience from "roaming freely" through the model, especially given that, during this later phase of the Les Halles project, the urban scale models were no longer publicly displayed. While relatoscopy does not limit participation when used as an additional means to allow access to the model itself, when, as in the case of Les Halles, the physical models are no longer displayed, it is my supposition that it inherently allows for more control and manipulation of the perspectives conveyed. Despite its original aims, relatoscopy seemed to narrow the audience's perspective and reduce public participation in the urban renewal debate.

As stated earlier, relatoscopy had a major effect on the way in which the public was involved in urban planning discussions concerning the redevelopment of Les Halles. The shift in perspective—from a holistic experience of the projects in the 1968 exhibition to a more orchestrated, "relatoscopic" experience between 1974 and 1982—led to the eventual decline of the models' public character. This resulted in a paradox. Ironically, while the initial intention was to increase the public's engagement with the redevelopment of Les Halles, a new distance was, in fact, created between the model and the public. Through this newly created distance, the focus could be directed towards certain urban moments, while omitting others. This allowed for greater control over the production of spatial representation and provided a mechanism through which to undermine fundamental and multifaceted discussions with the public concerning the future of Les Halles. This manipulative form of communication between professionals and the public can be recognized as the precursor of computer-animated visualizations of urban projects that followed the digitalization of urban scale models in the 1990s, thus evidencing the origins of almost total representational control of built form by architects, planners, and its commissioners.

Romanian shop in Berlin (photograph of a 1:20 model), 2022. [Ecaterina Stefanescu / Estudio ESSE]

Rooms

Modeling Migrancy in the Context of Berlin

Ecaterina Stefanescu

The image depicts an ordinary space in Berlin, the shop floor of a Romanian supermarket seen from the storage space at the back. Like most diasporic shops, it sells an array of Romanian produce, meats, drinks, sweets, and other groceries to the large Romanian diaspora in the area. It is also a place where the Romanian language is spoken, and where the jokes, conversations, and references are understood by all. However, this is not a real Romanian shop; it is a photograph of a 1:20 interior model, measuring about 100 by 90 cm.

This project considers the model as a tool for observation, documentation, and engagement; a slow, durational method of artistic and ethnographic research. It describes and defines ethnographic model making as a methodology that encourages access from the point of view of inhabitants, viewers, and makers. The research has been undertaken by me as part of the Urban Nation Museum for Urban Contemporary Art—"Fresh AIR" artistic residency in Berlin between October 2021 and March 2022. Titled *Rooms*, the project looked at the Romanian immigrant community inhabiting the city, the spaces they occupy and appropriate, and the objects that they surround themselves with. The final artistic output included three models of Romanian immigrant spaces—the shop and two domestic interiors—which were exhibited as part of a group show at the Bülow90 Gallery in Berlin between March and July 2022.

Ethnographic Research

As an immigrant myself, I have experienced the transient position and the sense of loss inherent to this condition. I was born and grew up in Romania, but I have been living abroad for 12 years and have a complex and hard to define relationship with my country of origin. Moving around so much meant that it was very difficult to carry many personal belongings with me, so the way I maintained connection to my country was through foods and drinks, searching for Romanian shops everywhere I would go to get a taste of home. For most passers-by, however, the shop is a place of mystery, and the people frequenting it are sometimes the subject of denigration.

I started the project applying the ethnographic and situated actions I was familiar with, being part of the Romanian diaspora: as part of my project, I visited Romanian shops and cafés I was interested in using, meeting and conversing with people there, and of course, participating in the acts of consumption. I bought Romanian foods and sweets, and I met the owners and employees in these places as well as regular customers. Returning again and again, I started using site sketching, drawing, and surveying as ways to embed myself in the spaces further. This durational method allowed not only a deep observation and documentation of the spaces but also enabled further conversations and informal interviews with participants in the project.

As architect Lee Ivett writes, by "participating in many aspects of a place through the act of making," local insight is gained through first-hand experience.[1] Ivett advocates for a performative act of making, which situates the artist/researcher as a participant, allowing one to register not only the physical, material environment but also the behavior within that environment. While his practice relies on collaborative making, directly with participants, in my case, the act of making was individual and objective. Through this situated practice, however, the daily activities and rituals of the people working or using the shop slowly revealed themselves, and the importance of the shop not only as a commercial amenity but as a social and meeting hub for the Romanian diaspora becomes apparent.

1 "I am from Reykjavik," Lee Ivett, accessed October 16, 2022, https://www.iamfromreykjavik.com/portfolio-item/the-act-of-making/.

Migrancy and the Romanian Shop

Sociologist Maurice Halbwachs talks about the home and the space occupied by an individual as bearing their imprint, through furniture, decorations, and objects.[2] He identifies the importance of objects as symbols of stability for migrants, and the personal uncertainty occurring when one's surroundings change or move. By clinging to objects that trigger nostalgia, individuals long for a sense of stability.

Moreover, these individual material possessions also bind members of a group to the group.[3] For the Romanian diaspora, therefore, the Romanian Shop constitutes a spatial repository for their identity and sense of self in a foreign context. As emotionally charged items and artefacts trigger feelings of nostalgia in the individual, so does the shop, at the scale of the locality, act as a place for the consumption of memory for the diasporic group.

The model of the shop, therefore, is not only a representation of the place but of the liminal condition of the migrants and their strong feelings of nostalgia triggered by the shop itself. The first act of participation uses the model as an environment through and within which the lived experiences of migrants are communicated. The focus on the mundane minutiae of the items on sale validates and renders this condition tangible and reveals the value that migrants can place on objects and artefacts that help them maintain a connection to back home.

2 Maurice Halbwachs, *The Collective Memory*, trans. Francis J. Ditter, Jr. and Vida Yazdi Ditter (New York: Harper & Row, 1980), 128.

3 Ibid., 129–130.

Making

Gaston Bachelard talks about the condensing of value within miniatures; he suggests that the scaled-down version of the object is richer and more packed with insight than the real object.[4] Bachelard proposes that by creating something small and gazing at it, the insight and understanding generated would not be possible by simply studying the real thing. Because of this, spatial interior models of contested spaces offer the chance to instruct the lives within them. But more than that,

4 Gaston Bachelard, *The Poetics of Space*, trans. Maria Jolas (Boston: Beacon Press, 1994), 150.

the miniature in fact increases the importance and value of the object being depicted, revealing it as a "refuge of greatness."[5]

The reproduction of the space as a 1:20 interior model is therefore another form of analysis: through physically re-making the shop, I was forced to re-inhabit it, embedding myself in the lives of the people using it, acquiring tacit, implicit knowledge through the process of making, as historian Ralf Liptau describes.[6] This represents the second act of participation, for the maker, through this deep involvement in the lives of the community I am depicting.

The level of insight amassed—about the visitors, the owner, people working there, as well as about the Romanian community as a whole—, by manually constructing the space and all the items within, could not be replicated by simply observing or documenting the space in two dimensions. And this necessarily takes a long time: the model of the shop took two months to build. Moreover, colored paper was chosen because of its tactile potential to simulate objects closely, but with a level of abstraction still present. Paper's fragility also conceptually denotes the transience and instability inherent in the migrants' condition, while the scale—1:20—is small enough to allow for the whole space to be modeled, but large enough for details to be captured and atmosphere recreated in a realistic way.

5 Ibid., 155.

6 Ralf Liptau, "R is for Representation," in *An Alphabet of Architectural Models*, eds. Olivia Horsfall Turner, Simona Valeriani, Matthew Wells, Teresa Fankhänel (London: Merrell, 2021), 82.

The Model

The public is encouraged to occupy and immerse themselves in the "ethnographic place" of the model by viewing it from multiple directions.[7] In this way, a third act of participation takes place, as the model becomes a dissemination tool for external observers. The miniature requires from its maker patience and, according to Bachelard, love.[8] The care and attention employed in the painstaking making of the models for *Rooms* implies an engagement and observation that goes beyond the ordinary. Therefore, the deep contemplation and empathy that is required of viewers through the extreme level of detail demands attention for the usually unfamiliar space itself and is intended to advocate for the lived realities of the individuals and the community depicted. The public becomes interested in the place and the lives contained in a way that they would not be if confronted with the real shop.

The photograph of the model then introduces an uncanny ambiguity, adding to the experience of participation by directing the gaze of the external viewers, instructing them on the most empathetic way of looking at the space: from within the model at eye level, embodying the real users of the space.

7 Sarah Pink terms the representations of theory, research, and reflections of a real place that are communicated to others in visual form as "ethnographic places." Sarah Pink, *Doing Sensory Ethnography*, (London: SAGE, 2009), 42.

8 Bachelard, *The Poetics of Space*, 159.

The Method

Rooms demonstrates the use and appropriateness of a novel ethnographic model making methodology within the study of marginalized communities. By "miniaturizing" the contested, transitory immigrant space, the maker comes to understand the space and the objects intimately and by making the art object by hand, gets to participate in the lives of the individuals and the community depicted.

This project and methodology can have wide applications in the field of participation in architecture and community engagement, as the ethnographic model offers simultaneous forms of access, as an environment through which participants can communicate their lived experiences; by the process of 'learning through doing;' and by engaging external viewers with the spaces and people represented. The Romanian shop in Berlin acts as a trigger and a vessel for the Romanian diaspora's consumption of nostalgia. Modeling the mundane of the space, furniture and produce reveal it as an object of atmosphere and beauty, that recognizes, acknowledges, and brings value to the feelings experienced by the community and their lived realities in this liminal, transitory condition. The visual ethnographic research and dissemination methods of the model encourage participation through the documentation of the real space and the creation of the "ethnographic space" for external viewers. This situates the model as a tool for observation and engagement, and describes the potential of ethnographic model making as a mode of practice to encourage access and elevate the existence of people and place.

Two young blind students stand by the window, their hands immersed in sand, 1892. [Courtesy of Perkins School for the Blind Archives, Watertown, MA]

Hands in Sand

Modeling (Inner and Outer) Landscapes

Tamar Zinguer

In 1892, two young blind students stood by the window, their hands immersed in sand. They were trying to form a volcano, judging from the mountain's shape and its mouth. At the Perkins Institute in Massachusetts, the oldest school for blind people in the United States, some lessons would first take place outside. The children would go on a walk, touch the terrain, feel the topography, then, back in the class, would attempt to precisely recreate their impressions of the land.

A *Boston Daily Globe* article told the story of five-year-old Tommy Stringer in 1891, Helen Keller, age eleven and a student at Perkins, had organized a fundraiser to support his schooling. Tommy, the article said, was "fascinated with the study of geography through the medium of sand."[1] He first represented the kindergarten grounds and its buildings in sand, then the adjoining streets and its homes, gradually modeling the entire neighborhood in sand and naming the streets of Jamaica Plains, expanding to include areas of South Boston, and their respective geographic locations. His teacher was convinced he could find his way around the neighborhood alone. To comprehend larger landforms, Tommy and other children would touch precise relief models of mountain chains and entire continents from the school's collection, which they then reproduced in sand. At the Perkins Institute, already at the turn of the century, before the advent of flight and global travel, children would grasp their place in the world and mold lands of possibilities.

Even before the study of elements of geography by touch was deemed necessary for the students at Perkins to find their grounding, Johann Heinrich Pestalozzi (1746–1827), in *ABC der Anschauung* (*ABC of Sensory Perception*) (1803), broke visual impressions of the world down to line segments, simplifying the multitude of images impacting young pupils, providing them with simple tools to recreate those views in drawing. Friedrich Froebel (1782–1852), student of Pestalozzi and inventor of the kindergarten, put crystalline solids in the hands of children, educating them to accurately gauge their *Anschauung*—or sense impression—of nature in three-dimensional form. While there were different approaches to touch as a didactic method, by the end of the 19th century, many blind schools had accumulated collections of objects for students, emphasizing tactility as an important source of learning. Samuel Neil, rector of the blind school in Edinburgh, called for an organization of such object lessons,

1 "Darkness to Light. Wonderful Work at Blind Kindergarten," *Boston Daily Globe*, February 12, 1897, in *Perkins Institution Scrapbook of Clippings*, vol. 15, March 1896–April 1897, 126.

that would distinguish tactile qualities such as texture, weight, and temperature. He advocated the development of an "ABC of touch sensations," an "Anschauung" of touch that would help reconstruct exterior objects distinctly in the mind.[2] The touch of sand, pliant and moldable, presented the world as a place that was flexible, accommodating, and with potential for change.

Ingraining a haptic connection to one's place was an aspiration of the pedagogical theories of Zonia Baber (1862–1956), the first woman Professor of Geography in the United States, at the University of Chicago. A pioneer of progressive education, she also emphasized touch and experimented with these methodologies by teaching geography with sand. In 1896, she patented a Sand Desk, whose wooden writing surface could lift to reveal a box, lined with zinc, inside of which the student could model topographies in moist sand. Throughout her career, Baber championed sand. In 1916, she spoke at a public hearing in Chicago in favor of the Indiana Sand Dunes to become a National Park, claiming that this place, where for years she had taken kindergarten children and graduate students alike, had the unique potential to inform students of the alphabet of nature, because of the special dynamic interaction between wind and sand. Her idea of holding sand in one's desk intimated this thought that the fluid patterns and formations accessed through touch—seen with one's hands—may leave a bigger imprint than a two-dimensional image of vast lands.

The concept of geographical imagination was also engaged by Margaret Lowenfeld (1890–1973), a medical doctor, who opened the Clinic for Nervous and Difficult Children in London, where, skeptical of language, she developed a playful technique based on nonverbal communication. There, since 1927, a tray of sand had become the ground for the construction of scenes by children, in a therapeutic setting. Lowenfeld would start a session by parting the sand in two, a river flowing in the middle, she explained to the child, where adults presumably lived on one shore and children on the other. Presented with a multitude of miniatures, such as figurines, animals, small houses, everyday objects, and imaginary creatures, the children populated the land and shifted the sand around. Spontaneously, she recalled, without her intervention, a technique developed, created by the children themselves, who repeatedly called their creations in the tray "the world." Jungian psychoanalysts adopted the World Technique, which allowed the player to concretize inner images and experiences, following Carl Gustav Jung, who wrote in 1916 that "often it is necessary to clarify a vague content by giving it a visible form... Often the hands know how to solve a riddle with which the intellect has wrestled in vain."[3] In trays full of sand, children, agents of change, would give shape to their wished-for social revolutions.

Until the end of the 20th century, armed battles—world wars even—were enacted on sand tables in preparation for actual deployment on land. In 1811, Prussian nobleman Georg Leopold von Reisswitz (1764–1827) invented a strategy game, *Kriegsspiel*, or *War Game*. On a bed of sand, modeling a terrain at a scale of approximately 1:2000, enemy armies could deploy forces, perform battles, endure casualties and loss of equipment—all enacted with place markers and wooden pawns. *Kriegsspiel* caught the attention of King Wilhelm III, when his sons then aged 14 and 16 asked their tutor to install the game in the Berlin castle. Von Reisswitz declined a private audience with the king, claiming he could not present his royal highness with mere sand. Nevertheless, the game became a popular training tool,

2 Jan Eric Olsen, "Models for the Blind," *Interdisciplinary Studies in the Long Nineteenth Century* 19 (2014): 7. http://19.bbk.ac.uk.

3 Carl Gustav Jung, *Collected Works Volume 8: Structure and Dynamics of the Psyche* (Princeton: Princeton University Press, 2014), 86.

educating troop leaders to confront the enemy's distribution of cavalry, artillery, and infantry units. Full-scale exercises in the field were very costly, limited in space and time, and difficult to undertake in winter. Most of all, planned maneuvers excluded the most important factor of real battle—the unknown, which was part of the chaos of any war. Having two teams engage in a game with rules yet without a premeditated plan added an element of chance; hence, *Kriegsspiel* became a tool to evaluate the decision-making acumen of officers poised to advance to higher levels.

The sand table, affording a bird's eye view of the terrain, entrenched the view of the topography in the minds of the soldiers who would spend most of the war in trenches. As Helmut Puff wrote, "certain vehicles of the imagination have the potential to catapult humans into a sovereign position, if only for a moment, allowing beholders 'to see the world' from an elevated perspective."[4] The use of topographical models in sand persisted well after aerial photography became available. And while these military preparations at the sand table anticipated a great tragedy and loss of life, the huddling of men around the wooden frame of a box of sand was reminiscent of instances of play and camaraderie inside the sandbox. War and play are related, wrote Johan Huizinga in his pre-World War II *Homo Ludens* (1938), as "[i]ndeed, all fighting that is bound by rules bears the formal characteristics of play by that very limitation."[5] Equal adversaries engage each other, common rules of behavior on the ground prevail, leading him to write that "[p]lay is battle and battle is play."[6] However, what could not be reenacted in battle was the reversibility of a war game: inside the sand table, a soldier could die over and over again.

Sand—the material—is porous, fluid, and malleable and allows for erasure and reversibility. With the slightest movement or wind, sand shifts. A model made of sand will always move and erode but will not tear nor break apart. It is not divisible in equal parts, nor is it ever precise. The tactile model in sand presupposes change, it is a model whose main referent is change. In a pre-digital era, this model could elicit constantly shifting conditions. Models of sand bridge the realm of what exists and what is imagined; they can seem authentic for both real landscapes and landscapes of the mind. Those models represent both outside and inside and conform to what Donald Winnicott has described as the "intermediate space of experience," a space of in-between, between the inner subjective world and the outer world that is objectively perceived. Just like the space of play, the sand table is a place in which inner life and external reality both participate.

Landscapes of sand are associated with play, but sands are also known to bury and hide; they suggest oblivion and death—burial grounds. In 1947, two years after the bombing at Hiroshima and Nagasaki and a year after his father's death, Isamu Noguchi (1904–1988) created a model in sand, called "To be seen from Mars." The thirty-centimeter square model is long gone, but an image remains of what was to be a ten-mile-long face of a man, to be seen from outer space, that was to attest to the humanity of Earth's inhabitants. The sand tables present sites of conflict—war, inner turmoil, the vision of a blind person confronted by a seeing eye—, but they are also sites of mediation. With hands submerged in sand, as solid structures flow and transform in search of the perfect model, we try to hold on to time, which, just like sand, is fleeting.

4 Helmut Puff, *Miniature Monuments: Modeling German History*, (Berlin and Boston, MA: De Gruyter, 2014), 174.

5 Johan Huizinga, *Homo Ludens: A Study of the Play-Element in Culture*, (Boston, MA: Beacon Press, 1955), 89.

6 Ibid., 41.

What the Hell Happened to Me?

On the Afterlife and Decay of Models

Teresa Fankhänel

1 Oliver Elser, "On the History of the Architectural Model in the 20th Century," in *The Architectural Model. Tool, Fetish, Small Utopia*, eds. Oliver Elser and Peter Cachola Schmal (Zurich: Scheidegger & Spiess, 2012), 11–22.

2 Walter Grasskamp, "Sentimentale Modelle," *Kunstforum International*, no. 2 (1980): 54–79.

3 A sample of recent case studies looking at individual historical models: Oliver Elser and Peter Cachola Schmal, eds., *The Architectural Model. Tool, Fetish, Small Utopia* (Zurich: Scheidegger & Spiess, 2012). Ralf Liptau, *Architekturen bilden: Das Modell in Entwurfsprozessen der Nachkriegsmoderne* (Bielefeld: transcript, 2019). Teresa Fankhänel, *The Architectural Models of Theodore Conrad. The 'Miniature Boom' of Mid-Century Modernism* (London: Bloomsbury, 2021). Matthew Wells, *Modelling the Metropolis. The Architectural Model in Victorian London* (Zurich: gta Verlag, 2022). David Lund, *A History of Architectural Model Making in Britain. The Unseen Masters of Scale and Vision* (London: Routledge, 2022).

4 Teresa Fankhänel, "Getting Comfortable with Loss," in: *Neue Nachbarn. Einblicke ins Archiv*, eds. Mariann Juha and Andres Lepik (Munich: Architekturmuseum der TUM, 2022).

When you google "architectural + model + destroyed," two of the first search results are YouTube videos in which architecture students delight in stepping on or dropping their meticulously fabricated miniatures. Other acts of violence against architectural models include rolling over them with your car, lighting them on fire, submerging them in water, shooting them with a crossbow, or having them eaten by a pet. Once you begin to think about it, there are innumerable ways to lose a model.

Models are rarely created to outlast their initial utility. To students, they are an exercise; to architects, they are a design tool and a means of communicating their work; to curators they are a medium of display. After their initial utility ends, they can become mementos or trophies;[1] they can be contractual items or ideal versions of reality;[2] they can be prized collectibles or traveling ambassadors of a design collection.

But, more often, they become deteriorating hinderances that occupy prime office real estate. In the realm of museums and collections, models are equally a challenge. Aging materials or fragile structural conditions never meant to be preserved are as much a threat to the objects as are accidents, infestation, or the occasional deaccession long after they have entered a collection. While research in the last decades has begun to uncover model histories of the recent past—of the 20th century especially[3]—much remains to be studied, not least because the farther back one looks, the fewer models there are. The passage of time leads to an exponentially decreasing number of surviving specimens.

Studies on the afterlife and decay of models uncover the opposite: the many ways in which models continue to exist after their initial purposes have been fulfilled. When the dust settles, models enter their afterlife; they endure on shelves in offices, are tucked away in basements, or proudly paraded behind glass in archives or museums. Others are stored virtually on hard drives. Some models survive by accident, losing the context of their making; others may take on a new role as (material or digital) spolia. Larger models, such as model parks or cities, might become ruins themselves or survive outside the controlled spaces of archives. Each model's materiality ultimately plays a decisive role in its fate: the resilience of glue and paper presents vastly different challenges than the upkeep of a digital model.[4] The preservation of models often includes an attempt to conserve not just material constructs or geometric shapes but sensorial and spatial insights of models past.

The contributions in this section examine the changing status of models as objects of value and the multifaceted reasons for why models are either archived or lost, restored or destroyed, filed away, exhibited, or reused. Three papers look at groups of physical models: Stéphanie Quantin-Biancalani explores French architect Paul Andreu's series of seven spherical exhibition models, Stefanie Brünenberg and Kai Drewes study public buildings and housing projects from the former German Democratic Republic, and Christiane Fülscher assembles student models made of the Weissenhof Siedlung in Stuttgart—whose original context has dissolved and can be reestablished only through meticulous research in order to find the future potential for the remaining objects. The authors dissect how the act of reimagining an object's or a collection's utility through positioning them in a new context can become a creative force. They ask how models could be regarded as spatial resources for a lost built environment and look for ways in which the disappearance of a collection could be compensated by reimaging or reassembling its original context. Each object's materiality informs the research and ultimately foreshadows what might be lost of physical models if they were to be digitized and the viewer relegated to a digital three-dimensional version of the object on a screen. A third contribution by Daniel Cardoso Llach examines how the reconstruction of born-digital models, which are no longer accessible because of the ephemeral nature of their early digital technology, can add new insights to our understanding of the original model's programmed context. It explores digital modeling as an archeological challenge and software and its underlying design strategies themselves as models for architectural thinking at large. Here, questions of sensorial and experiential reconstruction of not just the soft- but hardware merge with technological questions of what it means to reconstruct or recreate an "original" digital work in today's programming environments.

Common to all is a desire to show how the salvage or loss of models can affect the architectural histories we build and the stories we tell about architectural design, thinking, and culture. They ask which histories are edited out and why. To move beyond established certainties of architectural historiography, cracks in physical models, the fragmented nature of records, or the loss of a model's original environment and context are no longer just occasions to be lamented. They present singular opportunities to dig deeper and uncover mechanisms of model and world making that were hitherto hidden underneath an individual model's exterior or inside the intricate processes of modeling the very concept of model making itself.

Exhibition *The Metamorphosis of the Circle*, curated by Serge Salat, Asia, 1991. [Archives d'Aéroports de Paris]

Crossing and Transformation

About Paul Andreu's Sphere Models

Stéphanie Quantin-Biancalani

In 2021, an ensemble of architectural models by French architect and engineer Paul Andreu (1938–2018) was donated to the Cité de l'architecture et du patrimoine in Paris. Andreu was one of the major figures of the architectural scene in the second half of the 20th century. He started his career in 1963 as an engineer at Aéroports de Paris, then a public company dedicated to the management and construction of airports. At the age of twenty-nine, he was entrusted with the design of Terminal 1 of the Roissy-Charles de Gaulle Airport (1967–1974), thus becoming a prominent expert of airport architecture on a global scale. In 2002, he left the company to open his own studio after winning the competition for the Grand National Theater in Beijing (1998–2007) and made a rich career as an independent architect, especially in Asia where he was among the few French to make a mark.

One of the donated models was a mysterious sphere representing the Crater (1991–1995), a circular ascent via double escalators in an underground square in La Défense, lit by a large light well and connected to the very epicenter of the project, below the Grande Arche. This item shared many similarities with another spherical model from the collection of the FRAC Centre, which represented the central void of Terminal 1 at Roissy-Charles de Gaulle Airport, the very soul of the architecture, the symbolic beginning of the flight. The two objects had the same shape, dimensions, materials (plexiglass, plastics, metal), and concept. This comparison triggered an encounter with the former model maker, who had a photo of the original display, and research in the company archives of Aéroports de Paris.[1]

History and Symbolics

This model was made during a favorable period in Paul Andreu's career, when he was expanding in Asia in the late 1980s and early 1990s. Between 1987 and 1988, he took part in and won a decisive competition: the basic design for Kansai International Airport. At a time when the Japanese construction market was closed to foreign competitors and powerfully coveted by the American industry, Andreu's victory had a strong political and economic dimension, so much so that the French Prime Minister, Jacques Chirac, wrote to the president of Aéroports de Paris to congratulate the architect.[2] However, Japanese authorities

1 Archives of Aéroports de Paris, 2000388-6; 2000388-7.

2 Letter from Jacques Chirac, Prime Minister, to Bernard Lathière, President of Aéroports de Paris, March 28, 1988. Archives d'ADP, 2012341-1.

later decided to launch an international competition from which Andreu was excluded. Aéroports de Paris, as design engineering office, was credited the basic design. Renzo Piano's winning project outshone Andreu's earlier design as a complex 25-million-passenger airport that was supposed to be built on a 500 hectare artificial island. In 1993, Andreu was awarded the commission for the Maritime Museum in Osaka (1993–2000), whose bold architecture had the same spatial characteristics as Terminal 1 of Roissy-Charles de Gaulle Airport and the Crater of La Défense: a long and narrow underground tunnel, running under the sea, led to the main museum gallery, a circular and high glass dome, bright and semi-transparent, where the *Naniwa Maru*, a real-size replica of a ship of the Edo period, was to be displayed. In 1991, he took part in the competition for an airport in Hiroshima; the same year, a private Japanese client also asked him to design a resort including hotel, apartments, and a golf course in Kumihama Bay, in the northeast of Kyoto.

In this very favorable context, a series of touring exhibitions on his work was organized in 1991 and 1992, mostly in Japan. Hosted by the French cultural institutes, they were on display in Osaka, Kyoto, Tokyo, Seoul, Hong Kong, Taipei, Beijing, and then back in France.[3] The show was produced by Aéroports de Paris, clearly serving communication and commercial purposes. As Andreu's team was trying to conquer the Japanese market, the exhibition was supposed to be an advertisement for the company's expertise. The concept was conceived by Serge Salat, a chief engineer and a close co-worker of Paul Andreu. The show was entitled *The Metamorphosis of the Circle*, as was the exhibition catalog, one of the first monographs on Paul Andreu,[4] which was written by Salat together with Françoise Labbé. Despite the official context, this exhibition had an unexpected conceptual meaning. The series of models was designed by Philippe Cesse, the professional model maker of Aéroports de Paris. It included four spherical models measuring 60 centimeters in diameter and one square model, each set on an aluminum structure and a green marble base. The layout designed for a 100 to 150 square-meter space also included seven scanachromes (photographic enlargements as silkscreen prints on canvas) and 22 framed montages of Andreu's architecture.

These architectural projects, including Terminal 1 of Roissy-Charles de Gaulle Airport, the Transmanche (French terminal of the Channel Tunnel), Hiroshima Airport, and the Sea Sphere, were not necessarily the most famous; some were representations of parts of a project; some were not even built. The model of the Crater was left unfinished as the model maker was unable to complete it before the opening of the show in 1991. But all of them were about transformation, passages, transitions, from earth to air, from shadow to light, from west to east. Paul Andreu's architectures always had a strong spatial symbolism, with dark underground and narrow passageways leading to high circular volumes, dramatized by the expansion of space and the choreography of light. Circles were quite often the mark of the thresholds. Aluminum structures evoked an ancient astronomical instrument, the armillary spheres, which were designed to mimic celestial spheres in order to show the movement of the sun and the stars around the Earth. Moreover, models would occupy the center of the room, and its axis commanded the hanging of the scanachromes and the montages. As presentation models, these spheres were a crystallization of Andreu's work: like alchemy they encapsulated the very essence of his architecture—transitional spaces, passages, and movement—and distilled it in a very expressive way.

3 File of the exhibition *Metamorphosis of the Circle*, 1991. Archives d'Aéroports de Paris, 2000388-6.

4 Serge Salat and Françoise Labbé, *Paul Andreu. Métamorphoses du cercle* (Paris: Electa Moniteur, 1990).

A few years later, according to an undated inventory of Aéroports de Paris' models,[5] three spherical models were added, probably for another promotional exhibition abroad. Two identical ones represented the Kumihama Springs, whose aim was to integrate the building into the landscape. Paul Andreu attempted to "chop off" the top of the hills to rebuild them organically with architecture and blur the lines of the buildings in the shapes of the landscape. Another model showed a bird-like beacon, one of twelve blue-lit structures powered by solar energy, that would draw a circle with a 12 kilometer diameter on the coast of Kumihama. Like land art, no one would see the twelve lit beacons at one glance, but only part of them, as "the full circle would have existed only in the memory and the imagination of people."[6] The lesson learned in Japan was first and foremost the lesson of landscape that would matter increasingly in the work of Paul Andreu during the second part of his career. Once again, the spherical shape of the models reflected the conceptual importance of these projects and symbolized the renewed connection between his architecture and earth.

Reactivating Historical Models

In the course of their afterlife, these spherical models were modified or disappeared: they lost their metallic arches and bases, sometimes even one half of the sphere. Their history was unknown and their original meaning forgotten: they were considered individual pieces, without links between them. Research enabled to identify and locate most of them: one is in the collection of the FRAC Centre, two are held in the collection of the Musée national d'art moderne – Centre Pompidou, while one is in the collection of the Cité de l'architecture et du patrimoine. Two are part of private collections. One is known from a different and lower-quality version at the Centre Pompidou, and one is missing.

In the context of an upcoming exhibition on Paul Andreu in 2024, the goal is to reenact the connection between these models and reactivate their symbolism by means of a renewed spatial installation. The overall design, including the scanachromes and montages, has disappeared and there would be no point in rebuilding it today. The marble pedestals and the aluminum structures have also got lost. However, the 2024 show will reunite the sphere models, hang them from the ceiling, and connect them with two key installations of the show: dated from 1969 to 2018, the 69 notebooks of the architect, which motivated a thorough research on Paul Andreu's corpus of work and tell the whole genesis of his major projects, will be displayed as the backbone of the exhibition, as a story of creation. A collection of quotes, as Andreu had such a strong relationship to literature and wrote many essays as well as fiction, will create a parallel narrative about his architecture. Historical research will be developed through plans and archives in distinct side parts of the exhibition. The spatial symbolics of the spherical models does not serve a unilateral celebration of Andreu's work but a hermeneutic approach: models, sketches, and writings will give a comprehensive insight into Paul Andreu's design process, while archives will provide a contextualized and documented overview of his work in architectural history.

5 Inventory of models, model studio of PK (Architecture and Engineering Department), Aéroports de Paris, Orly, n.d. Archives d'Aéroports de Paris, 2000388-6.

6 Conference, Osaka, May 10, 1995. Collection d'architecture moderne et contemporaine, Cité de l'architecture et du patrimoine.

Two interior views of one building: on the left, the model of the rebuilt Schauspielhaus in Berlin—created for an exhibition—and on the right, an alternative design for the interior of the main hall, 1987. [IRS Erkner, Scientific Collections, E5-04 and E5-13]

How to Use Architectural Models

Connecting Archive and Research

Stefanie Brünenberg and Kai Drewes

Architectural models provide insights into the past, into alternative spatial concepts, and into an idealized built environment. In the scientific collections of the IRS in Erkner, there are models that illustrate these three characteristics in a special way: The architectural models of the GDR show spatial situations that no longer exist today, that were never built, or that were realized differently. The illustration shows two models of designs for the stage of the rebuilt Schauspielhaus at Gendarmenmarkt in Berlin. The exhibition model was made by a model workshop of the Building Academy of the GDR. The other presents a previously unknown alternative design, which highlights the possibilities of research but also the limits of archiving.

In the GDR, models—from architectural models to scaled-down agricultural implements—generally had a great relevance. This is shown by numerous documentations of exhibitions and political events at which the "construction of the socialist state" was demonstrated with the help of models,[1] as well as by contemporary newspaper reports in which model photos were shown to strengthen the public visibility of planning projects.[2]

Only few original models from the GDR have survived. A major reason for this is undoubtedly that a lot of models were destroyed around 1990 in the course of the rapid dissolution of East German offices and companies. For many models, the space they took up was the reason for their loss. A large number of models was likely also disposed of during the GDR era. This may have been partly due to changes in architectural policy—for example, the replacement of socialist classicism in favor of industrial building. However, it must be assumed that many models, especially larger ones, only existed for brief periods of time because of a lack of space.

1 Compare for example: *Architektur und bildende Kunst: Zum 20. Jahrestag der DDR im Bezirk Potsdam* (Potsdam, 1969).

2 For some examples see: "So wird es an der Stalinallee Ecke Bersarinstraße Ende 1955 aussehen," *Neues Deutschland*, November 12, 1954; Rei., "Neuer Omnibushof der BVG," *Neues Deutschland*, January 6, 1964; rdt, "Sowjetische Baumaschinenausstellung in Berlin," April 24, 1959, *Ein neuer Beweis deutsch-sowjetischer Freundschaft*, 253.

3 Allgemeiner Deutscher Nachrichtendienst, "Tanzpalast aus Hirnholzklötzen, Leim und Gips," November 10, 1954, Bild 183-27387-0001, Bundesarchiv.

4 Perhaps the only exception was a company in Leipzig which made a model for Berlin's city. "Ein Leipziger baut Berlin auf," *Neues Deutschland*, April 18, 1985.

Building Architectural Models in the GDR

State-run model workshops were responsible for the construction of architectural models: In the 1950s, one such workshop is documented, which was directly subordinate to the Ministry of Construction;[3] in addition, most of the district-owned planning offices likely had their own model making facilities and staff. Privately run modeling firms, on the contrary, were not envisaged in the socialist labor system.[4] Particularly for exhibitions and research, the German Building

Academy (Deutsche Bauakademie), as the GDR's most important research institution, operated at least one model workshop from the 1950s onwards.

By the 1980s at the latest, the Institute for Urban Planning and Architecture (Institut für Städtebau und Architektur, ISA) of the Building Academy had its own model workshop. It enjoyed a good reputation and carried out commissions for other GDR building institutions and even for clients in West Germany. In 1981/1982, a new building was planned and erected for the ISA model workshop and its model film simulation facility at Wallstraße in Berlin-Mitte.[5] In the last years of the GDR, according to personnel lists, a total of about a dozen people were employed in this branch of the institute, including four model makers and a technical assistant.[6] The department bore the name "Video Simulation" and was headed by architect Dr. Gerd Priese. The head of the model workshop since 1975 was Hans-Günter Zechert, a trained foundry model maker.[7] The most important models of the workshop that still exist include a detailed model of the Zeiss Major Planetarium in Berlin, the Lubmin nuclear power plant near Greifswald, and the above-mentioned cutaway model of the Schauspielhaus.

There was hardly any public reporting on the work of the model workshop. In an official account of the Building Academy from 1988, some models photos were shown, but the workshop is not mentioned.[8] On the other hand, an FDJ brochure from 1986, a publication geared toward East German youth, which presented the latest building projects in the capital of the GDR,[9] not only featured photos of models from the ISA workshop but also of employees at work.[10] It also pointed out the latest methods of model film simulation that were used in the workshop.[11] The necessary technical equipment was of high quality and correspondingly expensive—a fact that shows how highly valued the model workshop was. However, it had probably been closed down by 1990 already, and only few models could be saved.

5 Bauakademie der DDR Muster- und Experimentalprojekt, Bautechnischer Erläuterungsbericht, November 30, 1981, Gesellschaftsbau, 03891, BBSR Bonn.

6 Personallisten, May 1990, A1_40, A1_42, IRS, Scientific Collections.

7 Atelier 4 Modellbau, "Historie: Biografie Hans Günter Zechert," accessed October 21, 2022, https://web.archive.org/web/20061106063316/http://a4-modellbau.de/historie.php; Atelier 4 Modellbau, "Modelle bis 1990," accessed October 21, 2022, https://web.archive.org/web/20070125061910/http://a4-modellbau.de/modelle-vor-90.php.

8 Klaus Rummel and Bauakademie der DDR, *Bauakademie der Deutschen Demokratischen Republik* (Berlin: Bauinformation, 1988).

9 Klaus Taubert and Thomas Bencard, *Mensch, Berlin, wie haste dir vaändert!* (Berlin: Verlag Junge Welt, 1986). We would like to thank Volker Mende (Freiberg University of Mining and Technology) for the kind hint and for providing reproductions of the pages in question.

10 Ibid., 85.

11 "Mit Kamera und Bildschirm durch ein Modell," *Neues Deutschland*, August 17, 1984.

Alternative Spaces: A New Version of the Schauspielhaus

In the FDJ brochure, Hans-Günter Zechert is shown finishing the last details on a cutaway model of the Schauspielhaus in Berlin. This model can still be viewed today in the Scientific Collections of the IRS. It was possibly created for Berlin's 750th anniversary celebrations in 1987.[12] The Schauspielhaus had been partially destroyed in the Second World War and stood ruinous in the city center for decades. It was not until 1965 that it was decided to restore the buildings.[13] Work on the interior of the theater, as a faithful reconstruction of Schinkel's previous building, began in 1981.[14] Until recently, the neo-classicist reconstruction was believed to have been without alternative. However, a chance find proves that there were indeed alternative designs for its interior. A model from the estate of architect Heinz Dübel shows what seems to have been an internal competition entry for the company Ingenieurhochbau Berlin (IHB), which is not at all reminiscent of Schinkel: wood-paneled walls and boxes set off with shaped stones, a sophisticated acoustic ceiling design, and a new interpretation of a modern organ are distantly reminiscent of Hans Scharoun's philharmonic hall at the Kulturforum in West Berlin, built in the 1960s. The model is undated, yet its existence alone is reason to conduct further research into the planning history of the Schauspielhaus: Were there other alternative designs?

12 Daniel Hadwiger, "Architektur als Instrument der Außenpolitik. Unterlagen zur Ausstellung 'Bauen in der DDR' in Paris 1988: Fund des Monats Nr. 11 vom März 2021," accessed October 21, 2022, http://ddr-planungsgeschichte.de/bauausstellung-paris-1988.

13 ADN, "Platz der Akademie wird restauriert," *Neues Deutschland*, May 3, 1965.

14 Dieter Bolduan, "Berlin erhält seinen schönsten Platz und das große Schauspielhaus wieder: Vom Neuaufbau eines weltbekannten Schinkel-Bauwerkes," *Neues Deutschland*, January 23, 1981.

Why was a decision made in favor of reconstruction? Who were the decisive stakeholders?

However, the model also shows the difficulties of preservation: It is in poor condition due to years of improper storage; parts of the interior are detached, and since there are no further clues as to the design, restoration of the model is hardly possible. Moreover, due to the size of the model's box, it is not easy to store or to make available for possible users to view. Conservation is an important task for archives, but unlike museums, they have far less experience with three-dimensional objects such as models. Of course, models pose special challenges in terms of their materiality, but the combined knowledge of archivists and researchers about the creation and transmission of models is directly relevant to their restoration. This starts with seemingly banal questions about where to reinsert individual parts that have become detached from a model. But it is also important to ask: Do we want and can we afford the potentially significant expense of restoring models? Or is the condition in which models are decades after their creation not also authentic in its own way and possibly worth preserving?

The juxtaposition of these two models of the Schauspielhaus, which are very different in several respects, is well suited to reflect on some fundamental aspects of collecting, preserving, and researching architectural models in context: For what purposes were models made, by whom, and with what means? For what reasons have very specific models survived to this day, what role did individuals play and what were their intentions? Which questions can be answered (or are even newly raised) when we take an in-depth look at architectural models? And how can we ensure that these models remain preserved and accessible in the future?

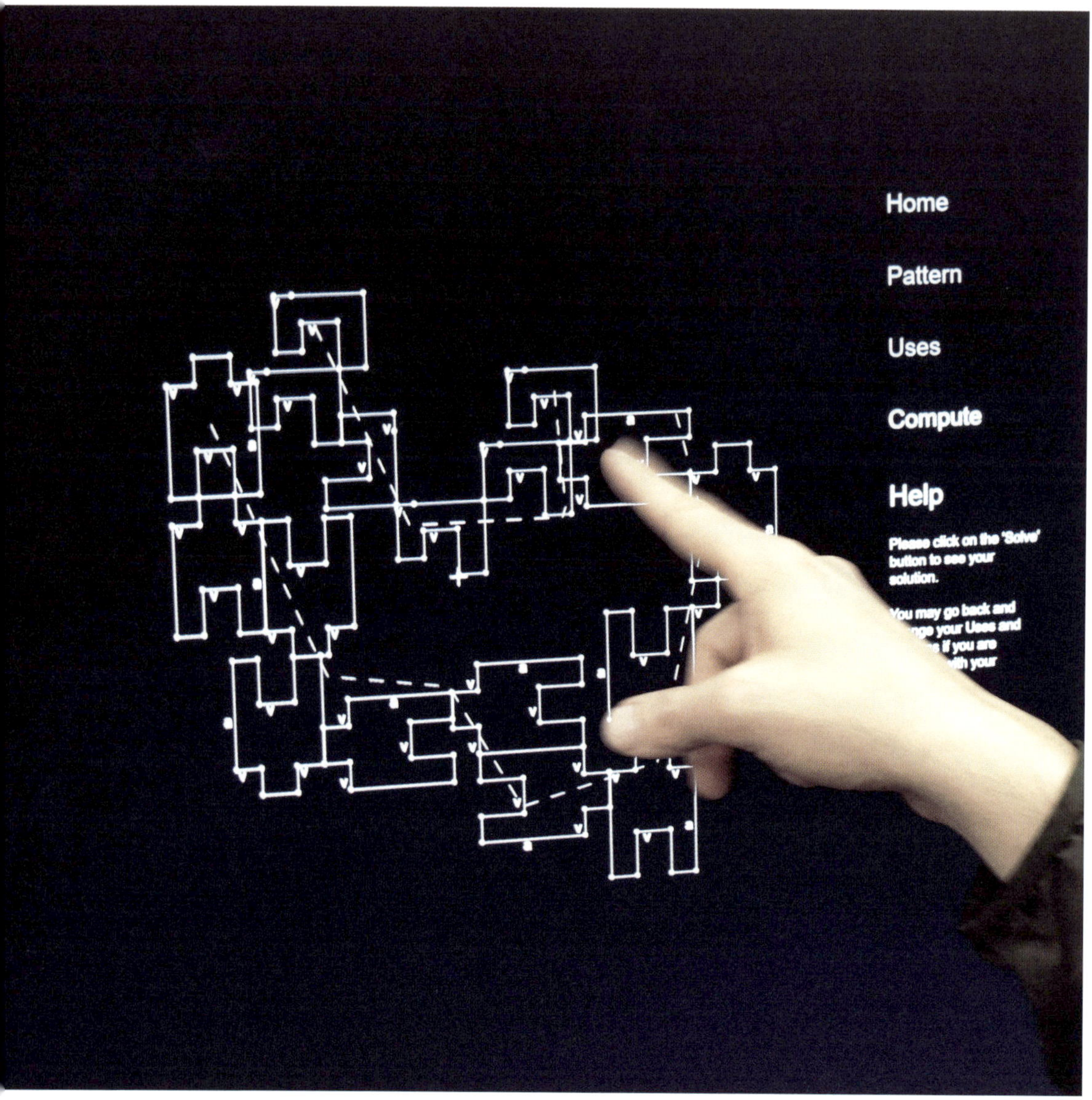

Architectural researchers have used software to model new conceptions of design. Under the advice of Charles Eastman and artificial intelligence pioneer Allen Newell, Chris Yessios developed an early software for urban design, called CISP, as part of his doctoral dissertation completed at Carnegie Mellon University in 1973. The image shows a 2019 interactive reconstruction of this system by the author, and Harshavardan Kedia. [Courtesy of the author]

Software Models Design

Daniel Cardoso Llach

Software is a vehicle through which technical knowledge, and ideas about design and its organization, travel into architecture, altering its fabric. Geometric engines developed for the aircraft industry undergird architects' modeling tools; computational modes of structuring information delineate contemporary architectural roles and sensibilities around the assemblage of ever larger building information models. The magnitude of these transfers over the last several decades has underscored the need for a critical reflection about "the digital" in architecture beyond proselytizing technologies' adoption and touting the purported advantages of a fully digitalized future. Aware of this need, recent architectural scholarship has interrogated software's intimacy with contemporary modes of architectural production and labor, as well as its importance as a domain for critical inquiry and creative intervention.

These efforts present a welcome challenge to the discipline's long-standing distaste for recognizing its own conditions of production. In diverse forms—dissertations, monographs, exhibitions, think-pieces, and even mockumentaries—, researchers interested in these questions have started to interrogate architectural software's intellectual and institutional histories, technical lineages, gender dynamics, and geographies. They have chronicled their insertion into architectural and design cultures and their role in fostering new technical and design roles in the discipline. The image of the digital currently emerging as a result is one not merely comprised of abstract, symbolic entities, monolithic turns, or of techno-utopian visions of automated design or managerial efficiency. Instead, software has started to appear as the site of important conceptual and methodological redefinitions in the discipline, and as a sociotechnical milieu that demands the field's attention through empirically grounded, critical scrutiny. Rather than an undesirable underworld populated by technicians solely concerned with the instrumentality of design, distant from discipline's higher pursuits, software is now starting to be seen as one context where key questions about architecture and its labors are negotiated. Recent scholarship has traced, for example, formal and conceptual shifts in design resulting from the creation and adoption of software;[1] or the role women digital pioneers played challenging narratives of architecture's "digital turn" as driven by mostly heroic, male figures;[2] speculatively explored epistemic

1 See for example Nathalie Bredella, *The Architectural Imagination at the Digital Turn* (London, New York: Routledge, 2022); Daniel Cardoso Llach, *Builders of the Vision: Software and the Imagination of Design* (London, New York: Routledge, 2015) and "Architecture and the Structured Image: Software Simulations as Infrastructures for Building Production," in *The Active Image: Architecture and Engineering in the Age of Modeling*, eds. Sabine Ammon, Remei Capdevila-Werning (Springer: Berlin, 2017); and Theodora Vardouli and Olga Touloumi, eds. *Computer Architectures: Constructing the Common Ground* (Milton Park, Abingdon, Oxon: Routledge, 2019).

2 See for example Shelby Elizabeth Doyle, and Nick S. Senske, "SOM's Computer Group: Narratives of Women in Early Architectural Computing," in *International Journal of Architectural Computing*, August 2020, 1478077120950713. https://doi.org/10.1177/1478077120950713.

questions or dystopias raised by mainstream software;[3] or used exhibitions to examine architectural software in new ways.[4] These works extend, and in some cases reframe, previous architectural scholarship that valuably charted the discipline's digital excursions.[5] And yet, the center of gravity of the part of the discipline concerned with computing still skews heavily towards techno-utopian fantasies or heroic figures.

Part of the trouble is methodological. In this book, the editors have fashioned a unique opportunity to playfully reconsider models, broadly understood, as architectural actors. How then might we make visible software not merely as an environment where architectural models are produced but itself as a model of design practice? How may we see it not simply as an "aid" but also, and primarily, as an infrastructure that models, conditions, and reorganizes architectural labor and understandings? How to approach the material and phenomenal aspects of software?

The image above is a photograph of an interactive installation that reconstructs a software system for urban planning originally developed in the early 1970s. The software, named CISP by its author, Christos Yessios, is no longer accessible, and its only remaining traces are written descriptions and line diagrams in contemporary research reports and in his doctoral dissertation.[6] The original system was programmed in FORTRAN in an IBM 665 machine. The reconstruction, part of a broader effort to reenact architectural software, was programmed in Processing, a programming language for interactive graphics geared to artists and designers based on the modern Java programming language, and runs on a Mac Mini, a smaller and more powerful computer compared to the significantly bulkier IBM 665 originally used. Importantly, it is the system's logic—the "algorithm"—and not the details of its technical implementation that is being reconstructed. This detail matters because it is precisely there, in the algorithm, that a historical software system can most clearly be read as a theoretical model of the design process—a model of design. What is it then that this software is modeling?

Software systems model by naming elements; by defining levels of dependency between those elements; and by differentially giving control over those elements and modes to the users. Rather than giving users access to digital versions of conventional drafting tools, the system we reconstructed allowed users to create a vocabulary of geometric elements representing the outline of an urban site and the contours of building units. It further allowed users to define constraints on how the units could be configured by, for example, establishing the desired placement of doors and windows in each unit. With these elements, the system attempts to semi-autonomously create design solutions that respect the constraints, resulting in different, and sometimes surprising, urban configurations. Important to our analysis is that the system models design as the definition of basic elements and rules; and it models the designer's role as one of rule-setting, constraint-defining, and evaluating automatically generated outputs. This model of design is enacted by the software, which might be seen as a theoretical artifact first and a functional system second. After all, CISP was never implemented except as part of its author's doctoral project.

The reconstruction of CISP is one of several interactive installations I have developed with my research group at Carnegie Mellon University as part of an ongoing project combining historical research and technological prototyping in order to recreate some of the earliest

3 Ng, "OOTB," in E-Flux Architecture (blog), 2019. https://www.e-flux.com/architecture/positions/280207/ootb/; and "Mockumentary by Office for Uncertainty Research," dir. D.I.A.N.A, 2023, https://www.officeofuncertaintyresearch.org/diana.

4 Teresa Fankhänel and Andres Lepik, eds. *The Architecture Machine: The Role of Computers in Architecture* (Basel: Birkhauser, 2020); Daniel Cardoso Llach and Theodora Vardouli, eds., *Designing the Computational Image, Imagining Computational Design* (San Francisco, CA: Applied Research + Design, 2023).

5 See for example Robert Bruegmann, "The Pencil and the Electronic Sketchpad: Architectural Representation and the Computer," in *Architecture and Its Image*, Eve Blau and Ned Kaufman, eds. (Cambridge, MA: MIT Press, 1989); Willam J. Mitchell, *The Logic of Architecture: Design, Computation, and Cognition* (Cambridge, MA: MIT Press, 1990); Kristine K. Fallon, *The AEC Technology Survival Guide: Managing Today's Information Practice* (New York: John Wiley & Sons, 1997); Mario Carpo, *The Alphabet and the Algorithm* (Cambridge, MA: MIT Press, 2011). Antoine Picon, *Digital Culture in Architecture* (Boston, MA: Birkhauser Architecture, 2010).

6 Christos Yessios, "Syntactic Structures and Procedures for Computable Site Planning" (Dissertation, Carnegie Mellon University, 1973).

CAD systems. A premise of the project is that while oral, archival, and other documentary sources provide invaluable insight into these technologies, they say very little about their gestural and sensual aspects, or about their specific modes of operation. Part of engaging with software as a primary material is to understand how it behaves visually, gesturally, and interactively, and this requires that we expand our methodological repertoire. As described above, software reconstructions offer access to historical software systems which are no longer accessible because of technological limitations—for example, many historical systems can't be emulated because they depend on hardware platforms that no longer exist. In addition, it can help approximate ergonomic and gestural particularities of historical systems that are no longer part of modern computing systems.[7]

These reconstructions make different theorizations of design evident. Using archival materials and technology prototyping, they enliven distinct understandings of design. Software systems are thus rendered in their fundamental ambivalence—at the same time as visual artifacts, modeling techniques, and signifiers for specific ways of imagining designing and building. At times, they show how software models an understanding of design founded on the geometric plasticity of computational descriptions; sometimes, on the possibility of physically realizing these descriptions via numerically-controlled manufacturing methods; sometimes, as the structured, hierarchical composition of artifacts as interlinked informational units. Reconstructing historical software thus offers a path towards performative accounts of these architectural technologies, their histories, and their contexts.

From here it is worth pondering what other overlaps and tensions we might productively identify between architectural and software theories. If software indeed models design, perhaps architects have been looking for architectural theory in all the wrong places.

7 See Daniel Cardoso Llach, "Reconstructing 'Sketchpad' and the 'Coons Patch': Toward an Archaeology of CAD," *Leonardo* 51, no. 4 (2018): 429–430; Daniel Cardoso Llach and Scott Donaldson, "An Experimental Archaeology of CAD: Using Software Reconstruction to Explore Early Computer-Aided Design Technologies," in *CAAD Futures 2019: Hello, Culture* (New York: Springer, 2019); and Daniel Cardoso-Llach, Eric Kaltman, Emek Erdolu, and Zachary Furste, "An Archive of Interfaces: Exploring the Potential of Emulation for Software Research, Pedagogy, and Design," in *Proceedings of the ACM on Human-Computer Interaction* 5 (CSCW2): 294:1–294:22 (2021). https://doi.org/10.1145/3476035.

Model Project Weissenhof Estate, scale 1:500, 1991. [Universität Stuttgart, Digitale Sammlungen der Universitätsbibliothek, https://digibus.ub.uni-stuttgart.de]

Same, and Yet Different

Eleven Realities of the Weissenhof Estate

Christiane Fülscher

The model collection of the Department of Architecture and Urban Planning at the University of Stuttgart comprises around 300 models, which were created exclusively in the context of teaching and mostly produced by students for exhibitions in collaboration between the Institute for Architectural History and the department's model workshop from 1980 to 2015. The collection contains a great number of highly appreciated models of architectural icons that were shown in exhibitions like "Soviet Avant-garde," "Neues Bauen International," or featuring Erich Mendelsohn, Alexander Melnikov, and others. This occupation with the Modern Movement followed the example of Jürgen Joedicke, founder of the Institut für Grundlagen moderner Architektur (Institute for Principles of Modern Architecture) in 1967. Correspondingly, the internationally renowned building exhibition of the German Werkbund on the Killesberg in Stuttgart in 1927—also referred to as Weissenhof Estate—was the subject of student projects on several occasions. The culmination was an exhibition on the houses by Ludwig Mies van der Rohe, Le Corbusier, Mart Stam, Walter Gropius, and others in 1985, commissioned by the Institut für Auslandsbeziehungen (Institute for Foreign Relations), which toured the world for decades as cultural ambassador. The single houses on a scale of 1:50 and the model of the site on a scale of 1:200 are still the most requested items of the whole collection.

Outside the Box

An exception to these sophisticated objects is a student project created in the summer term of 1991, which was never meant to be presented to a greater public. Under the supervision of the model workshop's master, Martin Hechinger, 27 participants created site models of the Weissenhof Estate at a scale of 1:500.[1] All models had the same dimensions, the same outlines, and showed the same group of buildings. In each case, the section of the terrain was chosen as if the model could be immediately inserted into a larger environment, as in competitions, but here, it was the defined outline of the settlement area and the surrounding streets. This is where the similarities of all models end. Each model was made of a different material and different formulations of terrain, buildings, and greenery. Not only traditional modeling materials like plaster, Plasticine, cardboard, and

1 Correspondence Christiane Fülscher with Martin Hechinger in 2022 and 2023.

wood or those popular since the 1960s such as aluminum and acrylic glass were used. Less established components like newspapers, lead, or cake were also employed. Eleven models of this assemblage showing the same object have survived the last 30 years, spread across different places. Seven models were kept safe yet dusty in numerous display cabinets and cupboards at the building of the architecture department. Four others were pinned to the wall in the dean's office and highly cherished. Hidden from the university's public, they blended inconspicuously into the built-in inventory. Being manufactured a decade before cutting and laser plotters arrived in model workshops, all eleven models impress with their manual craftsmanship.

Transition Processes

Creating a model is a design process. In transferring the two-dimensional idea of point, line, and area into three-dimensional rod, board, and volume, the choice of modeling material forms the individual model's character. The special features of a material and its natural or artificial coloration cause a distinct perception. Ideally, the material selection underlines the initial design idea, but it can also evoke contrary associations. Like a test track, the eleven objects celebrate the individual interplay of colors, textures, shadows, and lushness. The project's main theme of visualizing the same architectural complex in eleven material variations contradicts a fundamental position that institute director Wolfgang Knoll and his staff member Martin Hechinger phrased in their publication *Architektur-Modelle. Anregungen zu ihrem Bau* (*Architectural Models. Proposals for Their Construction*), published in 2006. In making the distinction between building reality and model reality, they state that the underlying architectural idea influences the decision to choose a certain material. Accordingly, there is only one appropriate solution for the material choice to highlight the existing project in line with the architect's intensions. To emphasize this statement, the authors present the models of the Weissenhof Estate by showing only one monochromatic example.[2] Classified as an urban concept model, its basic idea was related to a preliminary draft and should meet the requirements of changeability and variability.[3] This assumption is the opposite of presenting a model of an estate that has already existed for eighty years. Models do not only activate seeing as the sensory stimulus. The perception of a model and its intrinsic idea occurs through tactility, movement, and finally through the viewer's experience connoted with the individual material, depending on its cultural ties. Turning around the system of one single solution for building reality and model reality, the manner of material and priority setting changes the recognition of the Werkbund exhibition. Consequently, variations of materials and model realities associate—maybe unwittingly—variations of building realities just as several realities of the Weissenhof Estate.

2 Wolfgang Knoll and Martin Hechinger, *Architektur-Modelle. Anregungen zu ihrem Bau* (Munich: Deutsche Verlags-Anstalt 2006, 2nd edition), 17.

3 Ibid., 10, 13.

A Set of Realities

The monochromatic example shown in the book was made of Efaplast, an easily moldable and kneadable modeling compound that hardens in contact with air. Following its additive nature, baseplate, buildings, and trees merge into one homogenous mass. The only difference between trees and buildings is their size and the form contrast of square and round shapes. Streets, pedestrian paths, and plot boundaries are slightly pressed into the smooth surface. The warm white Plasticine shapes the hillside of the Killesberg, the buildings and trees growing out of it as a single unit. Scratches, grooves, fingerprints, and cracks evoke its unfinished appearance of a concept model. However, the seemingly conventional Plasticine is connected to the Modern Movement as a common modeling material in the 1920s and one of the first concept models for the Werkbund Estate by Ludwig Mies van der Rohe in 1925.

Another model in the university's collection boasts greater perfection with its cubes cast in plaster, while the terrain is formed from elevated aluminum sheets and the trees from rectangular, matte acrylic sticks. The production technique of the plaster cubes is elaborate, and this is probably the reason why these plaster houses were only on display once. The so-called white modern is also conveyed in a model using polystyrene for the terrain and houses. By working with thin strips, the building structures achieve a finer level of detail. Nonetheless, the use of round acrylic sticks for the trees seems necessary to contrast with the houses. Polystyrene is THE modeling material of the 1980s and 1990s and the most used material in the Stuttgart collection. Its stability and durability make it ideal for exhibition models that are frequently transported.

For the appearance, it makes a great difference whether a model is manufactured by hand only or machines are used. Thus, the wooden model of the Weissenhof Estate allows a first insight into the possibilities of processing materials by using three different kinds of wood to distinguish between terrain, nature, and building volumes. The base plate consists of thin, hand-crafted balsa sheets that contrast with the prefabricated beech spheres for the trees and the very hard, reddish-brown pearwood sawn to create the building cubes. The latter allows the addition of details like the roof garden and the brise soleil at Le Corbusier's duplex house in the front. Obviously, this ought to be the focus of the observer, so the receding surroundings emphasize them. But the use of wood creates a traditional impression that is connected to the history of the Weissenhof Estate, too. To promote the wood industry in the early 1930s, Richard Döcker planned a second building exhibition on the Killesberg. After the Nazis seized power in 1933, Paul Schmitthenner took over the project to realize the so-called Kochenhof Estate according to long-established craftsmanship techniques. This connotation concerns two other models with wooden building structures that compete with their metal environment. In one case it is rusted steel, in the other black-colored lead. However, even the soft construction material lead tells the history of the Weissenhof Estate. In the monochromatic lead model, the method of reduction is taken to the extreme. The material properties of formability and duration are employed on one single layer shaping the landscape and the outer walls of the houses. There are neither roofs, correct heights nor trees, the edges are rounded, sometimes dented. In a way, the model design corresponds with the toxic nature of lead—the black oxidized surface in combination with the display of the building outlines involuntarily recalls the destruction and loss of ten houses in World War II.

A real contrast in its characteristics, but also a transformation of the material properties into a design theme, can be seen in the fourth monochromatic model made of acrylic glass. The crystal-clear layers shaping the terrain are elevated by transparent acrylic sticks, whereas the houses—formed as opaque shimmering volumes—

4 When architectural theorist Julius Posener called the building exhibition a fraud in a letter to Jürgen Joedicke in May 1980, he referred to the overestimation of the importance of the Stuttgart sanctum, but the formalism debate and the ICOMOS critique of the 1990s were already resonating. Universitätsarchiv Stuttgart and Wüstenrot Stiftung, eds., *Jürgen Joedicke, 1925 bis 2015. Notes from the Archive* (Stuttgart 2020), 104–108.

stand out. The sanded surface corresponds with the necessity of working with a circular saw and its raw cut. Overall, the technological, polished appearance is punctuated by a lack of trees. The unaged acrylic model can be seen as synonymous with perfection and the conservation of the modern. In the early 1980s, the Weissenhof Estate had been refurbished and the surfaces were removed from the shell.[4]

In contrast to all others, the last three models seem to be indecisive, almost inconsistent. Due to the mixture of more than two materials, they appear homely, like model railway houses. But more than the abstract ones, these picturesque models are an attempt to approximate the existing contrast of the natural environment, of terrain and trees, and the hard edges of the buildings. Layers of newspaper or plaster blur the contours, and the streets and plots are set off by color. The trees made of sponge, white soaked paper, or steel wool reflect their grown structure and contrast with the buildings made of wood or Efaplast painted in white or gray, recalling a bon mot of one of Stuttgart's postwar professors, Günther Wilhelm: "Just take a cheeky gray."[5] While all models appear like a kaleidoscope of different identities of the Weissenhof Estate, these final models come closest to its current state of various conditions and conflicting interests: partly lost, partly modified or reconstructed, partly preserved in its original appearance, and extended by previously overlooked houses, the former building exhibition functions as an icon, a place to live in, a museum, and an important tourist attraction at the same time.

5 Kerstin Renz, "Nehmen Sie doch ein freches Grau. Günther Wilhelm und die 'Stuttgarter Schule' in den Nachkriegsjahren," in *Architekturschulen. Programm, Pragmatik, Propaganda*, eds. Kerstin Renz and Klaus Jan Philipp (Tübingen and Berlin: Wasmuth Verlag, 2012), 53–65. Translation by the author.

What Is My Act?

On Models as Actors and Stages

Lisa Beißwanger

1 Exhibition dates: October 4–November 18, 2022, Cooper Union Foundation, New York; Catalog: Cynthia Davidson and Anyone Corporation, eds., *Log 56: The Model Behavior Exhibition CataLog* (New York: Anyone Corporation, 2022).

2 Quoted from the exhibition guide leaflet.

3 Having a background in the field of performance studies, I am convinced that this methodological takeover holds great potential for architecture history and theory. For an attempt to bring both fields together see: Lisa Beisswanger, "Architecture and/as Choreography: Concepts of Movement and the Politics of Space," *Dimensions. Journal of Architectural Knowledge* 1, no. 2 (2021): 23–50.

4 Albena Yaneva, *Latour for Architects* (London: Routledge, 2022), 1.

5 Ibid., 76.

6 Thea Brejzek and Lawrence Wallen, *The Model as Performance. Staging Space in Theatre and Architecture* (London: Bloomsbury, 2018), 1.

7 Ibid., 3.

8 Erving Goffman, *The Presentation of Self in Everyday Life* (New York: Anchor Books, 1990 [1956]).

9 Annabel Jane Wharton, "Models as Ethical Agents," in *Log 56: The Model Behavior Exhibition CataLog*, eds. Cynthia Davidson and Anyone Corporation (New York: Anyone Corporation, 2022), 13–20, 13.

When in 1931 the Society of Beaux-Arts Architects held its annual ball at the Astor Hotel in New York City, one of the program's highlights was a performance by architects dressed up as models of their own creations. A hilarious picture from the event captures seven established architects imitating the New York skyline. Towering above all of them is William Van Alen in the guise of his recently completed Chrysler Building—at the time the tallest building in the world—, the building's impressive Art Deco crown so high that it pierces the image's upper edge. Merging into absurd versions of human scale models, these architects immerse in a play of identification and (self-)representation, demonstrating unity and competition at the same time.

Architects A. Stewart Walker, Leonard Schultze, Ely Jacques Kahn, William Van Alen, Ralph Walker, D. E. Ward, and Joseph H. Freelander dressed as their own buildings at the Ball of the Society of Beaux-Arts Architects at Hotel Astor, New York City, 1931. [Photographer unknown. Source: Open Culture, accessed October 30, 2023, https://cdn8.openculture.com/2014/03/03112824/buildingcostume.jpg]

The depicted scene demonstrates the most literal way to interpret the "performance" or "staging" of a model. However, as this chapter argues, there are many more. In recent years, scholarly engagement with architectural models has shifted toward the processual and performative. Instead of focusing on models as autonomous objects or secondary stand-ins for "real" buildings, there has been a growing interest in what models do, how and why they are deployed, and in what contexts they become effective. The recent *Model Behavior* exhibition at the Cooper Union, New York City, makes this shift particularly clear: models, the exhibition makers argue, are active agents in processes of meaning making.[1] More precisely, the exhibition examined "their role in projecting, eliciting, or even reinforcing social behavior,"[2] dealing with models not only in architecture but in all realms of science, the arts, and everyday life.

In accordance with the scope of this book, this chapter focuses on models in architecture and expands the view beyond their influence on human behavior. Posing the question "What is my Act?", it asks for a model's performative and theatrical qualities. This brief introduction aims to outline some of the concepts, tools, and perspectives for approaching architectural models in this way. Taking a cue from performance studies, the chapter proposes to think about architectural models through concepts of the theater.[3] Theater is a peculiar space, set between reality and the aesthetic realm. A place where realities are reflected, probed, and negotiated. It is exactly this performative negotiation of realities which is also highly relevant for the discussion of models and model making.

Among the fields of inquiry such a perspective opens are questions about "stage or staging" (or modes of presentation in relation to an audience); "plot or narrative" (or the stories models tell to pursue, convince, or to question); and "actress and performance" (or the roles models, architects, model makers, and their audiences play).

The chapter's subtitle "Models as Actors and Stages" suggests to consider models as active agents in performative processes of world-making and to study their relationships to external actors performing with or even inside them. Models, in this sense, also become visible as projections and projection surfaces. Owing to the theatrical double function as actor and stage, categories such as subject and object become blurred and the boundaries between the literal and the conceptual may at times oscillate, or even dissolve.

To discuss models as actors is to move away from an understanding of models as discrete objects to which meaning is ascribed from the outside. Two interdisciplinary theoretical concepts may facilitate this perspective.

The first comes out of disciplines such as linguistics, art, and performance studies and concerns the concepts of performativity and theatricality. Both help to understand models not only as signifiers loaded with a fixed meaning, but as producers of realities by means of their very relationships to other actors and the contexts in which they appear. This approach, derived from J. L. Austin's speech act theory, brings to the fore the formative potential not only of the spoken word but by extension also to human and non-human entities. Although Austin ruled out theater and art from his theory, cultural science has seen a shift toward studying objects—art or not—with respect to their performative qualities, in other words: to focus on the productive effects they have on their recipients and the world they inhabit.

A second trajectory is rooted in sociology, more precisely actor-network theory. Following Bruno Latour, architecture historian Albena Yaneva has introduced this theory into architecture discourse, observing "a tendency to acknowledge the active role of objects, materials and technologies [such as scale models] in the design process."[4] Focusing on the production of architecture, Yaneva points out that "[m]odels, software, sketches, and programming all make designers act, think and create in a specific way" and she stresses, that "[i]t is neither the model nor the designer but that very specific attachment between them that acts in a design process."[5] This focus on the in-between or interaction of human interlocutor and model comes into focus in Mara Trübenbach's "Conversational Essay". Going beyond conventional methods in architecture theory, Trübenbach reflects on her own role when observing a model maker at work. Her observations as a participating observer shed light on model making as a practice and process of many decisions and complex relationships between human and non-human actors.

Interpreted as stages or stage sets, models act as platforms for other players to act on. In doing so, they can create both actual and imagined realities. In their book *The Model as Performance*, Thea Brejzek and Lawrence Wallen stress this "potential for *cosmopoiesis*, or world-making."[6] Pointing at the narratives that are embedded in any model, they speak of models "as a space of action that may or may not require activation by the viewer."[7] While a stage-like quality is present in most models, the most obvious study case may be actual stage or film sets, modeling environments often as fragmented and immersing in a deceptive play of scales and sizes. In their contribution "From *Site* to *Set*: The Multi-Scalar Effect of Architectural Models in Crafting Gender and Sexuality in Postwar Italy", Giulia Amoresano and Christina Moushoul discuss a film set of Rome's EUR district in Federico Fellini's episode of the miniseries *Boccaccio '70* (1962). Navigating the complex and often self-referential relationships between architectural, human, and metaphorical or role model, the authors interpret models as "a social technology [...] of representation and self-representation [...]".

A stage, very generally speaking, is a place for the representation of reflections and projections of reality. The stage design, just like a model, generates an "as if" reality and enables to imagine "what if...". The proverbial fourth wall acts as the interface between audience and play, between the real and the aesthetic or theatrical realm. In modern times, this boundary has increasingly come under attack. The stage moved closer to reality, and reality in turn became visible as staged. Looking at architectural models as a stage may as well blur the threshold between model and built architecture. This is particularly true for 1:1 models. Walk-in models and mockups create a "real" sensual and bodily experience, often of projected environments, yet to be built. From these liminal spaces it is only a small step to recognize that also built buildings can be seen as models with stage-like qualities. This idea is at the center of Christian Janecke's contribution "Modeling Scenic Attitudes." Diving into postmodern architecture and the peculiar theatricality associated with it, he discusses architecture's various modes of staging, along with its stage-like qualities. This perspective conflates the model and its referent and stretches the definition of an architectural model to the breaking point. It thereby challenges the traditional understanding of a model in architecture and expands it towards a more conceptual one, sharpening the senses for the built environment as a constructed reality for the performance of everyday life.[8]

Finally, in a more figurative sense, any model in any scale or material form can become a stage. For example, for architects presenting their ideas in carefully scripted performances. This perspective asks for what purposes models are made or presented to whom, such as clients, the general public, or the researcher.

So, what does it mean to look at models from the angle of theater, performance, and the performative? Since all models are made to act and to be acted with, they are all actors and stages at the same time. The question "what is my act?" therefore does not lead to the discovery of a new type of models, but it offers a way of looking at their productive relationship with the world. Art historian Annabel Jane Wharton has rightly pointed out that, in addition to all the questions that can be asked of a model, it should be asked above all whether they are ethical agents.[9] The question "what is my act?" can possibly help to answer this question, although it does not necessarily draw a line between real and fake, good or bad. Putting emphasis on qualitative rather than normative questions, it brings to the fore how a model acts, how is it staged, by and for whom. It is therefore best suited to shed light on the highly political nature and agency of architectural models.

Mara and “Digital Mara” looking at the 1:25 model of the Warburg Renaissance made by Ellie Sampson, Oslo/London, 2020. [Mara Trübenbach / Ellie Sampson]

Sculptural Puzzles

A Conversation Essay about Model Making, Rituals, and Material Literacy in Architecture

Mara Trübenbach

The definition of a model as an object is increasingly disappearing in contemporary practice—models are no longer defined by "something else, instead the models become that 'something else' themselves," argues architect Pippo Ciorra.[1] Having said that, it confirms my observation that "making" models is not only about understanding the material and having the skills and tools, but more importantly about the shared experiences and responsibilities of actors involved in an act of collaborative meaning making. In this paper, I claim that models hold performative potential. I argue that relations such as emotions and trust are crucial to form knowledge around this "something else."[2]

From September 2020 to November 2021, I followed model maker Ellie Sampson's work. This project, in which I was most of all interested in the tactile, in the haptic, and in the material, was conducted under the extraordinary circumstance of a total ban on physical interaction. At the initial start of the study, in spring 2020, I was confined to my apartment in Leipzig. Sampson had been forced to move her entire model making activities for the architectural office Haworth Tompkins into her two-room flat in North London. Later, when I started observing her, she was allowed a small amount of physical interaction; I still had to participate at a distance, this time from Oslo. I negotiated with my research institution, Oslo School of Architecture and Design, to send Sampson an iPad, a device which became known as "Digital Mara." It became a kind of teleport that allowed me to observe advice/crit sessions, take screenshots of process, and conduct interviews with Sampson herself. Like a NASA Mars probe, but controlled by a very informal set of vocal exchanges between Sampson and myself. "Digital Mara" explored the (tacit) knowledge in model making, from planning to digital preparation files for laser cutting to considering material thickness, mocking-up 3D CAD models, and logistics related to storage and relocation. The combination of this strange and constant digital observation, which was accompanied by the sometimes intense, sometimes sporadic, sometimes silent exchange of thoughts, as well as my own reflections that steered and adjusted both processes, amounted to a form of ethnography.

Inspired by David Hockney's and Martin Gayford's book *A History of Pictures: From the Cave to the Computer Screen* (2016) and their

1 Pippo Ciorra, "Architectural Catwalks," in *Modelling Time. The Permanent Collection 1925–2014*, eds. Mari Lending and Mari Hvattum (Oslo: Torpedo Press, 2014), 13.

2 Adrian Johns, *The Nature of the Book: Print and Knowledge in the Making* (Chicago: University of Chicago Press, 1998), 42.

principle of getting inside the heads of art practitioners, this conversation essay, co-written by Ellie Sampson, from which I present excerpts, aims to find a productive interface between theory and how models can be performative in the architectural design process. The text aims to make visible the working processes around the model as an integral part of knowledge generation in model making.

Scene 1

Ellie Sampson: The current physical distance from the various teams I work with has had a big impact on the model making process, but it hasn't been wholly negative or overly rigid—it has simply changed the rhythm of the conversations surrounding a proposed model. I thought the fact that I was making things in my flat and that we could no longer huddle around a model making space, pointing at, picking up, testing, and sketching on the models we were collaborating on, would make my job extremely difficult. Not just for me trying to grasp the intricacies of each design proposal I was portraying but also for the team. An inability to play around with the models themselves throughout the making process and to change elements as we went along goes against many architects' hands-on design impulses.

Pre-lockdown, the model making area really felt like a hub within the studio that members of the team (or anyone really!) could stop by and comment on what was going on or make suggestions to both design or making technique. Depending on the stage of the design, it provided a chance for the team to get the design out of the computer and see the details and forms being manipulated in the real world. This is the sort of "control" I was referring to that architects enjoy—understandably so! It's fun! The chance to see if elements of their designs work in the real world, outside the sense of weightlessness you can sometimes feel in the CAD world. Making a model of a proposal gives the design some real-life weight and substance.

Mara Trübenbach: The "fun control" acts like a performance between architects, models, and their responsiveness to the "real world" through materiality. Architects interact with surfaces, light, scale, etc., as if the engagement (mental and physical) with the material triggers an identification with the design, almost like actors wearing costumes to better empathize with the desired character. When architects are aware of the involvement of materials as active agents, there is tremendous potential to engage in respectful dialogue, especially in light of climate change and diminishing resources. But do we need the physical encounter to get an inter-relational connection to the material? Are there other ways forward?

Scene 2

Ellie Sampson: [...] In a way, my position as an outsider to the team not knowing as much about the individual projects is a benefit, not the hindrance I feared. The team and I can concentrate on the information which best supports the views, details, strategy, or materials within the proposal that the model seeks to represent. For a 1:50 model of a scheme in Cambridge, I needed to absorb a lot of information quickly and unpick a dense layering of existing and proposed information. The scheme includes the heavy stone envelope of a church, updated circulation within existing Georgian townhouses, and the insertion of proposed entrances and communal spaces amongst this layered restoration of existing built fabric. For this, the team had to trust my understanding of the scheme, and I needed to trust their detailed stage 4 drawings. It felt like making the model was a dry run for constructing the proposal itself. I had to read the drawings as an instruction pack as a contractor would, which made it incredibly satisfying when the end result came together.

Mara Trübenbach: Odd though, that trust still seems to be an underestimated value in the design process. The architectural theorist Albena Yaneva conducted an ethnographic study of the Rotterdam-based architectural firm OMA (2009) to reconstruct how design is implicitly experienced and enhanced. By elaborating the reuse of both material and immaterial sources, Yaneva captured the motion of the design process that takes place within the office and that you describe as well. She demonstrated that design and design techniques are based on everyday routines and that "design never starts from scratch."[3] However, what I think Yaneva is missing is the sense of trust building that you describe, one's role in the collaboration, and, of course, one's trust in one's self.[4] In order to enter into a collaboration, a high degree of trust is needed to become accomplices. This kind of security that comes when you trust your counterpart in his/her area of responsibility is necessary to move the design forward. But trust is also critical in more non-explicit ways. Remember our conversation about your most popular posts on Instagram about model making and how the most popular images included both the work in progress and your hands touching the models. I don't think that's a coincidence. When people see your hands, they feel more connected to your model simply because of the fact that someone made the model, is holding it, and cares about it. People can better identify with hands touching the material than relating to a model standing on its own. If trust is part of the environment of learning and so of literacy, the hands in the image contribute to building that condition. They inject tactile experience and awake a recall of experience gained, of past encounters. Do you think architects could learn from craftspeople how they engage and speak *with* material?

3 Albena Yaneva, *Made by the Office for Metropolitan Architecture: An Ethnography of Design* (Rotterdam: 010 Publisher, 2009), 103.

4 Yaneva fleshes out the redefinition of the social link by the COVID-19 virus: "As design played an active role in regulating flows of movements, calibrating distances, impeding touch and dispatching energies, a new architectural sensitivity resurfaced." See: Albena Yaneva, *Architecture after Covid* (London: Bloomsbury, 2022), 148.

Conclusion

By reflecting upon interactions with material in a conversation, Sampson and I realized that the impact of digitalization on the understanding of material and the potential to connect haptic sensations with the visual impressions we encounter in our daily lives needs to be explored more deeply. There is a moment where the digital becomes more integral to a sense of haptic materiality. The related emotions evoked by hands-on work are linked to material knowledge that can be revealed in the design process when makers talk about their relationships with the objects they create. According to craft historian Glenn Adamson, "[i]t would be a mistake to believe that material intelligence is only applied through tactility, via making or touching."[5] It is not only hands-on engagement with the material that teaches material literacy but also mediation, which Sampson, her team, and myself had to learn very quickly during the restrictions caused by COVID-19. The digital, then, is intimately related to embodied experience and bodily memory. It forces one to get to the core of what is seen. This "new collage of communication," as Sampson calls it, has great potential to accompany, rather than replace, architects' usual work habits. Emerging from the digital, mediation itself serves as a key tool to reveal material knowledge by following not an object but the making of an object.[6] However, Sampson never makes actual buildings but instead produces avatars. Such avatars should not be seen as second-class. They do have a capacity to speak, even envision, some material world in the object being made. Models are not static but performative.

5 Glenn Adamson, *Fewer, Better Things: The Hidden Wisdom of Objects* (New York: Bloomsbury, 2008), 113.

6 Glenn Adamson, *Thinking Through Craft* (New York: Bloomsbury, 2013), 3–4.

Actress Anita Ekberg (as herself) chasing Dottor Antonio in a scene of *Le tentazioni del dottor Antonio*, directed by Federico Fellini, screenshot from the film, 1962. [Film still, screenshot by authors]

From *Site* to *Set*

The Multi-Scalar Effect of Architectural Models on Crafting Gender and Sexuality in Postwar Italy

Giulia Amoresano and Christina Moushoul

Anita Ekberg stands towering over the sidewalk almost as tall as the streetlights beside her. In the background, Palazzo dei Congressi looms, signifying that she is in the EUR district of Rome, an ambitious urban planning project initiated by Benito Mussolini. Illuminated by the neon store signs beneath her, Anita directs her gaze downward towards the camera with a flirtatious smile. The camera is placed particularly low, with a steep upward angel towards her imposing giantess. The shot takes the point of view of the protagonist, Dottor Antonio, who is being relentlessly pursued by Anita. Anita emerged from a provocative billboard advertising milk outside Antonio's apartment window who, scandalized by it, campaigned tirelessly to have it taken down, only to then witness it come to life.

Federico Fellini's *Le Tentazioni del Dottor Antonio* is a short film within the larger anthology *Boccaccio '70*, which brought together four of Italy's most prominent directors at the time. Conceived of as the contemporary counterpart to the work of medieval Italian writer, Giovanni Boccaccio, *Boccaccio '70* sought to criticize the moralizing attitudes and strict censorship brought forth by the post-Fascist Christian Democrats. Federico Fellini's contribution to the project was a retort against the moralistic attack on his earlier film, *La Dolce Vita*, in which he reinstated Anita Ekberg as the star to play herself in a struggle against Dottor Antonio, a man who represented the real-life critics the movie faced. Often surrounded by boy scouts and clergymen, Antonio becomes the model Christian Democratic citizen that abides by and even enforces the rules above all else. Antonio fights against his sexual temptations which are personified by Anita who, in playing herself, comes to represent more broadly the Italian film industry's sexualization and objectification of women. As film scholar Patrizia Carrano states on the Italian film industry at that time, "the female character [since 1960] is blurred, [it is represented] as a silhouette that can only appear as a backdrop, [...] or that can only occupy a role that solicits erotism for the male's consumption."[1] In other words: she is reduced to a depersonalized model, a blank canvas for male projections.

Although film historian Teresa de Lauretis acknowledges Fellini's use of women actresses, she argues that what is represented, and reciprocally asked to be reproduced by the female spectator, is an image of women that does not embody the feminist battles of the

1 Patrizia Carrano, *Malafemmina. La donna nel cinema italiano* (Rimini and Firenze: Guaraldi Editore, 1977), 74–75. Translation by the authors.

time.[2] Which is to say, Fellini's women still solely occupy the role of mothers, wives, or objects of desire for men rather than that of complete characters with desires of their own. As what can be considered abstractions of women, they became models for the projection of men's desires while also modeling men's desired roles for women. Both de Lauretis and Carrano thus depict Fellini's approach, and more broadly the Italian movie industry following the late 1940s, as a set of images that represent and construct the "unconscious and collective fears of men [about female sexuality]."[3] Although this approach at times acts to admonish Fellini's perceived false moralism of the Christian Democrats, it also helps fortify the conservative purview of abstention and puritanism. In either scenario, cinema continued to further impress the role of women as the projection of men, designed to satisfy men's suppressed temptations and erotic desires.

Having emerged from the flatness of her billboard, model now occupies model, as Anita simultaneously liberates the male gaze while maintaining the status of women-as-object. Anita is in fact not a character, she is an image come to life, an object of desire in Antonio's imagination without any of her own preoccupations, intentions, or internal forces. In order for Anita to continue to operate as image she had to remain at billboard-scale, which meant that Fellini had to shrink the EUR by building a 1:6 scale model. Originally designed as the grounds for the Esposizione Universale di Roma in 1942, the district functioned as an atemporal abstraction that linked the legacy of ancient Rome claimed by Mussolini with a modernized future for Italy under Fascism. Diane Ghirardo, quoting Mussolini's famous description of the EUR as the "Olympics of Civilization," explains how the objective of the EUR was to "set the standard towards which other nations could only aspire," using Italian civilization and its accomplishments as a model that linked the past, present, and future at home and abroad.[4]

While Anita's monstruous size informs us that this is not the true EUR, the model does a convincing job of portraying itself as such. In the Fascist regime's desire to create an atemporal model of Italian civilization linking Italy's former glory to its hopes for a modern and industrious future, they abstracted and linearized canonical Roman architecture, as seen most clearly in the Colosseo Quadrato (which literally translates to "Square Colosseum"). In so doing, the district appeared model-like, so much so that prior to its completion, the Fascist regime could convincingly use photographs of the district's models as propaganda. These qualities also led the district to become the favorite backdrop for some of Italy's most famous directors beyond Fellini, including Bernardo Bertolucci, Roberto Rossellini, and others. In a 1972 interview taken on the steps of the Colosseo Quadrato (or the Palazzo della Civiltà Italiana as it is formally called), Fellini states his reason for selecting the EUR as his filming location for *Le Tentazioni*:

> "[For my inspiration] I have chosen a neighborhood, not a piece of art; that is to say, I have not chosen the representation of an author or artist's world view, I have chosen the EUR! Why did I choose the EUR?...Above all, the EUR gives you back *leggerezza* (lightness, fluidity, malleability), it gives you the impression you are living in a painting, thus it provides a liberatory atmosphere, since in a painting, there are no rules if not those of aesthetics, no relations exist if not with yourself—thus the neighborhood stimulates a sense of freedom."[5]

2 Teresa de Lauretis, *Technologies of Gender. Essays on Theory, Film, and Fiction* (Bloomington and Indianapolis: Indiana University Press, 1987).

3 Carrano, *Malafemmina* (1977), 82.

4 Diane Ghirardo, *Italy. Modern Architectures in History* (London: Reaktion Books, 2013), 119.

5 Federico Fellini interview "Fellini e l'EUR" (1972).

The model-like essence of the EUR provided an anonymous backdrop upon which Fellini could stage his own views of modernity and society, and the ways in which women could operate within them. As the EUR would continue to demonstrate, its transition from the focus of the Instituto Luce's Fascist propaganda to that of a filmic backdrop for Italian and foreign directors further emphasizes that the project itself contained the model-like qualities that portability across mediums required.[6]

The end of the film sees Anita's return to the two-dimensional confines of the billboard, thereby no longer inhabiting a model but reprising the role of a model herself, while Antonio finally gives into his vices and admits what he truly desires. As a tool of mass-market consumerism, Anita maintains her larger-than-life status throughout the film in order to capture the attention of the male gaze and thereby potential consumers, while also continuing to advocate for men to liberate themselves. While advocating for the authorship and creative freedom of Fellini and thereby furthering his agenda toward the freeing of men from their false moralities, the model strips women of their agency and further objectifies them. The architectural model, in its multiple incarnations, thus becomes a social technology that informs, produces, and proliferates representations and self-representations of gender and society at large, while through the power of its abstraction depoliticizing the creativity of its authors.

6 Diane Ghirardo has shown how the EUR was used since the 1960s as a filmic backdrop to either criticize Fascism and/or modernization at large, or to celebrate Italian modernity using the district as proof of an alternative character of suburbia that differed from the North American model circulating predominantly across various media. Ghirardo, *Italy* (2013), 125.

Kunstmuseum Bonn, detail of the first floor plan (views from above and from below), Grand Staircase, 1992. [Charlotte Frank, ed., *Axel Schultes – Kunstmuseum Bonn* exhibition catalog (Berlin: Ernst und Sohn, 1994), 53]

Modeling Scenic Attitudes

On Funnels, Conical Stairs, and Caveae in Postmodern Architecture

Christian Janecke

The Kunstmuseum Bonn, designed in 1985 and subsequently modified by Berlin architect Axel Schultes and opened in 1992, is related to a series of new West German museum buildings of this era. The rooms are unadorned, uniform, and dedicated to the exhibition of art. Obvious architectural quotations were avoided, as were staged breaks or disparate stylistic heights. As the architect intended, one can admit that this is not an example of a programmatically postmodern building. This is true, if one applies the criteria of postmodern architecture put forward prominently and comparatively early by Charles Jencks. In this case, we would have to speak of a combination of late modern characteristics on the one hand and, on the other hand, of a building style that has lasted right up to the present day, which relies on certain parameters that are believed to be timeless—even superhistorical—such as light, mass distribution, and the language of materials.

The so-called "Grand Staircase," a stately, eye-catching, combined conical and inverse conical staircase that mediates between the two main floors, is also dedicated to clarity and transparency. Neither a foreign body nor an explicit quotation, its circular form seems to serve first and foremost the reception of visitors approaching from all sides. A round platform halfway up offers those ascending and descending a place for a respite, possibly also providing orientation as to the direction they should continue to take. However, the form chosen here is not only not neutral, it is definitely postmodern and, as I will show, in a specific way also an expression of a model- and stage-like quality that is now even inherent in the built architecture.

The peculiar combined conical and inverse conical staircase, reminiscent of the shape of an hourglass, has been known since the Renaissance. The upper, concave part of such a staircase, in the form of a halved funnel, forms the front edge of a painted scene behind it, or the tier of a terraced garden, such as at the Heidelberg Castle, or a proscenium in a theatre. The lower, massive cone of steps can, accordingly, mark the foreground in the painting, the audience area of a theatre, or the entrance to a lower plateau of a landscape garden.

More often, both in older and in postmodern times, architects confined themselves to either the upper or the lower half, whereby the upper, funnel-shaped part is formally congruent with the audience gallery of ancient theatres. Instead of continuing the semicircle to a circular arc of more than 180 degrees, at Kunstmuseum Bonn, only a smaller segment of the imaginary closed circle is left beyond its center for the lower, stepped cone. Consequently, the platform rounding off the center is almost entirely an intact part of the upper funnel, by which it is now also partially enclosed. The impression of a tribune along with the (almost) round orchestra is thus considerably reinforced.

Whoever descends this staircase to the pedestal changes *en passant* from the seating section to the stage, or rather from the status of a spectator to that of an actor. The importance of the pedestal—which simultaneously crowns the lower, convex cone of the staircase and monumentalizes what stands on it—is also evident from the fact that a sculpture by Markus Lüpertz was initially placed there. Except that it probably stood in the way of the actual staging, that of the users of the architecture!

And here they are, the postmodern characteristics *par excellence*: the indecisiveness, at first between the banal function of the stairs and the noble place of residence; then between a seating section and a stage; finally, there is the quote of form in the emphasis on the antique-like part of the stairs. Furthermore the dimensional relationships are shaken, namely between the stairs in the everyday sense (i.e., with dimensions adhering to physical aspects of accessibility and safety) and the evocation of something much larger (here, the ancient theatre setting). Such a de-proportioning, of course, corresponds excellently to the half-hearted theatrical allusion in post-theatricalized times. (In retrospect, we may find some of the theatre, film, or art of the 1980s mannered and theatrical, but we cannot assume that the museum visitors were indeed conceived of as performers strutting along instead of simply walking).

This leads us to the role of the model: it does not precede the built form here but rather is inherent to it! For whoever does not completely thoughtlessly experience the Grand Staircase in the Kunstmuseum Bonn takes part in an obvious illusion. With this staircase, which is emphatically not identical with itself, an antique-like theatrical setting opens up like an unstable image, of course, in no other way than in the state of being a mockup, a model. With the model, however, no practically relevant interaction is possible from the outset. Whatever one tries to accomplish on or with it, one will still only be performing—not necessarily in front of third parties but always according to principle.

Such figurativeness of use was programmatic at the time: the user of postmodern architecture was conceived as a distant recipient of scholarly allusion and at the same time producer of his or her inevitably staged appearance in public. This dual role of a "reflected self-existence," however, had long been intended for him or her by the visual arts of those years, there, by the way, in an explicitly model-like manner. In the works of Thomas Schütte, Bernhard Prinz, and the so-called "model builders" (Wolfgang Luy, Harald Klingelhöller, Ludger Gerdes), the ontological status of the exhibited works was sometimes vacant in three respects: between, first, a sculpture that presents itself to the viewer; second, a model for architectural realization (but typically in a provisional material that emphasizes the provisionality); third, a walk-in building, albeit one that appears small and like a proxy.

Whereas it was once a matter of baroque staging to lend a stage-like effect to entire streets, architectural ensembles, or interior sections, such as a niche or an apse, by means of foreshortening, it should be the merit of postmodern staging, by means of quotation, fragmentation, and playful handling of both materials and scale, to introduce moments of de-essentialization in precisely those places where prima facie essentialist pathos—classicizing in the case of tribunes, conical staircases, or rotundas—prevails.

The rhetoric of seriousness, long since passé in the visual arts with good reason, has survived in architecture, in its rhetoric of legitimation. It is true that in recent years, for example, the performative character of architecture and other "softeners" have been put forward as arguments against the power of built-up stone. But in my opinion, it is precisely here that we should insist on a specific heritage of postmodern architecture, which is otherwise often berated: namely, the escalated moment of the model-like. For the architecture saturated by it is vacant between real and implied extension, with its elements, despite all concreteness, nevertheless aiming at something prototypical. The space of the stage, as the transformative space it is, becomes their paradigm.

Am I the Real Thing?

On Copies and Casts

Christiane Fülscher

1 Michael Stöneberg, "To the stars and back. The plaster model of Erich Mendelsohn's Einstein Tower," in *The Architectural Model. Tool, Fetish, Small Utopia*, eds. Oliver Elser and Peter Cachola Schmal (Zurich: Scheidegger & Spiess, 2012), 29–37.

2 Cf. Doris Reisinger, *Was ist ein Original? Eine Begriffsbestimmung jenseits genieästhetischer Stereotype* (Bielefeld: transcript Verlag, 2020).

3 Heinrich Hübsch, *In welchem Style sollen wir bauen?* (Karlsruhe: Verlag der Chr. Fr. Müller'schen Hofbuchhandlung und Hofbuchdruckerey, 1828).

4 Cf. Alexander Nagel and Christopher Wood, *Anachronic Renaissance* (New York and Cambridge, MA: Zone Books, 2010)

5 Mass production of architectural models like Walter Benjamin describes it in "The Work of Art in the Age of Mechanical Reproduction" is rarely seen. Walter Benjamin, "The Work of Art in the Age of Mechanical Reproduction," in *Illuminations, Essays and Reflections*, ed. Walter Benjamin (New York: Houghton Mifflin Harcourt, 1968). For the idea of the mass production of copies cf. Winnie Wong, *Van Gogh on Demand: China and the Readymade* (Chicago: University of Chicago Press, 2013).

6 Ines Weizmann, "Mimesis and Copyright, or the Rights of Copies," in *Mimetische Praktiken in der neueren Architektur: Prozesse und Formen der Ähnlichkeitserzeugung*, eds. Eva von Engelberg-Dočkal, Markus Krajewski, and Frederike Lausch (Heidelberg: arthistoricum.net, 2017), 54–63, here 55.

7 Mari Lending, *Plaster Monuments: Architecture and the Power of Reproduction* (Princeton: Princeton University Press, 2017).

8 Ines Weizman, "Architectural Doppelgängers," in *AA Files 65*, ed. Thomas Weaver (London: Architectural Association, 2012), 19–24.

The production of plaster models is a complex technique. Unless a cast is to be made of an object, a preliminary model must first be built showing all the details of the later finished model. It is carefully covered with a silicone layer, and the hardened mold serves as a negative for all subsequent casts. Plaster casts are an integral part of numerous collections in museums and archives worldwide. They show miniatures, cutouts, or fragments of valuable historical buildings and their remains. In the 20th century, plaster models also became fashionable in the field of competition. There, they were used to reproduce identical base plates as models for use in larger urban contexts to be distributed to all participants, who later completed them with their design.

At first glance, cast plaster models may look like two peas in a pot. But just as each pea differs from the other in terms of size, surface texture, color, and chemical composition, plaster casts differ in the details: small irregularities on the surface due to casting, bubbles that occur during carbonizing, slightly varying differences in the composition of the mixture, and thus also the shades. The single detail might or might not make the model exceptional.

In this vein, the Deutsches Architekturmuseum in Frankfurt am Main thought for a long time that it owned one of six original plaster models of the Einstein Tower from 1919. The museum even had two replicas made in 1997 and 2005 to preserve the valuable unique item. Michael Stöneberg describes in his essay "To the stars and back. The plaster model of Erich Mendelsohn's Einstein Tower," how laboratory analyses and a computer tomography uncovered that the supposed "original" model was in fact created in the 1950s.[1] The following assignation as a "copy" was immediately accompanied by a loss of value, just as the prefix "original" had been accompanied by an increase in value in the beginning.

But what is the difference between both models? On the one hand, there is the esteemed "original" that is one of six, on the other, there is the faithfully produced newer "replica" as a reference of the lost series. Which one is the copy and which one is not? Or, vice versa, is the designation of originality in the case of architectural models appropriate at all?[2] We don't even know if the latter reproduction was cast from the older one or recreated from scratch. Nevertheless, it is the remaining evidence that allows us to discuss what might be lost, the model techniques of the 1950s, as well as present and future issues concerning the object on display.

In architecture, the act of copying has been a method for thousands of years: even the Romans copied parts of the architecture of the ancient Greeks but generated something completely new from it. All of historicism is based on the idea of the value of a copy to transfer the former attributes to the newly developed draft. Heinrich Hübsch's question "In which style should we build?" has affected generations of architects.[3] The traditional and highly influential academic education at the École des Beaux Arts in Paris is based primarily on the act of copying, repeating, and reproducing. And even today, more than a century later, reminiscence is one of the prominent design principles in architecture.

The act of replicating iconic role models serves as design and intellectual inspiration,[4] while the historical evidence is applied to the new object, which, however, is produced differently, shows changes, and is adapted to contemporary needs. One famous example for this transition is the Walhalla in Regensburg (1830–1942) by Leo van Klenze as a not quite precise likeness of the Parthenon on the Athenian Acropolis. It could hardly be further from imitation,[5] as the "diasporic model" achieves not only a value of its own but a "new originality."[6]

However, copying in architectural model making should be seen as a power,[7] as a tool of generating knowledge and achieving advancement. This understanding is the basis of all contributions in this chapter. By unfolding the investigation process on the 19th-century model of the Royal Albert Hall, Simona Valeriani displays the act of copying as a scientific approach to gaining comprehensive references. The process of multiple reproduction in different sizes, scales, shapes, materiality, or physical state supports the preservation and understanding of the remains of the older one as well as expands the possibilities of its presentation to a greater public. In Le Corbusier's oeuvre, the act of copying is already programmatic, his idea of the Unité d'Habitation exists in Marseille, Rezé-les-Nantes, Briey-en-Forêt, and Firminy (France) as well as in Berlin (Germany). By studying one-to-one reconstructions of iconic architecture fragments in museums like the duplex unit at the Parisian Cité de l'Architecture et du Patrimoine, Ana Carolina Pellegrini takes this concept of the "architectural Doppelgänger" to new dimensions.[8] The intrinsic role of these full-scale models as mediators is also seen in Diana Cristobal Olave's research, which demonstrates that architectural models have much more than just a physical role. The exhibition of the Idea Houses at the Walker Art Center in the 1940s simulated a vision of living to educate and to give the opportunity to live it, even if it was just one weekend in the visitors' live. And finally, the act of copying as an artistic approach to finding the most appropriate solution is presented by Chae Wonseok in his paper on the library in Marl, serving as the long-overseen prototype of the esteemed city hall. In all contributions, a copy is not just a copy; they redefine the categorical role of the architectural model as a mere referent.

Architectural models are always the result of previous decisions concerning their scale, of course, as well as their materiality and, as the most important criterium, their function. They do not result from a design's pure end in itself but take on a concrete task. Architectural models are created on the basis of an idea, a building, preserved photographs, another model, but in turn they develop new dimensions: in knowledge gain, in narrative, in experientiality, and above all as a partial step within a holistic design process. Every single object has a unique story, a value, and thus its right to exist: Am I the real thing?

The 19th-century Royal Albert Hall model fragment on show as part of *Shaping Space – Architectural Models Revealed* (Building Centre, London, September 2021–March 2022). Next to the historical artefact are its physical copy and a device to interact with the digital replica. In the foreground, model makers Scott Miller and Saul Parker-Backhouse of the B.15 Model making Workshop at Manchester University. [Simona Valeriani]

Copying, Building, Sharing

Multiple Approaches to the Study of a Historical Model

Simona Valeriani

An Unexpected Find and an "Ecology" of Models

In 2018, the fragment of a large 19th-century model of the Royal Albert Hall (1867–1871) was found in the back of a cupboard. This artefact augmented an already uncommonly rich set of models documenting different stages of the Royal Albert Hall's design process. While the other specimens present themselves as polished end products, the newly discovered model is simpler in appearance and bears traces of several modifications.

An analysis of the extant archival resources led to the conclusion that this model played a crucial role in the design process. The first mention of this "tool" dates back to the summer of 1866, when the Provisional Committee (the group of "notables" in charge of pushing the project forward) appointed a Committee of Advice. This comprised two engineers and two architects, as well as two artists and art critics.[1] These professionals were assembled to support and oversee Henry Y. D. Scott, the Royal Engineer in charge of the project, and to "afford a stronger guarantee to the public than exists at present that the architectural character of the building and the artistic elements generally will be satisfactory."[2] Minutes of the committee's meetings reveal that discussions about ways to improve the design happened around a "model of wood prepared by Colonel Scott", a model which was modified between meetings to incorporate the committee's advice.[3]

The materiality of the surviving model confirms its role as a design and discussion aid. For instance, despite its current fragmentary state, there is clear evidence that it was constructed so as to be taken apart easily to see the interior. Moreover, one could enter the space and "stand" in the model shoulder high, mimicking—to a certain degree—the perspective of a visitor to the actual building. A similar effect is obtained through "relatoscopy" as discussed by Maxime Zaugg in his paper. Throughout history, with different means, artificers sought a way of using models to offer stakeholders a means to "experience" the building before it had actually been built. While Zaugg's examples speak of widening participation in the design process to a diverse audience, in the case of the Albert Hall, this remained the purview of a selected few, deemed to be "authorities."

In line with the "experimental" ethos of the group in charge of the Royal Albert Hall's construction, who argued for architecture to be

1 John Fowler (1817–1898), Sir John Hawkshaw (1811–1891, FRS FRSE), William Tite (1798–1873), Sir Matthew Digby Wyatt (1820–1877), Richard Redgrave (1804–1888), and James Fergusson (1808–1886, FRS).

2 Herbert Fisher to General Grey, December 12, 1865, Archive of the Royal Commission for the Exhibition of 1851, RC/H/1/21/40. When the design of the building for the 1862 exhibition was entrusted to Fowke, great criticism was expressed about the fact that a Royal Engineer, rather than an architect, had been given the job.

3 Minutes of the Committee of Advice, July 26, 1866, Royal Albert Hall Archive, RAH/1/2/1/15, 57–58.

"scientific" and intended the Hall to be a place where the arts and sciences would come together, models were used at South Kensington as tools to carry out what they called "experiments" at different stages in the design process.[4] This attitude was influenced by practices characterizing the Royal Engineer's training, highly dependent on the use of models. It is interesting to draw a parallel with Heinz Isler's use of physical models as described in Giulia Boller's paper in this volume.

The Royal Albert Hall's model fragment was part of an "ecology" of models in different scales and materials. Mockups were also created, both to answer technical questions (the whole circumference of the Hall was built at the terracotta works to check the fitting of the façade pieces) and to support compositional choices (the scale of the figures in the mosaic frieze, for example). Full-scale models are not uncommon in the history of architectural design and represent an attempt to make a direct physical experience of the "building-to-be" possible.

4 Simona Valeriani, "Life and Afterlife of a Design Process: Models and Drawings of the Royal Albert Hall," in *The Routledge Companion to Architectural Drawings and Models: From Translating to Archiving, Collecting and Displaying*, ed. Federica Goffi (Milton Park, Abingdon: Routledge, 2022), 157–171. See also Simona Valeriani, *The Royal Albert Hall—Building the Arts and Sciences* (Turnhout: Brepols, forthcoming 2024).

Making Sense of the Evidence

The desire to understand the complex genesis of a 19th-century model fragment and to make the object intelligible to viewers led to the development of two projects: one involved the construction of a physical copy of the Victorian architectural model fragment, complemented by a reconstruction of the missing parts. The other project consisted in the production of a digital copy of the historical artefact. The aim was to investigate the potential of digital and physical copies of architectural models, both in terms of research methodologies and as tools for engagement and fruition. At the same time, the *Shaping Space—Architectural Models Revealed* exhibition, to be held at the Building Centre in London from September 2021 to March 2022, was being prepared.[5] This provided a forum for sharing the results of this investigation with a wider public, while creating a context which, inevitably, contributed to informing the process. For the first time, visitors had the opportunity to observe the 19th-century fragment and make sense of it through the nearby physical "replica." Moreover, exhibition goers could interact with an annotated digital copy to access a wealth of information in different formats, supporting a historical understanding of the artefact.

The physical copy was built in collaboration with the B.15 model making workshop at Manchester University, led by Scott Miller. The virtual model was produced in collaboration with the Laboratory for Models and Simulations for Architecture and Heritage (MAP) of the French National Centre for Scientific Research (CNRS) in Marseille, led by Livio DeLuca.[6]

5 "Shaping Space—Architectural Models revealed," under the heading "Architectural Models in Context," accessed October 19, 2022, https://archmodelsnetwork.com/shaping-space-architectural-models-revealed/. See also the publication accompanying the exhibition: Olivia Hosfall Turner et al., eds., *An Alphabet of Architectural Models* (London: Merrell, 2021).

6 The model was produced by Théo Zanetti in collaboration with Livio DeLuca (Director of Research, CNRS Heritage Digitisation) and his team at the MAP Laboratory.

Copying and Re-Making as a Research Methodology

The haptic engagement with the 19th-century model and the production of its physical copy were fundamental aspects of the research into the Victorian design process, towards a better understanding of the Royal Albert Hall's building. They provided insights into the techniques used and a heightened understanding of their "fitness for purpose." The materials and techniques—invariably low cost due to the transient nature of the object, which was modified constantly—were chosen for their aptitude to model the aspects at the center of discussion with efficacy and easiness of construction.

The process of creating the replica emphasized the patchy character of the historical record. We found ourselves faced by three sets of "evidence": the design drawings, the model fragment, and the finished building. They were, in many cases, not telling the same story. In fact, the model fragment incorporates traces of different design solutions trialed by Scott and the Committee of Advice. In this sense, it is many models in one, and its fragmentary nature complicates the interpretation of the evidence. Determining what should be copied was clearly a delicate issue. Each model is made for a purpose and with an audience in mind, both of which shape the makers' choices, including scale and materials. In our case, the replica model was built as a tool for research but also to equip exhibition goers to better understand the significance of the 19th-century fragment. It presents an easily comprehensible view of one specific stage of the design process, where some aspects had to be inferred. In its univocity, however, the reconstruction runs the risk of being taken as a statement of truth, as the last interpretative word. The many questions that remain open for future research and engagement, as well as the richness of discoveries, are concealed.

Exploring the Digital Dimension

The problem of providing critical tools was addressed by exploring the virtual dimension. The interactive digital model, enriched with annotations, presents information on the physical features of the 19th-century fragment. It enables users to discover the material clues it contains and to explore their significance in relation to the different stages of the design process. It explores what the material evidence reveals about the way the wooden model was used in its original context. Moreover, the digital copy allows the viewer to navigate the whole landscape of models produced during the Royal Albert Hall's design and building phase, and to understand how the fragment fits within this group of artefacts.

The virtual copy of the historical Royal Albert Hall model also contributes to ongoing research into the digitization of physical models in historical collections with the aim of making the many models hidden away in museum stores available—to a certain degree—to the public. We wanted to reflect on the opportunities offered by this format, which could at least in part "offset" the disadvantage of not having access to the physical artefact. The system used in our case is Aïoli, a reality-based annotation platform, which "aims to bring together the actors involved in documenting, safeguarding, and sharing our cultural heritage through new practices for a better understanding of heritage objects."[7] Its intent is to enable a simple process of digitization which would be easily implemented and offer a simple platform for sharing information on the physical artefact, between professionals and with the public. However, the difficulty of producing a high-quality digital replica of architectural models with limited investment of resources remains. The 3D representation obtained through the process we chose is useful as research and learning tool, but it is not highly refined aesthetically.

The Royal Albert Hall project was particularly interesting because it involved the parallel creation of two copies of the historical artefact, one physical and one digital. This spurred reflection upon the strengths and weaknesses of these different formats and processes.

The context in which the project took place obviously informed some of the choices made and the degree of accuracy adopted in the

7 "Aïoli," accessed October 19, 2022, http://www.aioli.cloud/. Aïoli is a non-profit initiative, developed by the MAP Laboratory of the French CNRS.

copies. The process highlighted the slippages of meaning intrinsic in the practice, if not the concept, of what a copy is. Copying, in most cases, focuses on some characteristics of the "original" that are deemed crucial in a specific context or for a specific purpose. In our case, the purpose was twofold: understanding a complex historical artefact and sharing with a large public the knowledge gained.

Following this project, the Royal Albert Hall decided to showcase its historical model through our replica, which has been placed on permanent display in the Hall. It's not yet clear if access to the digital copy will also be provided. It's an unexpected turn of events, which further stimulates considerations around the life cycle of a model and its various uses and interpretations in different contexts. How much will the models be able to speak for themselves? How is the copy of a working model going to be understood in its new context? We created a model and sent it into the world, but we have limited influence on how it is used. This is not uncommon for models, but we look with trepidation to the next stage of our model's life, which was conceived as a fruit of research, as a copy of sort, strongly linked to its model, but has taken on a life of its own.

Photographs of "Idea House II" staged as if being used. Ezra Stoller (left) and George Miles Ryan Studio (center and right), 1948. [Walker Art Center]

The Witness-Visitor

Dishwashers, Thermostats, and Garbage Chutes at the Walker Art Center's Model Homes, 1941–1947

Diana Cristobal Olave

Vegetables in the sink as if ready to be cooked, cupboards full of silverware, the dishwasher full of dishes, and the pantry doors open to proudly display a wide range of cleaning products. This is how "Idea House II"—one of the model houses built by the Walker Art Center in Minneapolis in 1947—appeared as photographed by the museum and represented in the media. This could be considered a rare staging choice, particularly when comparing these photographs to later examples of museum houses elsewhere, such as the Museum of Modern Art's House in the Museum Garden (New York, 1949–1954). Unlike these other model homes, which were built as stage sets for the simulacra of the everyday life, the Walker Art Center ensured that House I and II were fully equipped, fully functioning houses.[1]

The question of why a fully functioning dishwasher and cleaning products were seen as required to ensure this form of domestic simulacra becomes even more enigmatic when reading the material presented by the Walker Art Center's curators. These exhibitions were conceived as spaces where visitors could come and learn new concepts in design, building materials, furnishings, and technology, applying them as desired to their own homes, preferably with the help of an architect. Rather than a prototype to be replicated, these exhibitions were advertised as a repository of ideas that could potentially be applied to any home and modified by users and builders alike: "The theme of the Idea House is ideas. The house is not presented as a model or ideal plan for any given family nor for any average family."[2] Its plans were never made available to purchase; and when the media, visitors, and commercial sponsors alike wrote to the Walker Center to request blueprints, they were systematically refused. Plans, sections, and details were neglected as documents for media transmission:

> "This house was built by us purely as an educational exhibition of ideas and not as a model home. We believe that every house, regardless of the price, is an individual problem for owner and architect. We have not wished, therefore, to encourage the reproduction of this house."[3]

This provocation establishes this article's point of departure: If the Idea Houses were abstract concepts, why would their designers invest such effort in ensuring their physical integrity? When this question was posed to Walker Art Center Director Defenbacher, his

1 For a review on model homes built as stage sets see Ana Carolina Pellegrini's contribution in this volume, "Unstuck Architectures: When the Building Becomes a Model," 128–133.

2 "An Explanation of the Idea House," *Minneapolis Tribune and Star Journal*, June 1, 1941.

3 D. S. Defenbacher to A. W. Ross. Letter, July 9, 1941, Walker Art Center Archives.

response was clear: "Because we are trying to develop a new type of civic museum, one that is actually—not mythically—interested in art in everyday life."[4] Conceived against the backdrop of the Great Depression and the postwar housing crisis, Defenbacher reimagined the museum experience as an active event, one that could engage with pressing, everyday issues by encouraging close interaction between exhibition and visitor. In other words, he claimed that a 1:1 scale model home—rather than a set of drawings—could transform the museum from a potentially elitist cultural institution with a specialized audience into a popular institution organized around everyday issues and accessible to a broad public.

To that end, the Walker model homes operated as "probatory" technologies.[5] They persuaded the exhibitiongoer through their physicality, their seemingly unmediated (but staged) modes of inhabitation, and through visual and written testimonies disseminated in mass-media publications. The houses needed to not only showcase their exterior appearance, but to also demonstrate their structural, mechanical, and economic viability. As Defenbacher argued, "Idea House II was built to demonstrate the most advanced ideas in home planning and equipment."[6] Visitors had to be able to turn on any faucet and verify the supply of hot water, test the instant power of the modern gas kitchen, listen to the modern radio, the phonograph, and the silent gas refrigerator, and experience the comfort of the air conditioning and thermostat. As carefully described by the Walker Center's publications and by the media, technological innovations were considered integral to the success of the project. *The New York Times* called attention to the garbage chute connecting the upstairs bedroom to the utility room;[7] *Progressive Architecture* referred to a "factory-fabricated, one-piece unit"[8] that included all the usual fixtures in one piece of equipment; and *Everyday Art Quarterly* called the gas equipment one of the "greatest advances in comfort"[9] for modern housing. Invisible things, such as the ambient temperature or the noise of the appliances, were important in constituting a collective agreement upon the correct functioning of the house. Among the senses, sight was dominant but not unique. The Idea House needed to be seen, but also sensed, heard, and tested.

If the criterion for certainty was empiricism, then eyewitnessing was an important source of evidence. In 1947, the Walker Center held a series of contests to invite people to spend a full weekend in the house. Beyond advertising the project, the goal behind these uncanny experiences was to get personal feedback from the "testing" of the house. The article announcing the competition, published in the *Minneapolis Sunday Tribune* in September 1947, described the contest as an opportunity to try out the livability of the house:

> "Each group may move into the house on a Sunday night, stay that night, all day Monday and move out the following Tuesday morning. During that time, each group will have a maid at its disposal, will have all their meals prepared and served for them, the dishes washed, the beds made. There'll even be between-meal snacks furnished. The institute would like to get reactions from those who 'try out' the house."[10]

The test was, however, a highly mediated experience. Included was an organized tour of the house; meetings with a newspaper columnist, a radio commentator, and a photographer; and prearranged times for meals and parties with friends. A tight schedule defined the sequence of events that were programmed to happen in the house, who would they be meeting, and what was expected of them. In other

4 D. S. Defenbacher to Mary Davis Gillies, interior decorating editor at the McCall Corporation. Letter, July 23, 1941, Walker Art Center Archives.

5 For an extended discussion on the probatory technologies used by the Walker Art Center see Diana Cristobal, "One-to-one scale: Witnessing the Walker Art Center's Idea Houses I and II (1941–1947)," *Bitacora*, no. 44 (2020): 84–99.

6 D. S. Defenbacher, "A Man's House Is His Art," *Everyday Art Quarterly*, no. 5, autumn 1947, 10.

7 Mary Roche, "New Ideas," *New York Times*, November 2, 1947, 44.

8 "House," *Progressive Architecture*, February 1948, 39.

9 D. S. Defenbacher, "A Man‘s House Is His Art," 10.

10 Cedric Adams, *Minneapolis Sunday Tribune*, October 5, 1947, 3.

words, the selected witnesses were required to report the livability of an experience that was prearranged and therefore performative and extraordinary. When D. S. Defenbacher sent the future guests the official invitation, he wrote:

> "All you need to bring is yourselves, a spirit of adventure, and the usual street and lounging clothes. There will be no activities requiring long dresses. Obviously, you should bring along some eye appeal in night wear. If you don't wear any, I'm the last to object, but you might look amazing in the newspapers."[11]

Indeed, being photographed was an important part of the experience. The Walker Art Center compiled around one hundred photographs of these experiences, including very intimate ones. An old woman bringing breakfast to her husband in bed, a young couple eating grapes while gazing at each other, children playing with their toys, etc. Everyday life was being performed for the gaze of the media. These moments, carefully recorded through photographs, became detailed and vivid images of the type of domestic environment promoted by the U.S. postwar suburban housing boom campaign:[12] Informal meals at a snack bar that separated a clean kitchen and a neatly organized living room, large sliding glass doors and open living rooms that promised a new type of visibility (so that the mother could watch her children playing safely outside in their fenced-in garden), children having their own private space for their activities, and technologies such as the radio and the phonograph organizing everyday life. The photographs from the Idea House weekend contest aimed to reveal a seemingly unmediated depiction of such "family togetherness."[13] By featuring subjects that appeared to be unaware of the camera and who never looked directly at it, these photographs portrayed the camera as a self-acting machine capable of producing images, uncorrupted by human manipulation. Seen from this perspective, the photograph was an ideal record of events: mechanical, seemingly self-acting and not subject to human biases.

To study the dominant modes of observation and truth that were developed around Idea Houses I and II is to pay attention to the ways in which a museum promoted a shift from older forms of spectatorship, based on the passive and distant reception of information, to an active and probatory form of cognition. These houses utilized complex material, literary, and social technologies to convince museumgoers of the role of architecture in encouraging a new way of life for the suburban American family. Such "convincing" was built around the illusion of creating an unmediated and unbiased visitor experience through full-scale, fully-functioning models, photographs showing evidence of the space being used, and testimonies collected through the publicity contests, which together shaped a visitor experience based on empirical experience. In other words, the full-scale, fully-functioning model was at the center of a complex process of "consensus gathering"[14]—to use the concept developed by Simona Valeriani to explain the models of the Royal Albert Hall in the context of 19th-century experimental culture. Rather than a passive spectator carried away by dramatic, dazzling forms of entertainment, the subject of these exhibitions was a *witness* that provided testimonial evidence. The witness categorized certainty and veracity as derived from sense experience. In turn, this information was made accessible to a broad public and transformed into collectively agreed-upon evidence by virtue of visual, written, and oral testimonies. To this end, the houses were used, seen, touched, heard, and felt.

11 D. S. Defenbacher to Miller, Trully, and Vine. Letter, October 23, 1947, Walker Art Center Archives.

12 See Gwendolyn Wright, "The New Suburban Expansion," in *Building the Dream: A Social History of Housing in America* [e-reader version] (New York: Pantheon Books, 1981), 3884–3984.

13 This was the slogan that the magazine *McCall's* coined in 1954 to embody the "ideal of domestic social relations and priorities to which responsible Americans aspired." See Dianne Harris, *Little White Houses: How the Postwar Home Constructed Race in America* (Minneapolis: University of Minnesota Press, 2013), 121.

14 See Simona Valeriani, "Copying, Building, Sharing. Multiple Approaches to the Study of a Historical Model" in this volume, 118–123.

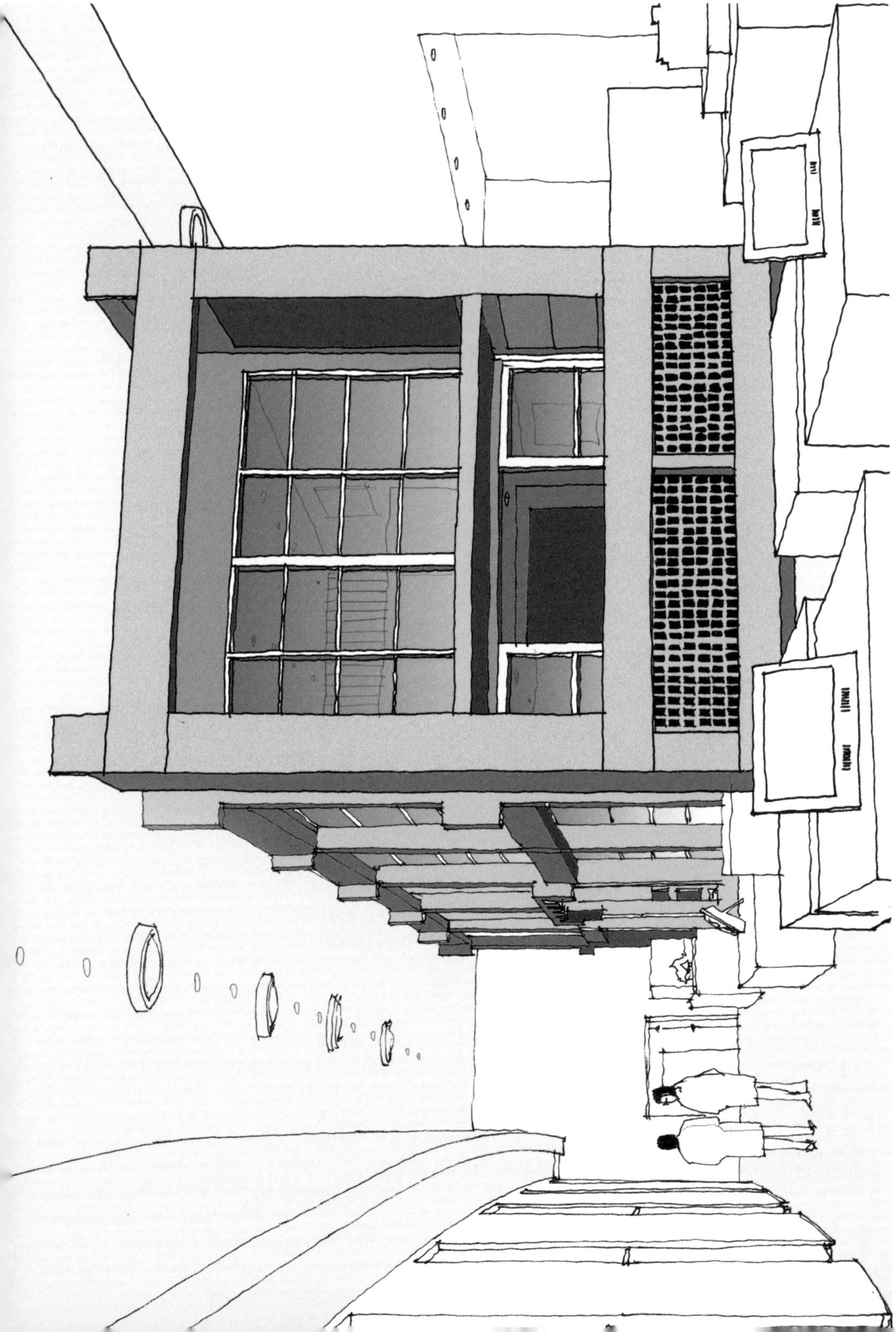

Reconstruction of the Marseille Unité d'Habitation's apartment in the Cité de l'architecture et du patrimoine, 2023. [Daniel Pitta Fischmann]

Unstuck Architectures

When the Building Becomes a Model

Ana Carolina Pellegrini

So it Goes

Billy Pilgrim is the protagonist of *Slaughterhouse 5*, a famous science fiction-infused anti-war novel by Kurt Vonnegut, first published in 1969. Billy lives a life oddly detached from time and space and does not control the back and forth between past and future. Sometimes he may start the day in the 1960s, at his ordinary optometry office, but shortly afterwards finds himself unexpectedly transported to the horrors of World War II. From there, he may be suddenly abducted to Tralfamadore—the planet where he became an aliens' guinea pig and got unstuck in time. At all times and situations, Billy seems to have every single memory at once—including the ones about the future. His inability to control the order of events leads to a sort of omniscience about the effects of time and subverts the relationship to time and space.

An examination of architectural history demonstrates that chronology subversion is not an exclusivity of fiction. Sometimes the usual order of events from which a building results is changed, giving way to less common and more polemical operations, such as building more than a version of the same design—coexisting with or replacing the original. Architectural reconstructions challenge the *Zeitgeist* and are often accused of being falsely old and falsely new. Both the lack of authenticity and the intent to deceive are persistent arguments against operations aimed at rebuilding old architectures in a new time or place.

True Copies

Copying, replicating, and duplicating architectures are polemic operations because they call into question modern concepts such as authenticity, originality, and authorship. More than 80 years since Walter Benjamin wrote about the consequences that mechanical reproduction technologies would bring to the "aura" of artworks, architecture reconstructions are still frowned upon.[1] However, when reconstructions are detached from their original sites, devoid of their utilitarian purpose, criticism may be mitigated. In an exhibition context, reconstructed remarkable architectures become models of themselves and are free from the label of forgery. Devoid of its utility, they are exposed to public visitation as full-scale models, inverting the usual pre-figurative role

1 See Walter Benjamin, *The Work of Art in the Age of Mechanical Reproduction* (New York: Penguin, 2008).

of this means of representation. Unlike a sculpture replica, a 1:1 scale architectural model deceives no one, even if it results from the same design or from a survey of the original building itself. Furthermore, detached from the primordial project's context, a real scale model not only does not threat its original but also reinforces its value, granting it the status of a museum masterpiece. Examples are, firstly, the Maison Tropicale, designed by Jean Prouvé and adapted by Rirkrit Tiravanija as the artwork "Palm Pavilion." It is currently exhibited outdoors at the Brazilian Inhotim Institute. Secondly, the living room of Francis Little House II, designed by Frank Lloyd Wright and rebuilt inside the Metropolitan Museum of Art. And thirdly, the Aldo van Eyck and Gerrit Rietveld Sonsbeek Pavilions, both reconstructed in the Kröller Müller Museum Sculpture Garden—the first one in 2006 and the last one in 2010. All these examples are analogous to the ones this paper will address: the indoor reconstructions of two projects by Le Corbusier regarding domestic architectural programs: the Marseille Unité d'Habitation apartment and the Cap-Martin Cabanon, both architectures out of their time and place, deprived of their function.

A full-scale model of the Marseille Unité d'Habitation E2S typology was inaugurated in September 2007 at the Cité de l'architecture et du patrimoine, the French Monuments Museum, in Paris. The construction works were curated by Robert Dulau and Pascal Mory.[2] Although the Cité was founded only shortly before in 2004 under Jean-Louis Cohen's direction, the Museé de Sculpture compareé of the Trocadero Museum had already been established in 1882 in the same place by Eugène-Emmanuel Viollet-le-Duc. At that time, the idea was to collect reproductions made during restorations of medieval monuments; a museum of casts of the most beautiful French medieval monuments. Systematically displayed together, the full-scale plaster monuments would allow the visitor to appreciate and compare sculptures and architectures of different places. The reconstruction of the Unité apartment more than two centuries after this, therefore, was not a novelty in terms of museography, but it was indeed a newness in terms of collection, since it was the Trocadero's first 1:1 scale model of modern architecture.

Although well-known, this was not the only full-scale reproduction of the apartment with a view of being visited by the public. In 1950, Le Corbusier himself, on the occasion of the Salon des arts ménagers, arranged a wooden model, aiming to publicize the construction work on the Unité, which was in progress at that time. The initiative was not uncommon in this kind of exhibitions. The following year, in the same exhibition, Jean Prouvé built a prototype of one of his prefabricated houses. In 1955, Ionel Schein also presented a full-scale model of his project for a house entirely built of plastic. In 1986, architect Ruggero Tropéano assembled part of the split-level Unité apartment for the exhibition "Synthesis of the Arts" in Karlsruhe. In the following year, Tropéano took part with Jean-Louis Cohen in the exhibition *L'aventure, Le Corbusier*, held at the Centre Pompidou in Paris, for which another real scale model was made. Finally, in 2007, the Japanese exhibition *Le Corbusier - His life and work - a life of creativity*, held at the Mori Art Center in Tokyo, featured a recreation of the Unité's apartment made of stucco and plywood, in honor of Le Corbusier's 120th birthday.

The Unité apartment was not the only reconstruction of a Corbusian project at the aforementioned Japanese exhibition, which featured two other full-scale replicas. The section "Live the Art" presented older paintings by Corbusier and a replica of the architect's

2 For further information about the reconstruction works, see Robert Dulau and Pascal Mory, *Le Corbusier Echelle 1* (Paris: Editions PC, 2007).

Paris studio at the Immeuble a la Porte Molitor from 1933. The visiting route, which included design drawings, models, paintings, sculptures, tapestries, etc., ended with the section "Return to the Sea," a recreation of the Petit Cabanon in Cap-Martin, originally built in the French Riviera. Designed in 1951, the 15-square-meter shelter was built the following year in Roquebrune-Cap-Martin, adjacent to the *Étoile de Mer* restaurant, owned by Thomas Rebutato, a friend of Le Corbusier. Lodging in the Cabanon, by the way, depended on its proximity to the restaurant, with which it shared both the kitchen and the bath. The original simple wooden building still exists and can be visited as a museum in its own right. As in the case previously examined, the Japanese replica was not unique. The Cabanon had already been completely rebuilt in 2006 in Milan, during the Salone del Mobile. Sponsored by the Cassina furniture factory, it remained at the Triennale garden from April to June.[3] The visitors, while experiencing the spartanly furnished space, were faced with odd landscapes pictures fixed on the windows, which were intended to simulate a view of the sea.

The several opinions against the Milan reconstruction did not prevent another initiative by Cassina in London. A third version of the Cabanon was built in a partnership with the Royal Institute of British Architects, RIBA. The English exhibition lasted from March to April 2009; featuring the rebuilt shelter inside Florence Hall, the institute's luxurious cafeteria, further detaching it from its original condition but keeping the landscape reproductions pasted on the windows. In all its versions, the reconstructions of the Cabanon were more criticized than the copies of the Unité apartments. It should be noted, however, that the negative opinions were not centered on the convenience or relevance of the reconstruction operation itself but on the quality (or lack of quality) of the result achieved.

Flawless and Timeless

Far from being unprecedented, reconstructing architectures is still controversial, mainly when it involves notable heritage. The most important international document that guides preservation and restoration—the Venice Charter—recommends to avoid any work of reconstruction. Since it was enacted in 1964, the stance against the so-called "historic forgeries" has become institutionalized in the field of heritage preservation.[4] Architectural full-scale models, in turn, do not usually arouse controversies about the validity of reconstructive operation or about the lack of authenticity, even if emulating a notable piece of architecture.

Unstuck in time and place, and deprived both of their function and use, they do not defy the exclusivity of their originals and do not mislead anyone. Besides, in an exhibition context, both the nature and the purpose of the architectural copies are clear, avoiding the fear of deception. Furthermore, reconstructing a notable piece of architecture in a safe and controlled space, protected from the elements, makes it possible not only to avoid the patina of time, but also to restore—and to maintain—an ideal state of its existence. The set of design documents allows revisiting the past recorded on drawings, pictures, and models, even if the original building is aged, damaged, or has vanished. In these cases, a copy may be more faithful to design intentions than the building itself. Defying the linearity of time, full-scale models can grant some architectures a permanence that their originals will never have.

3 For further information about the Milan reconstruction of the Cabanon, see Fillipo Alison, *Le Corbusier: L'interno del Cabanon* (Milano: Mondadori Electa, 2006).

4 "All reconstruction work should however be ruled out '*a priori.*' Only anastylosis, that is to say, the reassembling of existing but dismembered parts can be permitted. The material used for integration should always be recognizable and its use should be the least that will ensure the conservation of a monument and the reinstatement of its form." Venice Charter, accessed February 26, 2024, https://www.icomos.org/images/DOCUMENTS/Charters/Venice_Charter_EN_2023.pdf.

Regarding the subversion of the timeline, Billy Pilgrim states:

> "The most important thing I learned on Tralfamadore was that when a person dies he only appears to die. He is still very much alive in the past, so it is very silly for people to cry at his funeral. All moments, past, present and future, always have existed, always will exist. The Tralfamadorians can look at all the different moments just that way we can look at a stretch of the Rocky Mountains, for instance. They can see how permanent all the moments are, and they can look at any moment that interests them. It is just an illusion we have here on Earth that one moment follows another one, like beads on a string, and that once a moment is gone it is gone forever.
>
> When a Tralfamadorian sees a corpse, all he thinks is that the dead person is in a bad condition in that particular moment, but that the same person is just fine in plenty of other moments. Now, when I myself hear that somebody is dead, I simply shrug and say what the Tralfamadorians say about dead people, which is 'so it goes'."[5]

5 Kurt Vonnegut, *Matadouro Cinco* (Rio de Janeiro: Intrínseca, 2019), 46–47. Translation by the author.

Children's Library on the left and the city hall on the right. [Wonseok Chae]

The Mockup of the City Hall in Marl

The Grammar of Prototypes

Wonseok Chae

A Mockup

Approaching the city center, a building, half hidden behind bushes, distracts the eye from the landmark of the city hall high-rises with its strange resemblance to these towers. "Insel-Kinder- und Familienbibliothek Türmchen" is a two-story structure in Marl, Germany. The small tower, or "turret,"[1] has a square volume. The overall shape is reminiscent of Villa Savoye built in 1931 by Le Corbusier, except for the flat roof without a roof garden. The main volume is raised to the height of the first story by pilotis. The façade has an all-round ribbon window made up of horizontally lined-up window elements. The lifted square volume is accentuated by the artistic graffiti works that dematerialize the concrete core in the center. A transparent glass volume encapsulates the staircase core, providing the main access and a reception room for the visitors. Above all, the turret features distinctive structures that protrude from the façade just like those at the city hall towers nearby, which could be seen as the result of the multiple stacking of the turret. In 1960, the structure, which now houses the Turret Library, was constructed as a mockup for the city hall of Marl by the Dutch architecture firm Van den Broek en Bakema.

Although transformed into a library, the mockup never existed as an independent entity in the last 40 years.[2] At all times, the library was still seen by the city council as a leftover from the design process of the city hall towers, and councilors constantly asked for its demolition due to a lack of both necessity and budget.[3] The city hall towers, on the other hand, were highly valued as the original building, and every effort has been made to maintain them by reinforcing structures, which cost more than a possible construction of a new tower in the mid-1980s.[4] Finally, in 2015, the city hall was listed as a national monument.[5] While the city hall towers are seen as symbols of societal, cultural, and technological achievements of the postwar democratic West German state, the mockup is still overlooked.[6]

In general, a mockup is a full-scale preparatory model whose primary purpose is to test the original idea of the building performance or simulate building aesthetics in reality.[7] The meaning derives from the French word "maquette," which means a model of sculptures or buildings.[8] From the typological perspective, a mockup is a model whose physiognomic characteristics are molded exactly with structure, form, or materials.[9] This is in contrast to the concept of prototype, which

1 Cambridge German-English dictionary, "Türmchen," accessed October 7, 2023, https://dictionary.cambridge.org/dictionary/german-english/turmchen.

2 Frank Bergmanshoff, Norbert Feyerabend, and Maria Poll, "Der Lesegarten im 'Türmchen'," in *Freundeskreise und Fördervereine: Best Practice in Öffentlichen Bibliotheken*, ed. Petra Hauke, (Berlin, Munich, Boston: De Gruyter Saur, 2015), 179, https://doi.org/10.1515/9783110421996.

3 Ibid.

4 Stefan Kleineschulte, *Das Rathaus in Marl*, (Bochum: Ruhr-Universität Bochum, 2003), 88.

5 Denkmalliste der Stadt Marl, Listenteil A, as per November 30, 2022.

6 HPP Architekten, *Baubeginn bei der Rathaussanierung in Marl*, November 3, 2020, accessed February 26, 2024, https://www.hpp.com/aktuelles/baubeginn-bei-der-rathaussanierung-in-marl.

7 Cambridge dictionary, "mock-up," accessed December 21, 2022, https://dictionary.cambridge.org/dictionary/english/mock-up.

8 Etymologeek, "mockup," accessed September 21, 2023, https://etymologeek.com/eng/mockup.

9 Leandro Madrazo, *The Concept of Type in Architecture*, (Zurich: ETH, 1995), 171.

focuses more on a design scheme or methodology as an essential principle of a group of forms.[10] In his 1965 book *The New Architecture and the Bauhaus*, Walter Gropius defined the overall meaning of "prototype models" as "type-forms" that are the results of collaborative work between individual craftsmanship and mechanical mass production in the context of the mass production culture in the inter-war period.[11] In 2019, anthropologist Susanne Küchler compared the prototype and the preparatory model in her paper "The Prototype in 20th-century Art" on the concepts of both. According to this investigation, the specific characteristics of prototypes are as follows. First, a model is prototypical if it further develops independently from the rest of mass-produced models beyond the final construction.[12] Second, prototypes have their own optimized form that differs from the designated final output.[13] Third, prototypes are defined by a series of works.[14]

A Mockup as a Prototype

Questions arise when it comes to the identity of the mockup. What is the true purpose of the city hall's mockup? Does it simply belong to the design process of the city hall as a preparatory model? The mockup seems to raise specific questions regarding its identity. This is not only because a preparatory model turned into a library, but also because a model has specific formal characteristics that underlie the architects' other design projects from the late 1950s to 1960s.

First of all, a mockup represents a temporary model for the architectural design process. A mockup is usually built before the final construction on the same building site. As a preparatory model, its temporary life usually ends before the final construction of the actual building starts.[15] However, the mockup of the city hall survived after the physical test and was turned into a building in its own right as a library with significant changes. Once the city hall was finished in 1967, the mockup was converted into a place for children and families by installing additional building elements such as toilets, kitchen, interior walls, and floors in 1969.[16] In addition, the children's and family library was extended with a glass box on the ground floor for handicapped children.[17] Consequently, the mockup of the Marl city hall cannot simply be reduced to being a dependent model for the final construction; instead, it represents an independent prototype that was developed further for a unique purpose.

Second, the shape of the external structures are optimized only for the mockup. Its structure is one of the most significant characteristics of the city hall towers. The structure is an extension of the massive truss construction from the rooftop level. The whole tower volume is suspended by means of a group of thin cables consisting of precast concrete and steel wires inside.[18] Unfortunately, this contradicts the nature of precast concrete, which is usually optimized for compression forces. In 1986, the two towers had to be reinforced internally with the same amount of tensile steel structures placed right behind each precast concrete component, which were deteriorating significantly.[19] However, this was not the case for the mockup. Its precast concrete elements sit on the ground, supporting the entire volume in a structurally logical manner without any problems for more than 50 years. In addition, unlike the city hall, the mockup does not require a massive structure on the rooftop. Furthermore, this solution is unique in all projects by the authors.[20] The physiognomic features indicate that the shape and structure of the mockup is more authentic and purer than that of the city hall.

10 Ibid., 240.

11 Walter Gropius, *The New Architecture and The Bauhaus*, tr. P. Morton Shand, (Cambridge, MA: MIT Press, 1965; 1971), 53.

12 Susanne Küchler, "The Prototype in 20th-century Art," *Visual Communication 9* (Los Angeles, London, New Delhi, Singapore and Washington DC: SAGE Publications, 2010), 301–312, here 303.

13 Ibid., 308.

14 Ibid., 306.

15 The *NEST* research building of Empa and eawag could be one of the exceptions in which mockups live after the final construction.

16 Bergmanshoff et al., "Der Lesegarten im 'Türmchen'," 177.

17 Ibid., 179.

18 Kleineschulte, *Das Rathaus in Marl*, 87.

19 Ibid., 88.

20 Ibid., 87.

Third, the mockup is not fixed to the city hall but is circulated through a series of works. Chronologically, after the city hall design was selected from the competition in 1958, the mockup was built in 1960, and it seemed to be a preparatory model only for the city hall towers. Although eventually only duplicated and stacked 12 times in the city hall project in 1967,[21] the mockup has also been used for other projects beyond the city hall. According to Stefan Kleineschulte, there are another six projects designed by Van den Broek en Bakema from 1956 to 1965, all of which are "fundamentally identical"[22] to the design of the Marl city hall towers with their square plans, rectangular façades, and glass podiums.[23] On the other hand, when remodeled with the ground floor extension in 2010, the mockup took the aesthetic reference from the fundamental identity shared by the seven tower designs. The "glass box volume under the tower"[24] was the one thing that the mockup was missing for the fundamental identity of the authors' tower design.

These formal characteristics show a specific state of a mockup beyond a representational model only for the final construction in the architectural design production. The mockup for Marl's city hall opens up a possible interpretation of the mockup from preparatory model to prototype. In this sense, a mockup is not simply a partial fragment of the final construction but a typological essence that provides a design principle for other projects beyond the designated one. The example shows the potential of a mockup produced in the context of postwar industrialization in Germany. The prototypical mockup is open to further development for adaptive reuse while communicating with diverse societies as a formal language. This manifests in a collective idea that transcends a specific project.

21 The mockup was duplicated and stacked 12 times to create two towers. The original plan with four towers includes 30 copies of the mockup.

22 This is an English translation of the original text written in German: "Alle Projekte weisen eine grundlegend gleiche Gestaltung bei den Hochhäusern auf, die der Marler Vorgabe entspricht," from Kleineschulte, *Das Rathaus in Marl*, 142.

23 The six projects are: the Rotterdam office for "Nievelt, van Goudriaan, and Veder" (1956), the Amsterdam Newspaper office "Het Parool" (1957), "The Offenburg city hall" (1962), "Jerusalem city hall" (1964), "Ashad highrise residence" (1965), and "The Frankfurt am Main multi-complex" (1964). Ibid., 141.

24 Bergmanshoff et al., "Der Lesegarten im 'Türmchen'," 182.

Do We Look Alike?

On Digital Multiples, Twins, and Simulation Processes

Chris Dähne, Roger Winkler, and Andreas Noback

1 Olaf Sauer, "Digitaler Zwilling – das Schlüsselkonzept für Industrie 4.0," accessed Februar 26, 2024, https://www.iosb.fraunhofer.de/de/geschaeftsfelder/automatisierung-digitalisierung/anwendungsfelder/digitaler-zwilling.html.

2 Providing a framework for the publication, sharing, and reuse of different models is one of the main tasks of the Specialised Information Service (FID) BAUdigital. For this purpose, a repository is being developed which, in addition to the general objectives of cataloging and archiving, takes into account the above-mentioned domain-specific characteristics of models and the resulting requirements of research in architecture, civil engineering, and urban planning.

3 A development of the Fraunhofer Institute for Computer Graphics Research in Darmstadt IGD/CULT-LAB3D, accessed February 26, 2024, https://www.igd.fraunhofer.de/de/branchen/Kultur-und-Kreativ/3d-scanning.html.

4 The Getty Research Institute began digitizing the work of Frank O. Gehry and Associates, architect in 2017. See: Emily Pugh, "Slides, Software, Data, Drawings: The Frank Gehry Papers as Hybrid Architectural Archive," in *Building Data. Architecture, Memory and New Imaginaries*. Proceedings of the 9th Annual Conference of the Jaap Bakema Study Centre, ed. D. van den Heuvel (Rotterdam: TU Delft and Het Nieuwe Instituut, 2022), 68–73, accessed November 7, 2023, https://www.getty.edu/projects/understanding-architectural-model-research-applications-3d-imaging/.

5 Deutsches Architekturmuseum, Modellsammlung, "Oswald Mathias Ungers," accessed Februar 26, 2024, http://archiv.dam-online.de/handle/11153/264-001-523.

In architectural design, models—whether physical or digital—take on the role of a manipulable "twin." A twin that is not so much an exact replica of a physical object as the classical "digital twin," but rather a "concept," which is modeled using digital tools and including geometric, kinematic, and logical data.[1] Until this concept takes shape in a built architecture, the digital model undergoes several transformations and lifecycle phases in an iterative process in which several twins are created. The advantage of these twins is that they can be used—in conjunction with the real requirements and data—to experimentally test the development states (of the architecture) within dynamic interrelationships between the physical, the real, and the modeled, the digital. But what happens when a digital model experiences the materialization of its data, or vice versa: when a physical model, or even the built architecture, is transformed back into a digitalized proxy?

Model Deutsches Architekturmuseum by Oswald Mathias Ungers, working model of the overall building (model I), 1980. [TU Darmstadt]

These questions are explored in the contributions to this section, which focus on the emergence of digital multiple twins and their role in the development and research of design processes. We would like to present two use cases from the knowledge and research fields of computational design and construction and architectural history that we have explored as part of the DFG-funded BAUdigital project.[2]

The first use case is the wooden pavilion for the BUGA Heilbronn 2019 (Federal Garden Show), which has become known for its innovative design reflecting new approaches in digital timber construction: segmented shells were assembled in a puzzle-like and automated manner according to the biological construction principles of the plate skeleton of sea urchins. For this architecture, which was designed, planned, and manufactured in digital process chains, the Institute for Computer Aided Design and Construction (ICD) at the University of Stuttgart created a variety of data-driven models that simulated the structural optimization of the architecture and the development of robotically manufactured component systems. These computer simulation models form the basis for the design and production of the research pavilion in order to map the entire manufacturing and construction process, as well as the expected structural and environmental behavior. Numerous models/multiple twins ultimately led to the construction of the pavilion, the materialized 1:1 model. The process chain for this building does not end there: the 3D scanning process and sensor technology have transformed the structure into a digitally enriched replica. This replica—which Christiane Fülscher's section "Am I the Real Thing!" focuses on—now serves as a platform for experimental tests similar to those carried out during the design and planning process. What has changed, however, is the focus, which is now on investigating the actual material and structural behavior and performance of the building. In particular, the data collected by the sensors on the physical behavior of the building is documented and recorded over time to identify innovative solutions for resource-efficient construction. The models created in the production and lifecycle of this architecture could be said to provide insights into the future of multiple twins in the context of such digital design, fabrication, and evaluation processes.

This is followed by our second example, which takes a look back at architectural history. Thanks to an autonomous scanning device based on photogrammetry, the CultArm3D,[3] it has become possible to convert physically built models, such as the BUGA pavilion, into a digital copy. The device first captures the geometry and texture of the models from different angles. Special reconstruction software then converts the raw images into 3D spatial data in the form of point clouds and textured meshes. In collaboration with the Deutsches Architekturmuseum (DAM) in Frankfurt am Main, we used the robotic 3D scanner to capture and analyze around 30 physical architectural models from the museum's collection, most of which were made between 1960 and the present day. We wanted to find out to what extent the retro-digitization/digital twin could open up new approaches to architectural history. After all, the physical working, design, measurement, and presentation models act as contemporary witnesses of built and unbuilt cultural artefacts and therefore offer incredible insights into architectural ideas and concepts.[4] Physical models usually consist of multiple and movable parts—such as Oswald Mathias Unger's five-part working model of the building of the Deutsches Architekturmuseum (1980)—which can rarely be exhibited for conservation reasons (box within a box).[5] The (retro)digitized twin of Unger's model was able to illustrate the concept of a 'house within a house' in the simple creation of interactive, kinetic 3D models and animations. The digital twin could be transformed through media processing into a digital explanatory model and virtual demonstration of the design concept. In contrast to the physical model, its twin is not subject to any conservation constraints and restrictions (conservation, durability/storage in the archive). A digital model can be accessed, experienced, and made comprehensible throughout the world but requires a virtual environment, in which it can be visualized and explored on a screen, VR or AR application. In addition, analytical transformations, modifications, processing, and annotation of its 3D data is possible, as are links to other digital sources within the Semantic Web that can be used to "edit" the model. It this sense, the retro-digitized model represents a new type of source for architectural research that opens up new possibilities for scientific or museal use.

Although some interesting measurement models, e.g. by Frei Otto, are available at the DAM, with the CultArm3D technology it is not possible at the time of our study to accurately capture, e.g., fine wire meshes, and the capturing campaign had to focus on more classical architectural models. However, Baris Wenzel presents a method for digitally preserving Frei Otto's surviving construction and measurement models in his article "Digitally Recreating the Mannheim Multihalle Model. Exploring the Simulation of Physical Form-finding in the Tradition of Frei Otto." In a reverse-engineering process, he succeeds in reconstructing the existing structure of Otto's model of the Multihalle. The twin created in a mix of retro-digitization and parametric modeling corresponds to an abstracted model allowing to trace and verify the static behavior of both the physical measurement model and the built object. In this respect, the digital model provides information about Frei Otto's innovative optimization of form and construction, which would otherwise remain trapped in a fragile artefact—one of the last remaining exemplars of this cultural heritage.

In the ethnographic study "The Model Multiple. On Approximation Work in Digital Models and Twins," Yana Boeva describes an approximation to the physical model that can be multiplied by certain interactions between human and non-human actors. Multiples generated in [computer] simulation, a mixture of instincts, anticipations, and interpretations of software, parameters, and data are the result of different planning teams and constraints acting on the design processes. For Boeva, the digital multiples are merely "approximate models" that can be used to visualize and communicate the computational designs of different actors, technologies, processes, and interests.

Another role played by the digital twin is an emergent expression of complex real-time systems. Yana Boeva understands computer models as changeable and dynamic due to the actors and production processes involved. In "Models in Reality – Dynamic Real-Time Systems in Architecture," Caroline Höfler adds that their geometric-mathematical relationships and material properties are relevant dynamizing factors. When these basic elements and variables are given as numerical values, they have an operative effect on the creation of a specific form design that is in exchange with its environment. Changing environmental influences and reactive material structures, 3D and robotic technologies, which generate moments of material unpredictability, create models as "digital-material events in real time." They act and change in time, so that for Höfler they are like an event that takes place in reality but is represented as a virtual idea of complex, medial, and material interactions of highly heterogeneous factors.

As a virtual representation of dynamic processes and concepts, the model, a digital multiple twin of dynamic processes and concepts, is replacing the conventional, object-like, and static model concept in architecture. The research projects outlined by the authors are exemplary of this change. The new role and function of the digital model is similar to that of an interpreted and abstracted model, as well as an approximation model, and also a real-time event that generates creative ideas and a variety of new applications.

Gramazio Kohler Research, ETH Zurich, Remote Material Deposition Installation, Sitterwerk, St. Gallen, 2014. [Gramazio Kohler Research, ETH Zurich]

Models in Reality

Dynamic Real-Time Systems in Architecture

Carolin Höfler

Model of Being a Model

One of the most enduring narratives about architectural design is the simplified ideal scenario according to which the design process is a chain of modeling stages that lead from the large to the small, from urban design to detailed structural planning.[1] According to this scenario, at the beginning of each modeling stage there is an architectural hypothesis with its respective specific subject promise. The final modeling stage at the end of the chain then results in the specific construction. However, computer-based design seems to interrupt this supposed sequence of design operations. With the help of 3D modeling and simulation software, the design is developed less in successive stages that build on one another and more in a single stage that theoretically includes all other stages. Scales are blurred, designing in discrete scales is weakened: digital process chains eliminate the traditional separation between the intellectual act of design and the material act of manufacture, and production technologies directly intervene in the design processes.

In light of these fundamental changes in design processes, drastic crisis scenarios about the loss of importance of architectural design as theory building have been drawn up in recent years (Mario Carpo spoke of the "obsolescence" of the Albertian paradigm),[2] whereas the consideration of the active potentials of computer-based models have remained rather underexposed. The question regarding the active potentials of digital models picks up on model-theory considerations developed by mathematician and scientific philosopher Bernd Mahr. He developed a "model of being a model," for which the double reference of being a model "for something" and "of something" is constitutive.[3] According to him, models are fundamentally in the field of tension between representation and production, depiction and enabling; they show something and at the same time are oriented towards exploring and designing possibilities.[4] This text will therefore focus on digital models and modeling practices that can be considered as emergent expressions of complex real-time systems. They have their own active life with a function that gives meaning and guidance for action. Modeling material systems and force fields in digital 3D space, as has been tested in experimental architectural practice, abandons the notion that the model is merely an abstract

1 Jörg H. Gleiter argues that with the introduction of scale drawing by Leon Battista Alberti, the architectural design process takes place in a chain of discrete modeling steps from the largest to the smallest scale, with the 1:1 scale representing the final model range. See Jörg H. Gleiter, "Gegenstandsversprechen: Entwerfen als Prozess der Theoriebildung," *Wolkenkuckucksheim | Cloud-Cuckoo-Land | Воздушный замок, International Journal of Architectural Theory* 25, no. 40 (2021): 11. In contrast, Albena Yaneva characterizes the architectural design process as a multi-layered rhythm based on multiple ups and downs between small and large models, each used for different aspects. See Albena Yaneva, "Scaling Up and Down: Extraction Trials in Architectural Design," *Social Studies of Science* 35, no. 6 (December 2005): 867–894.

2 In the Albertian tradition, an architect is particularly defined by their ability to model a future structure in abstract scale drawings, which would later be implemented by the qualified skilled worker on the construction site. See Leon Battista Alberti, *Zehn Bücher über die Baukunst*, tr. Max Theuer (Vienna and Leipzig: Hugo Heller & Co, 1912), 20; Mario Carpo, "Revolutions: Some New Technologies in Search of an Author," *Zona* no. 3 (2009): 15. http://pro.unibz.it/library/bupress/publications/fulltext/Zona3.pdf.

scheme. In the digital model, a multi-layered event is made tangible in actual execution, which is essentially determined by its relationship to matter and material.

Gatherings of Materials in Movement

Such a modeling approach is exemplified in the works of architects like Michael Hensel and Achim Menges, Fabio Gramazio or Matthias Kohler. Taking up the ecological paradigm in systems theory and cybernetics, Hensel and Menges refer to their designs as "material systems," which develop an activity that allows them to be processual and relational. The systems become active through a structure composed of elements that simultaneously generate space, dissipate force, and conduct and store energy.[5] These elements develop from the specific qualities of the materials and the production processes used; ideally, they have an undisturbed, reciprocal relationship with their environment.

Hensel and Menges produce their models in two ways: on the one hand, a structural element is developed from a specific material, and on the other, the properties of this element are reproduced in a parametric computer model. Analogous to Frei Otto's models of "natural constructions," they mainly use flexible, elastic, and unstable materials such as wood veneer, textile fabric, or plastic fibers, which form themselves automatically as a result of the forces inherent in and exerted on them. In this process, the material is no longer conceived as a passive carrier of an idea of form but as an operative structure in exchange with the environment.

The notion of the self-formation of form is not only fundamental to the material structural element but also to its digital model. Instead of a final form, the computer model defines a provisional scheme of mathematical relationships described with variables and constants. The generic model, in which geometric relationships, material properties, and production processes are inscribed, then forms the basic element of a composite. In the composite, the individual elements are interactively linked with each other, creating flexible structures of mutual dependencies. A specific shape design is only created when numerical values are assigned to the variables. As soon as the element enters into a reciprocal relationship with other elements and is to fulfill certain functions, it receives its specific, individual form.

The notion of self-regulating form becomes especially vivid in those models that react to alternating environmental influences with changes. For example, the reactive material structures that Achim Menges developed together with product designer Steffen Reichert in recent years are based on the shaping behavior of thin plywood sheets. An example of this is the installation *HygroScope: Meteorosensitive Morphology*: an architectural system that is sensitive to changing humidity.[6] When humidity is high, the veneer elements bend automatically, causing the structure to partially open. When the humidity decreases, the surfaces close again. These changes are caused by the hygroscopic properties of the wood used. Such projects are based on an understanding of modeling that focuses primarily on material transitions and transformations. Modeling in this case refers to the development of a material interface, a transition medium between inside and outside, a membrane that plays an active role in selectively transmitting natural movements such as light, air, and sound. No longer do models of this kind see themselves as statuary coagulated results or objects that depict a temporally fixed

3 Bernd Mahr, "Ein Modell des Modellseins: Ein Beitrag zur Aufklärung des Modellbegriffs," in *Modelle*, eds. Ulrich Dirks and Eberhard Knobloch (Bern: Peter Lang, 2008), 187–218.

4 The difference between models "of something" and "for something" has been discussed in: Carolin Höfler, "Modelloperationen: Zur Formierung gesellschaftlicher Wirklichkeiten," in *Was ist Public Interest Design? Beiträge zur Gestaltung öffentlicher Interessen*, eds. Christoph Rodatz and Pierre Smolarski (Berlin: transcript, 2018), 283–311. https://doi.org/10.14361/9783839445761-020.

5 Michael Hensel and Achim Menges, eds., *Morpho-Ecologies* (London: AA Publications, 2006); Michael Hensel and Achim Menges, "Performance als Forschungs- und Entwurfskonzept: Begriffe und Bezugssysteme," *ARCH+* 41, no. 188 (July 2008): 31.

6 Achim Menges, Steffen Reichert, and Oliver David Krieg, "Meteorosensitive Architectures," in *Alive: Advancements in Adaptive Architecture*, eds. Manuel Kretzer and Ludger Hovestadt (Basel: Birkhäuser, 2014), 39–42. https://doi.org/10.1515/9783990436684.39.

state of form. Rather, they gain in dynamism, become changeable at any time, and adaptable to alternating environments or changing requirements.

This understanding of a model as a digital-material event in real time becomes more evident when the model is a direct expression of a dynamic and adaptive fabrication process that is unpredictable: Gramazio and Kohler experiment with precisely operating robots to foam, cast, or shoot flexible materials in form of projectiles. Technical systems of traceability, reproducibility, and measurability are used to deliberately create structures that are unpredictable, unrepeatable, and transient. Here, 3D and robot technologies act as generators of moments of material incalculability. In the project *Remote Material Deposition*, Gramazio and Kohler explored the idea of robotically positioning material in space from a distance by throwing loam projectiles directly to its target position.[7] This approach was tested and validated through a series of prototypical structures. Despite digital control, it is difficult to fully predict and simulate specific deformations upon impact and the resulting local construction patterns to their full extent. Therefore, visual object tracking and real-time feedback as integral parts of the model setup ensure that those components that have already been physically created are related to and continuously alter the digital model in real time.

These models are "things" in the sense of Timothy Ingold. The British anthropologist calls them "gatherings of materials in movement" in order to emphasize their constant mutability and permanent mobility.[8] Ingold pleads for a shift in perspective with his "ecology of materials"—away from form as a fixed and final material entity and toward a modeled environment as a force field and a circulation of resources, energies, and materials.[9] Of central interest here is the temporal dimension of models, which heralds a transformation of the conventional object-like static model concept in architecture.

Such concepts of material agency aim to activate the model as a creative instance. They pursue the assertion of a new, active paradigm of model as real-time system, which has many preconditions, as it presumes both the undisturbed functioning of the system and an intact relationship to the environment. Its definition as an ecosystem assigns the model the status of a living being.[10] By implication, models that are characterized by inactivity are considered deficient.

7 Kathrin Dörfler, Sebastian Ernst, Luka Piškorec, Jan Willmann, Volker Helm, Fabio Gramazio, and Matthias Kohler, "Remote Material Deposition: Exploration of Reciprocal Digital and Material Computational Capacities," in *What's the Matter? Materiality and Materialism at the Age of Computation*, ed. Maria Voyatzaki (Chania: European Network of Heads of Schools of Architecture, 2014), 361–377.

8 Timothy Ingold, "An Ecology of Materials" in *Power of Material/Politics of Materiality*, eds. Susanne Witzgall and Kerstin Stakemeier (Zurich and Berlin: diaphanes, 2014), 65.

9 Ibid., 60, 64–65.

10 Carolin Höfler, "Model Operations: Morphogenesis and the Design Process," *Perspectives on Science: Historical, Philosophical, Social* 29, no. 5 (September/October 2021): 602–626. https://doi.org/10.1162/posc_a_00386.

A Generative Process in Its Own Right

The computational material systems are not conceived as works of artistic imagination but rather as seemingly objective results of reciprocal interactions between material, structure and environment, and thus as artificial forms analogous to nature that are detached from any cultural or architectural historical context. Differences between living and non-living, analog and digital, past and present forms are thus deliberately obscured. Modeling in this sense can be understood as a technique—a cultural technique or technology—that relates to processes of hybridization: It produces phenomena of the supposedly living that defy established patterns of interpretation such as the nature/culture difference.

These model approaches provide important impulses for a renewal of design practice, but also for an alternative theory of architectural form that sets itself apart from the relevant provisions of the aesthetic tradition. Like the polemics of the architectural avant-garde in the early 20th century, the criticism of the computer pioneers at the turn of the 21st century is directed against generally accepted styles and design systems and is part of a paradigm shift from predetermined, transcendent to self-generated, immanent form. Drawing on material and digital processes of self-formation, architects are working on the development of dynamic, time-based concepts of form that seek to counter the tradition of static spatial orders with a pliable and flexible architecture.

In the course of this paradigm shift, the weighting of the architect's individual work phases is shifting in favor of modeling, which is no longer just a stage on the way to the realized building but has become a generative process in its own right. It is not least the concept of the architectural model that undergoes a fundamental reinterpretation in this way. The presented works provide examples of this change: For as modeling gains in importance as an open process, normative models in the form of ideal types or exemplary blueprints become obsolete. They are replaced by dynamic models that appear as a material event of a real milieu, without the result being foreseeable from the outset. The material components and the techniques of their digital processing form a heterogeneous structure that is designed by the architects but not completely determined. Their responsibility is thus partially ceded to an emergent, independently acting model. The model literally steps into action to give an idea of itself in two respects: On the one hand, it appears as an event that takes place in reality; on the other hand, it enables an idea of the complexity of the medial and material context of effects, which includes a multitude of highly heterogeneous factors. In this perspective, models are understood as technical-ecological assemblages that set spatial, material, and atmospheric processes in motion, thereby giving rise to a wide range of new ideas. They thus directly contradict the notion of the computer model as a "digital twin" as negotiated in the current debate about the "metaverse."[11] The digital twin represents an intended or actual physical product, system, or process of the real world. It is understood as an indistinguishable digital counterpart used for simulations, testing, and monitoring. But how helpful is it to recognize in models merely advanced illusionism? Ultimately, models never represent *real* phenomena—they are themselves and they generate new reality relations and phenomena.

11 Gabriele Gramelsberger, *Philosophie des Digitalen zur Einführung* (Hamburg: Junius, 2023).

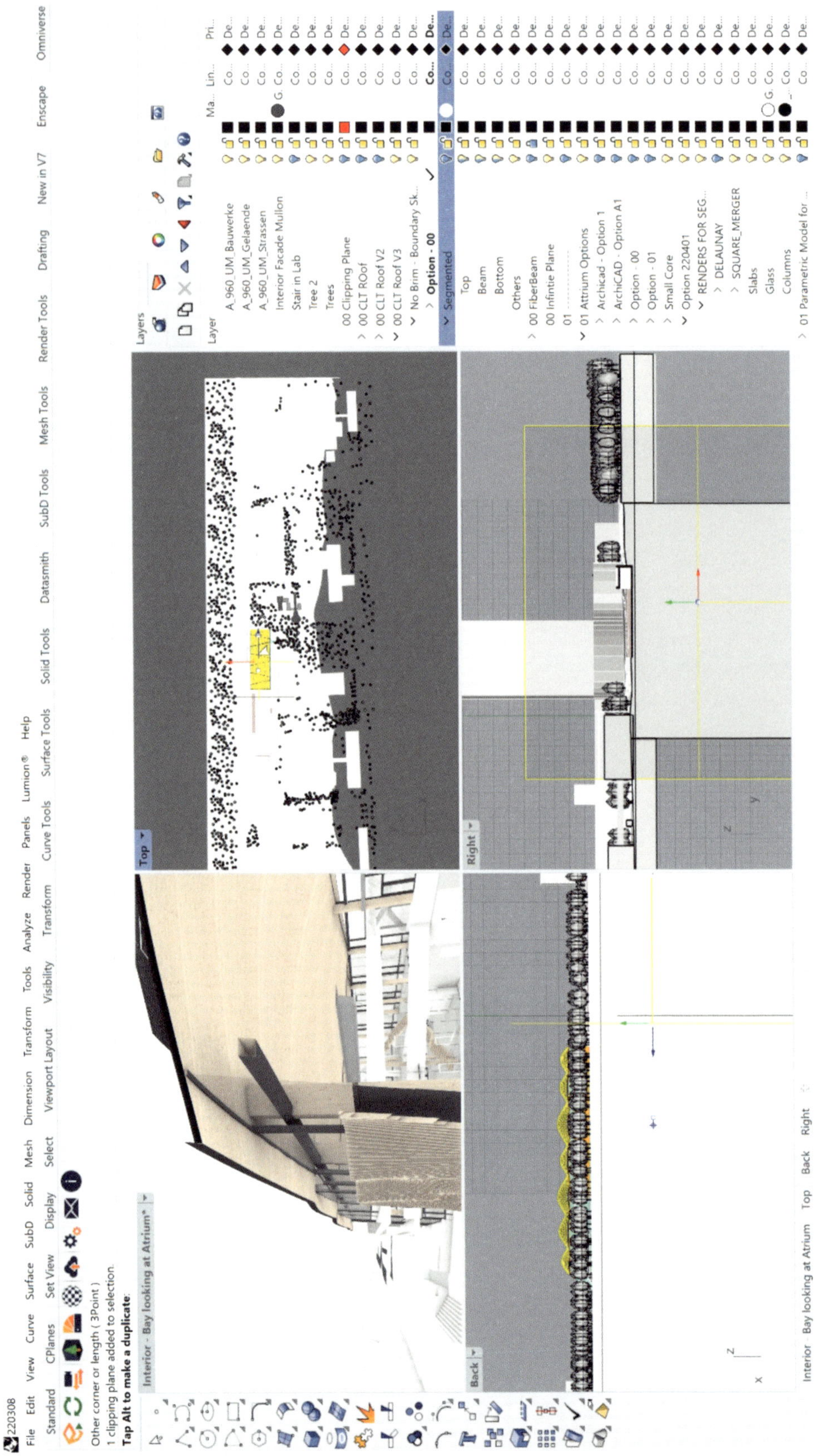

Exemplary preview of a roof simulation in Rhinoceros 3D, 2022. [IntCDC University of Stuttgart]

The Model Multiple

On Approximation Work in Digital Models and Twins

Yana Boeva

Introduction

Digital models and workflows have become ubiquitous in design, engineering, and construction practice, and in some instances, they even produce (their) digital twins. Broader representations of digital models and their production are regularly presented as integrative approaches to a particular design problem, leading to unified and "seamless" versions of the building-in-the-making.[1] The reality, however, consists of ruptures and multiplicities between digital modeling epistemologies, practices, processes, and technologies. The supposedly *one* digital model of a building and its potential twin turn out as multiples with every other actor involved in the design process and every additional condition to be achieved. As ethnographically informed research on design and architecture has shown, the multiple existence of digital models is rarely discussed due to the preference in design and architecture to present and discuss final results rather than processes that created them.[2] These presentations hide the approximation and anticipation work that goes into creating a digital model, which on little occasions remains a singular one, as this paper discusses.

In her ethnography of a disease, anthropologist Annemarie Mol argues that a specific disease and the respective body become a "composite whole" due to the coordination work performed between different experts, treatments, instruments, technologies, and places.[3] For Mol, reality multiplies "since the object of manipulation tends to differ from one practice to another," while keeping the relations between them intact.[4] Mol's concept of the "body multiple" proposes a praxeological perspective that allows reflection on the approximation work performed by many visible and invisible human and non-human actors in creating a digital model.[5] Approximation work in design and architecture captures ways of knowing and doing, particular around uncertainty.[6] Approximating the model of a building involves "overlapping, nonfungible, and messy work processes of anticipation" that remain unnoticed.[7] However, "approximation is part of the 'ambulatory' nature of design processes," as Brett Mommersteeg points out in his ethnography of architectural acousticians.[8]

Design practice, as described in scholarship, recounted by practitioners in interviews, and observed in the design meetings that led to the model discussed in this paper, is full of approximation work that mends ruptures and multiplies. In the following, I discuss observations

1 Daniel Cardoso Llach, *Builders of the Vision: Software and the Imagination of Design* (New York: Routledge, 2015).

2 See Cardoso Llach, *Builders of the Vision*; Albena Yaneva, *Made by the Office for Metropolitan Architecture: An Ethnography of Design* (Rotterdam: 010 Publishers, 2009); Thomas Yarrow, *Architects: Portraits of a Practice* (Ithaca: Cornell University Press, 2019).

3 Annemarie Mol, *The Body Multiple: Ontology in Medical Practice. Science and Cultural Theory* (Durham: Duke University Press, 2002), 9.

4 Ibid., 5.

5 The practice turn in the social sciences has shifted attention to the work of science and technology in terms of both the processes of production and the resulting products. It foregrounds who does what in a model, who knows what, and who can actually say what they know.

6 Brett Mommersteeg, "Approximations: On Some Ways to Listen to a Building 'in the Making'," *Science, Technology, & Human Values* (August 2022). https://doi.org/10.1177/01622439221116964.

and accounts of practitioners' approximation work that is always situated and emerging through particular interactions.[9]

The Invisibles of a Digital Model

Spring of 2022, a Friday afternoon. I am participating in a bi-weekly meeting of the design team during the final design phase. On a large screen in the middle of the room, a preview of today's agenda and documents are shared for everyone to follow. The senior architects discuss the segmentation of roof elements with the computational designers in the team. One of them handles the parametric model of the building-in-the-making on their computer. This designer is then asked to switch the preview to their Rhino model of the roof segmentation—a comparable perspective to the image addressed here. They respond to different requests by the architects and adjust some parameters. And then, we wait for a live preview of the rendering. As everyone looks at the new rendering of the roof segmentation, the senior architects, the computational designer in charge, and the structural engineers figure out something is odd with the model. Conversations between individuals begin across the room. At one point, I overhear one structural engineer pointing out that the parametric model is based on calculations combining outdated elements. The engineer adds that the computational designer needs their calculated version from that morning.

As the team continued to discuss other design issues, similar situations repeatedly happened—either with the Rhinoceros 3D (Rhino) parametric model or the many 2D CAD plans of sections previewed for discussion. The digital model addressed in this image and the ethnographic account multiplied across timescapes but also through the many human and non-human actors involved in its making. With every decision and at any moment, these actors performed approximation work to ensure its digital creation and subsequent existence and maintenance. The future building "in the making," shown in the image, is developed by two different design teams simultaneously but in distinctive ways. A research-based team introduces emerging developments, while a professional studio ensures that building codes are fulfilled and user expectations are taken into consideration. Instead of working with a BIM model that coordinates in the center of all actors and trades, the dual design team uses a temporary parametric model of the building, created and persistently maintained by one of the computational designers.

This parametric model has a twofold purpose. It visualizes and communicates the computational designs of the research team to the professional studio. It also aligns the advanced designs to the boundary conditions and regulations that inform the professional studio's designs, represented in 2D CAD drawings and, on occasion, as hand-drawn sketches on paper or a tablet. As Mommersteeg holds, referring to noise as an element of design, "in the [computer] simulation [it] is approximated as a mixture of instincts, anticipations, and interpretations alongside the regulations, software, parameters, and given data."[10] Similarly, the computational designer approximates the building's model, as the incorporated layers in the image of the Rhino preview suggest. An "ArchiCAD Option A1" coexists with an "Option 00", and so on. For instance, the Rhino model of this roof becomes an amalgamation of computationally designed and calculated elements by the research design team, elements designed by the professional studio, and standard, commercial building elements

7 Adele E. Clarke, "Anticipation Work: Abduction, Simplification, Hope," in *Boundary Objects and Beyond: Working with Leigh Star*, eds. Geoffrey C. Bowker, Stefan Timmermanns, Adele E. Clarke, and Ellen Balka (Cambridge, MA: MIT Press, 2015), 85–119, here 85.

8 Mommersteeg, "Approximations," 18.

9 I join previous research on the situational character of design work contingent upon local conditions. See Sophie Houdart, "Copying, Cutting and Pasting Social Spheres: Computer Designers' Participation in Architectural Projects," *Science Studies* 21, no. 1 (January 2008): 47–63; Mommersteeg, "Approximations"; Yarrow, *Architects*.

10 Mommersteeg, "Approximations," 16.

chosen by them. Except for the standard ones, the other elements become approximations in a digital model through simulation, prototyping, and fabrication.

Articulations by practitioners reflect digital models' situated and transient state, depending on their specific trade or phase in the design and construction of a building they are involved in. Unlike popular narratives of digital models about their value and potential, their real value is contingent upon initial objectives and interests pressed by clients and designers alike, the practical experience of actors handling it, as much as the importance and prestige of the built object. The continuous development of a model—the building's lookalike—is often said to stop when architects have tendered 2D CAD drawings from a 3D model and continue to work with those instead. The 3D model needs reconstruction by fabricators, other specialists, or the BIM coordinators in a team, thus implicitly including their values, objectives, and interpretations of what it looks like. This becomes possible because 3D models are "infinitely and instantly manipulable," as anthropologist Keith Murphy observes.[11] As a result, a model is never the same for each party and may not mirror its "lookalike" but instead multiple and approximate it.

These conditions also emerge from local modes of project development and regulations. Building contractors seek to integrate designers or other trades with less digital aptitude, such as building services planners or electrical planners, into the digital modeling process as early as possible. For example, contractors perform approximations by offering to produce highly detailed and functional BIM models for fabrication based on the minimal information provided by designers and others. Moreover, the performance of this invisible approximation work in the digital model allows to enroll actors and thus strengthens power relations. The idea of BIM models enabling seamless collaboration and intra- and inter-organizational design equally neglects their disciplining and processual character.[12] What sounds like multiple participants shaping one digital building model also means that, in reality, the building model multiplies by overlaying each actor's contribution. As Mol writes: "Singularity can also be deliberately strived after. It can be produced. The *result* of addition is a single object."[13]

In conclusion, this leads us back to the proposition to acknowledge the existence of the digital "model multiple" and what it does for discussions of hidden work. Revealing a model's multiplicity means to "restore agency" of everyone and everything managing the model's existence.[14] Approximation work performed in digital models and equally part of digital twins is always distributed between actors, technologies, processes, and interests. Thus, in the long run, as software and technology companies strive for more automated digital twin solutions, extending the techno-utopian idea of a singular digital model and promoting it to clients, big architectural firms, and urban developers, a closer inspection of the careful manual and crafted processes behind automation to actually approximate models continues to be necessary.

This work was supported by the Deutsche Forschungsgemeinschaft (DFG, German Research Foundation) under Germany's Excellence Strategy – EXC 2120/1 – 390831618.

11 Keith M. Murphy, *Swedish Design: An Ethnography* (Ithaca: Cornell University Press, 2015), 145.

12 Yana Boeva, Kathrin Braun, and Cordula Kropp, "Platformization in the Built Environment: The Political Techno-Economy of Building Information Modeling," *Science as Culture* (July 19, 2023): 1–28. https://doi.org/10.1080/09505431.2023.2237042.

13 Mol, *The Body Multiple*, 70; original emphasis.

14 Susan Leigh Star, "The Sociology of the Invisible: The Primacy of Work in the Writings of Anselm Strauss," in *Social Organization and Social Process: Essays in Honor of Anselm Strauss*, ed. David R. Maines (Hawthorne: Aldine de Gruyter, 1991), 265–283, here 267.

Collage, on the left the original measurement model built at the Institut für leichte Flächentragewerke in 1972, on the right its digital twin, 2022. [Baris Wenzel]

Digitally Recreating the Mannheim Multihalle Model

Exploring the Simulation of Physical Form-Finding in the Tradition of Frei Otto

Baris Wenzel and Eberhard Möller

This work is part of the DFG-funded research project Last Witnesses, which is dedicated to the preservation of the last few surviving physical measurement models. Digital twins of the models are created and used for damage mapping but also as part of the conservation strategy, since they offer a multitude of possibilities, such as VR exhibitions or virtual testing.

For the 1975 Federal Horticultural Show in Mannheim, Carlfried Mutschler's architectural office won the competition for the construction of a pavilion with a lightweight structure. Since this construction turned out to be very complex, Frei Otto, an experienced planner in this field, was consulted, and several measurement and form finding models were built. The filigree measurement model examined in this article was built to create the complex free form of the hall. The model was built in a simplified way due to the large number of parts. Only every third member of the roof was represented in the model. The net of the model consists of 15 millimeter long chain links made of 1 millimeter steel wire with rings, 2.5 millimeters in diameter. And it is precisely these properties that make retro-digitization considerably more difficult. A laser scan cannot image the filigree reflective parts, and manual recording of all intersections would be very time-consuming. Therefore, the author opted for a hybrid process in two phases.

First, the boundaries were modeled. The second step was the modeling of the wire grid using parametric design tools. This process is described in detail in the next sections. As it would have been impossible to capture all individual intersections of the wires using photogrammetry in a reasonable amount of time, I tried several shape-finding methods in order to replicate the wire grid. To have as similar boundary conditions as possible, I decided to divide the grid, as in the physical model, into the parts *restaurant*, *banana*, *Multihalle*, and *link*.

Retro-Digitization

To reverse engineer the preserved form-finding and measurement model, the existing structure was photogrammetrically recorded as a basis for the 3D modeling. Pictures from various positions were taken with a DSLR. Later, in photogrammetry software, the pictures were overlaid and 333 points were extracted. The modeling process that followed can be described in two parts. The first part, in which the masts and boundaries are modeled explicitly (by hand), and the second part, consisting of modeling the chain grid.

For every mast, three points were extracted to establish a local coordinate system, as well as one point determining the height and one point indicating the rotation angle of the bent arm on top. With this information, the parts can be placed by a script.

The arches, which are chains in the original model, were obtained by simulating a hanging chain. The concrete boundaries, in the original model represented with thin bent acrylic plastic strips, were modeled as surfaces, using several points obtained by photogrammetry. The laminated timber beams were modeled as polylines. For the cables, the endpoints of the masts as well as several additional points, all obtained by photogrammetry, were used to be combined in a Bézier curve.

With this method, the first step was to create a rectangular and equidistant base grid in the global XY coordinate system. Then this grid was divided by the closed boundary curve, and the exterior part was removed. The following steps were done using Grasshopper's physics engine Kangaroo 2: The anchor points were moved to their final position and fixed. Now the line segments were relaxed. The line segments that touch the boundaries are able to change their length, simulating the springs in the original model. The inner edges remained at a fixed member size of 15 millimeters.

To begin with, a regular triangulated mesh was created, with the boundaries projected onto the global XY coordinate system. This mesh was then relaxed using a particle spring system to create a 3D shape. This shape was used to drape the final quad mesh over it, simulating the way it was done by hand in the original model. After that, the protruding line segments were removed.

The basis for this method is described by Frei Otto in the IL booklet number 10.[1] It uses a compass to generate equilateral square stitches on an arbitrary surface. To create the grid shell of the digital twin, this method was implemented in C#, which can be described as followed: First, a surface is created from the relaxed mesh, similar to method 2. Then, any two planes are chosen and intersected with the surface to create four parts. Now the four resulting curves are divided into segments with the length of the desired mesh width. Two branches are selected to start with, and a sphere with the radius of the desired mesh width is placed at each first point. These spheres intersect each other. The resulting circle is now intersected with the surface, resulting in the new vertex. First, this is repeated for the whole quadrant and then for the other three quadrants. The resulting arrays are connected to lines in warp and weft direction. In a last step, the grid is trimmed using the boundary curve.

1 Burkhardt Berthold, Takeschi Hasegawa, Jürgen Hennicke, Kazunori Matsuschita, and Frei Otto, “Die Zirkel Methode,” in *Gitterschalen Gridshells, IL 10 Mitteilung des Instituts für leichte Flächentragwerke* (Stuttgart: Institut für Leichte Flächentragwerke, 1974), 140–141.

Do We Act/React Alike?

Almost all mathematical disciplines are based on the so-called *Zermelo-Fraenkel* set theory:
$\forall x\,(x \in a \iff x \in b) \implies a=b.$
The complicated-looking formula states that two sets A and B are equal if they contain the same elements. That sounds quite simple, but even with numbers this becomes more difficult if the observer is included: $f(x)=2x+4$ and $g(x)=2(x+2)$.

For any numerical value of x, both figures produce an identical result. However, the outer form of the equations is definitely different.[2] So things can be(-have) the same, even if they do not appear to be. In model statics, it was quite common to use acrylic resin to simulate reinforced concrete. If you look at the materials, they don't seem very similar, but, more importantly, they behave similarly. Key is that they have a similar elasticity (Young's modulus) and a similar Possion's ratio (Hooke's law) and therefore behave similarly.

Although the studied measurement model certainly cannot be denied an aesthetic value, less emphasis was placed on external appearance than on functionality. Due to the lack of time in creating the digital twin of this model, little attention was paid to the representation of colors, weathering, oxidation, and similar aesthetic features, whereas greater attention was paid to more important aspects: its technical functionality and the correct location of the vertices of the wire grid.

I would like to start this section with a famous quote from George Box: "All models are wrong, but some are useful."[3] Tolerances already played a role in the making of the physical model. Due to the usual inaccuracies of man-made objects, wear of the tool, and the minimal length differences of the members when added together, the model no longer corresponded to the desired scale of 1:100 but to 1:98.5.[4] Likewise, in the creation of the digital twin, there are several possible sources of error; the question is always how much is still acceptable, which in turn is often determined by the subsequent use. For example, one can check whether two points are identical in order to determine which of the form-finding methods leads to the best results by comparing a reference point from the photogrammetric recordings with one calculated by the algorithms. The individual components of a point (X, Y, and Z values) are floating point numbers and are rounded to the 8th decimal place. To compare two floating point numbers, a tolerance variable is usually used, considering the tolerance of an absolute value: $x=y\leq$. But how to define this threshold? This is certainly to be evaluated differently depending on the situation. Here, one should probably weigh the costs and benefits.

There is certainly no globally correct answer to the question "Do we act/react alike?" Rather, you always have to weigh up how much time you are willing to invest in order to be able to satisfy a lower threshold value for the deviations. A more precise question might be: "Am I reacting similarly enough?", addressing how similar the model needs to be. A final verification of the accuracy of the digital twin is difficult due to the large number of elements of the model, as well as the possible sources of error, and is still pending in its completeness. The digital twin serves its purpose, but we had to make compromises for the creation, for example regarding the visual appearance of the parts.

The next step, as suggested by Giulia Boller in her remark during the conference discussion, is definitely to implement the force-density method developed by Klaus Linkwitz in C# and apply it to the model.

2 Florian Freistetter, "Freistetters Formelwelt: Ist gleich immer gleich gleich?" *spektrum.de*, 16.10.2022, accessed September 27, 2022, https://www.spektrum.de/kolumne/gleichheit-in-der-mathematik/2065647.

3 Guillem Barosso, "All Models Are Wrong, But Some Are Useful," George E. P. Box, accessed September 27, 2023, https://www.lacan.upc.edu/admoreWeb/2018/05/all-models-are-wrong-but-some-are-useful-george-e-p-box/.

4 Burkhardt Berthold, Max Bächer, and Frei Otto, "Die Formfindung der Gitterschale," in *IL 13 Mitteilung des Instituts für leichte Flächentragwerke* (Stuttgart: Institut für Leichte Flächentragwerke, 1976), 88–89.

What Can You Learn from Me?

On Model Didactics

Christina Clausen

1 Jean-Luc Nancy, *The Ground of the Image*, tr. Jeff Fort (New York: Fordham University Press, 2005), 36.

2 Reinhard Wendler, *Das Modell zwischen Kunst und Wissenschaft* (Munich: Wilhelm Fink, 2013), 25.

3 Ibid., 23.

The manner of reception and the visualization potential of a model diverge substantially from the perception of constructed architecture, yet this need not be considered a drawback; in fact, it contributes to the distinctive quality of models. An architectural model can be readily observed from a distance and from an elevated vantage point, offering a unique and privileged perspective. When models are simplistically viewed as a means of representing or simulating reality, these distinctive attributes often go underappreciated, but representation goes beyond mere depiction; it involves revealing and even shaping meaning, which is something models also achieve. Therefore, it might be beneficial to utilize Jean-Luc Nancy's perspective on representation when discussing models:

> "Representation [...] does not present something without exposing its value or sense—at least, the minimal value or sense of being there before a subject. It follows that representation not only presents something that, either by rights or in point of fact, is simply absent: in truth, it presents what is absent from presence pure and simple, its being *as such* or even its sense or truth."[1]

In other words: Representation doesn't just display something missing, it also lays bare its significance or essence, even if that something isn't directly there. Essentially, it unveils what's lacking in straightforward presence, be it its existence, meaning, or truth. Isn't this a crucial aspect of teaching or learning with models? Using models in educational settings also comes with challenges because they are not always as straightforward to understand as commonly believed. Models are frequently linked to the idea of instant clarity due to their physical resemblance to actual structures. However, their connection to what they represent is more autonomous and distinct. The medialization of a building always initiates a process of transformation, and the newly created object has a "material and medial sense of its own" that goes beyond a function of representation.[2] Reinhard Wendler speaks of an "unfolding of the active potentials of the models," in other words, they "become involved in thinking and acting."[3] This can be seen both in the form-giving effect of materials in the design process and in the historical, theological, or physical knowledge that always remains connected to the concrete form of the model in memory.

The four contributions presented in this chapter address various inquiries related to the didactic utilization of models. While these papers represent individual viewpoints within this extensive subject area, they collectively underscore the resurgence of specific questions across different historical epochs and contexts. Notably, they center on the materiality and tangible existence of models and their significance in generating knowledge, both in the context of observation and production, as well as their adaptation to the digital domain.

Holger Zaunstöck's article delves into the model of the Halle orphanage within the Francke Foundations, crafted in 1719/1720. This model serves as a compelling manifestation of Pietist ideals, specifically the aim to address societal disparities through a combination of devout piety and structured pedagogical practices. Functionally, this model serves as an invaluable educational instrument, revealing intricate structural and operational facets when disassembled. Its inherent potential extends across a spectrum of applications. In particular, it assumes a role in architectural representation, explicating the existing structures as well as blueprints for future expansions. Pedagogically, it functions as a repository of knowledge, vividly illustrating diverse aspects of daily life and the institutional organization. In the realm of image building, the model becomes a convincing vehicle that brings the ethos and mission of the foundations closer to a broad audience. Within the context of the Cabinet of Artefacts and Natural Curiosities (CANC), it serves as a didactic tool to impart experiential knowledge to visitors, although even in the first half of the 18th century it could only be touched by educators and guides as a valuable museum object. Zaunstöck portrays the Halle orphanage model as an emblematic embodiment of Pietist educational ideals, transcending disciplinary boundaries and combining model materiality with a variety of academic and cultural functions.

Alberto Calderoni's research focuses on the role of physical models in contemporary architectural education. It addresses the challenges in teaching architectural design due to the abstract nature of architectural theories and the underestimation of architects' expertise by the public. The use of physical models as cognitive and pedagogical tools bridges generational and linguistic gaps in architectural education as well as in the planning of and communication about architecture. In his paper, Calderoni discusses the pivotal role of physical models in architectural design studio courses at the University of Naples Federico II. These models help students analyze the built environment, explore narratives in domestic architecture, and understand urban design elements. They also promote haptic learning, a fundamental aspect of architectural education. Physical models enable the discretization of reality and provide a means to translate diverse problems and conditions into architectural form. They foster the synthesis of volumes and spaces mediated by formal sensitivity. According to Calderoni, models serve as irreplaceable pedagogical tools, encouraging formal recognition and disciplinary procedures in architectural design education.

The contribution authored by Salome Schepers, Orkun Kasap, and Silke Langenberg again delves into the physical manifestation of models, focusing on a collection of mockups exhibited in Zurich in September 2021. The 1:1 scale models, in particular, exuded a unique and compelling presence, offering a distinctive form of persuasion and suggestiveness. The research projects considered the efforts, material, and energy involved in building, the status of construction in Swiss society, the ambiguity between temporary construction sites and intended permanent buildings. The projects also examined the gap between administrative regulations and actual demand in construction projects and highlighted the contrast between luxury and refugee accommodations. Finally, they explored the architectural expressions of office buildings and single-family houses, revealing shared interests and ideals among powerful societal groups. The research raises questions about documenting and archiving the diverse interests and stories behind mockups, the potential shift in the mockup's role from symbol to laboratory, and how altered attitudes towards material and space could impact general building activities. It also suggests that mockups can serve as agents to communicate the existing qualities of the building stock and proposes that transformations begin with mockups to evaluate existing potentials and propose sensible interventions.

Andreas Pilot's paper introduces the digital component into the wider context of the didactic section, which is essential in the contemporary use of models. He investigates the integration of digital modeling and interdisciplinary collaboration in educational settings, with a specific focus on a case study implementing a pedagogical framework. A consortium of academic experts from various institutions developed and implemented this approach in a workshop during the summer semester of 2022. The paper addresses the challenges associated with model usage, creation, verification, coordination, and communication within the context of digital building design models. It introduces the Technology Acceptance Model (TAM) to demystify the process and encourage technology adoption. The workshop underscored the value of early exposure to digital modeling within the context of collaborative education, demonstrating that simplifying the task to a creative endeavor empowered students to swiftly develop self-efficacy in model-based collaboration. The findings suggest the potential applicability of this approach in various educational contexts.

Team play in digital models, 2022. [digiLEARNbim research group]

Built Together!

Digital Models and Teaching Team Play

Andreas Pilot

The field of architecture and design is undergoing a transformative change with the extensive integration of digital modeling methods that depict objects or components combined with information. Often it is integrated into the academic landscape on a knowledge-based concept with a practical experience at the end.[1] A novel pedagogical framework commences with practical application in an interdisciplinary seminar to impart basic skills and competences for interdisciplinary collaboration, as opposed to prioritizing knowledge acquisition.

In architectural education, digital models typically adopt an object-oriented approach, allowing for a detailed examination of building components, which enhances the learning environment. In this context, the use of models as teaching aids becomes crucial, as they serve as fundamental tools for collaborative learning, offer a realistic representation of designs, and promote interdisciplinary collaboration in planning.[2] The consortium of architects, engineers, and psychologists from the Technical University of Darmstadt, the University of Applied Sciences Erfurt, the Leibniz-Institut für Wissensmedien, and the University of Tübingen designed a workshop to reduce technical barriers and encourage collaborative involvement. The students collaborated in teams to co-create a concept for a 3D puzzle, individually designing each piece as simple geometries. They then assembled the pieces in a common data environment (CDE) to explore and present them in virtual reality (VR). The conceptual underpinnings, practical implementation, and outcomes of the workshop will be explored, focusing on the key challenges of collaboration as well as the creation and use of digital models.

1 Yilei Huang, "Developing a Three-Level Framework for Building Information Modeling Education in Construction Management," *Universal Journal of Educational Research* 6, no. 9 (September 1, 2018): 1991–2000.

2 Ruoyu Jin, Tong Yang, Poorang Piroozfar, Byung-Gyoo Kang, Dariusz Wanatowski, Craig M. Hancock, and Llewellyn Tang. "Project-Based Pedagogy in Interdisciplinary Building Design Adopting BIM," *Engineering, Construction and Architectural Management* 25, no. 10 (July 31, 2018): 1376–1397.

Methodology and Its Challenges

The teaching concept was applied for the first time in the summer term of 2022. The structure of the workshop, the composition of the teams, and the evaluation criteria were designed to measure the effectiveness of interdisciplinary collaboration and to gain insights into technology uptake, barriers to entry, and collaboration outcomes. Several challenges have been identified in areas such as model use, model creation, model checking, and model coordination as well as management and communication.[3] These challenges revolve around knowledge gaps, technological limitations, coordination issues, and problems arising from the unpredictability of creative processes. The workshop approached each challenge strategically, ensuring a balanced distribution of skills within the teams, reducing the task to sculptures with simple geometries to avoid overwhelming detail, and encouraging the competitive yet collaborative nature of the task to inspire creativity and originality. The primary approach was to opt for open BIM as the method and technology enabling students to choose from a broad range of software for model creation. Additionally, the task was structured in such a way that only fundamental features were necessary for collaboration in the CDE and presentation through VR.

Influences and Outcomes of Technology Acceptance Model Integration

In the quest to integrate digital modeling into teaching methods, the workshop was met with an initial wave of uncertainty among participants. There were inherent reservations about the feasibility of designing, modeling, and presenting a sculpture within a VR tour in just a few hours. To overcome this, the Technology Acceptance Model (TAM) was used to both demystify the process and communicate its inherent benefits.[4] Therefore, the pedagogical concept is modeled according to TAM's factors of "perceived usefulness," "perceived ease of use," "attitude towards use," and "behavioral intention to use" which lead to the "actual system use."[5]

Regarding the "perceived usefulness," participants were made aware of the end game—a compelling VR presentation of their sculptures that would be anonymously voted on by peers and educators. Utility was further enhanced by the revelation that this kick-off workshop would lay the groundwork for the upcoming Tiny House co-development phase, highlighting the continuity of learning. To reinforce the accessibility of the task at hand, defined as the "perceived ease of use," the educators staged a 20-minute live demonstration. This playful walkthrough demonstrated the simplicity of the overall workflow and provided practical workarounds where necessary. Interestingly, the participants realized that their skills were already surpassing those of the trainers in certain areas of the workflow, particularly model creation. This demonstration was made readily available as a recorded resource, extending its reach. The streamlined nature of the workshop meant that students only needed to understand a subset of the tools' functionality. This reduction in the skills required, coupled with the ongoing technical support provided by the trainers during the subsequent group activities, further reduced anxiety.

In addition to establishing the usefulness and simplicity of the system, there was a concerted effort to foster a forward-thinking technology mindset according to TAM's "attitude to use." Educators advocated an agile approach to technology adoption, fostering a culture where mistakes were not shamed but seen as opportunities for growth. This was further reinforced by endorsing workarounds as a core principle, encouraging adaptability. Regarding "behavioral intention to use" and "actual system use," as the workshop progressed, there was a palpable sense of competition between the teams. Even as the time limit approached, the teams showed an unwavering enthusiasm to improve their sculptures. Analysis of the data collected within the CDE documented this continued drive and was testament to the perceived benefits of refining individual

3 Tim Lemmler and Andreas Pilot, *Implementierung von BIM in der Lehre* (Berlin: bSD Verlag, 2021), 42.

4 Felix Andrian Prihatono and Tri Joko Wahyu Adi, "Building Information Modeling (BIM) Technology Acceptance Analysis Using Technology Acceptance Model (TAM)," *IPTEK Journal of Proceedings Series,* no. 1 (2020): 81.

5 Viswanath Venkatesh and Fred D. Davis, "A Theoretical Extension of the Technology Acceptance Model: Four Longitudinal Field Studies," *Management Science* 46, no. 2 (February 2000): 188.

model components and the newfound ease with which they could navigate the workflow. This culminated in repeated and intensive use, underlining the success of integrating the TAM into the fabric of the workshop.

The workshop highlighted the value of early digital modeling in collaborative education. It demonstrates that simplifying the task to a creative one empowers students to experience self-efficacy in model-based collaboration within a brief period. However, these study findings may require further validation through expanded research that concentrates on a range of variables and larger participant demographics. Individual creativity, background, and attitude towards technology are significant factors influencing the outcomes and levels of acceptance, and thus necessitate further inquiry.

Exploring Diversity in Teaching Technological Skills

This workshop as part of a teaching framework reinforced the transformative potential of integrating digital models with teaching strategies in interdisciplinary education, echoing broader discussions on future model-based practices. The collaborative development of an innovative teaching concept has successfully reduced entry barriers and promoted effective interdisciplinary collaboration through digital models. This approach avoids the traditional knowledge-based learning method and instead utilizes a practical and competitive workshop at the outset, followed by reflection and adaptation to other tasks like designing and planning a tiny house by collaborating in the fields of architecture, interior design, landscape design, construction, and MEP planning (Mechanical, Electrical, Plumbing). The workshop's knowledge and experience have significant repercussions for integrating digital models in future educational and professional practices. This provides an alternative to knowledge-based concepts presented in the guidelines, such as VDI/BS-MT 2552 sheet 8.1 "BIM - Basic Knowledge," VDI/bS 2552 sheet 8.2 "BIM - Qualifications - Advanced Knowledge," and VDI/bS-MT 2552 sheet 8.3 "BIM - Qualifications - Skills."

The findings from the workshop suggest that reducing the technical demands to a creative activity facilitated the participants' swift development of self-efficacy in model-based collaboration. Nonetheless, careful examination is necessary for the generalization of these findings. The results primarily capture the observations and input of attendees exclusively from a workshop, underscoring the necessity for future studies to validate these perceptions amongst diverse contexts and demographics. The technological prowess, innovative flair, and strategic approach of each participant are critical factors influencing technology adoption and outcomes, necessitating a broader and all-encompassing investigation. However, transferring these insights to wider educational or professional settings requires a thorough comprehension of diverse contextual influences and individual disparities. Hence, further research should concentrate on assessing the enduring effects of incorporating digital models in varied learning environments and examining their adaptability and efficacy in diverse educational contexts. Exploring diverse teaching methodologies while progressively integrating advanced skills is crucial to ensuring the holistic development of students.

By re-drawing and re-building various mockups in Zurich, students of the master thesis studio at the Department of Architecture at ETH Zurich explored the narratives hidden behind the construction projects. [Salome Schepers]

Let's Begin at the End

The Mockup as a Tool to Re-Examine Building Projects

Salome Schepers, Orkun Kasap, and Silke Langenberg

In September 2021, the students of the master thesis studio de Vylder/Delbeke/Langenberg at the Department of Architecture at ETH Zurich counted a total of 23 mockups in Zurich.[1] As a common planning tool in the building process in Switzerland, this type of 1:1 model placed on the construction site announces the forthcoming transformation of the built environment, while its omnipresence in Zurich hints at the brisk and excessive construction activity of recent years.[2] As architects, we are heavily involved in the extensive process of transformation and therefore need to understand the mechanisms steering the building industry. By closely analyzing the mockup as the harbinger of imminent construction, the master thesis studio aimed at understanding the interests and stakeholders involved in the building process in order to propose sustainable alternatives.[3]

1 The RE-NOW-RE studio was a master thesis studio led by professors Jan de Vylder, Maarten Delbeke, and Silke Langenberg in the autumn semester of 2021. At the beginning of the semester, the students together with 8000agency (assisting the chair of Jan de Vylder) went on a collective walk within the city of Zurich. The walk was based on the field research made by the students beforehand.

Are You a Mockup?

A "mockup" is a model built at a scale of 1:1. It is a critical proof-of-concept tool to test an idea, scenario, material, form, or technology in many disciplines, not just in architecture. For example, the airline Swissair used mockups of planes in the early 1990s for training their cabin crew in case of emergencies. Rather than a complete aircraft, the mockup included only specific elements necessary for the exercises.[4] Like any other model, the mockup concentrates on a particular question and consciously omits other aspects. In architecture, it enters the stage at a critical moment of transition—from conceptual design to the material construction—and thus depicts the compromises emerging due to the translation from an idea on paper to the physical implementation of the project.[5] It can also serve as an assessment instrument, as is the case in Zurich, where high quality architecture is required by law for public and high-rise buildings or large-scale developments, while mostly focusing on the facade of the future building.[6] Situated on the plot rather than at the architects' office, it brings together various stakeholders involved in a project. It consists of specific elements that are of particular interest—to the architect, to the client, to the builder, or to the administration—, presenting a valuable insight into the intentions of a project, while equally casting light on aspects disregarded.

2 Part of the collective research was a visit to the exhibition *MOCK-UP* at the Swiss Architecture Museum (S AM) in Basel, Switzerland, which ran from August 28 to October 31, 2021. The exhibition included photographs of mockups by David K. Ross. The photographs were shot at night with a spotlight directed on the mockup, leaving out the surrounding context. Contrary to these representations, the master thesis studio aimed to reveal the context of the mockup in order to analyze and critically evaluate current construction projects.

There is a direct correlation between the current transformation of the building stock in Zurich and the mockup as its proclamation. This observation led us to examine five mockups found in Zurich during the master thesis studio in the autumn of 2021, with the goal of assessing present forces within the building industry. Each of the five students chose one mockup for closer investigation.[7] By thoroughly observing, re-drawing, or re-building the mockup, questions began to surface: What does the mockup show? What does it not show? Who has been involved in the construction of the mockup? Whom does the mockup address? During the process of critically reading the model, the students retraced the objectives of the architectural project behind it, gaining insight into the mechanisms shaping the transformation of Zurich's built environment. Finally, this investigation led the students to explore alternative solutions for a more sustainable building practice in the future.

In one case, a chosen mockup showed a fragment of the future facade for a large-scale development on the outskirts of Zurich. The building project intended to replace the existing properties of a housing cooperative in order to respond to the urgent need for more housing in the city. The mockup was found installed in-between the existing properties, directly confronting the old with the new. But the three-meter-high and four-meter-wide mockup representing one corner of the facade failed to convey the extensive scale of the new development. Rather, it resembled the children's playground situated next to it on the green lawn between the houses. Based on this observation, the student decided to challenge the envisaged replacement of the existing buildings and alternatively propose an additive system, based on the fragmentary character of the mockup.[8] Other students investigated questions regarding the temporality of construction material or the imbalance between economic speculation and actual necessity for space.

The following description of a selected student project aims to illustrate how the reading of one particular mockup, in this case constructed for a new office building in the center of Zurich, resulted in a critical analysis of the appropriation of architecture and thereupon turned into a starting point for an alternative proposal for the entire development.

3 Jan De Vylder, *universum carrousel journey. RE-NOW-RE 3,33% 33,3% 333%* (Zurich, 2021). https://ethz.ch/content/dam/ethz/special-interest/arch/department/Studium/PDF/masterarbeit/themen/Themen_HS21/De_Vylder_Delbeke.pdf.

4 Swissair, "Mock-up der Swissair für Evakuations-Übungen des Kabinenpersonals in Zurich-Kloten," ETH-Bibliothek Zurich, Bildarchiv, accessed November 12, 2023, http://doi.org/10.3932/ethz-a-000268697.

5 Reto Geiser, ed., *Archetypes* (Basel: Standpunkte and Zurich: Park Books, 2021).

6 In the Planungs- und Baugesetz (PBG) of the canton of Zurich, §71 and §284 respectively demand the architecture of large-scale developments and high-rise buildings to be "especially well designed." A phone call with the building department confirmed that the mockup hereby serves as an instrument to control the quality of such developments.

7 The following five students were part of the master thesis studio in the autumn semester 2021: Manon Zimmerli, Kunqi Hou, Tom Mundy, Miriam Tröndle, and Salome Schepers.

8 This master thesis project was developed by Kunqi Hou under the title "The overlap of time.", accessed February 15th, 2024, https://works.arch.ethz.ch/thesis/the-overlap-of-time-2.

What Do You Mask?

The examined mockup was made for an office building on the shore of Lake Zurich. The new building for an insurance company replaced a previous one on the plot which combined both residential and commercial use. The new building is part of a row of office blocks lined up along the lake, and the mockup temporarily acted as the final structure in the sequence. Situated on a small meadow and isolated from the construction site, the model did not immediately reveal its connection to the development a few blocks away. The two-story model represented the corner of the facade proposed by the architects, which consisted of red prefabricated concrete elements and large windows. Together with two white rendered walls at the back, the facade enclosed an interior space which was used to test interior design concepts.

The position of the mockup on the meadow, its height, and interior space differentiated the model from the others found in the city. Instead of a fragment, this particular mockup appeared as a finished building. And yet, the two different expressions of the facade and the surrounding context of the office buildings revealed inconsistencies, generating interpretations that alienated the mockup from its original purpose.

The starting point of the analytical exploration was a short story speculating on potential interpretations of the mockup. In this fictional story, the white rendered back walls were associated with the stereotypical appearance of single-family houses, as they can be found outside of the city. After a road trip to the periphery of Zurich, eight single-family houses in Fehraltorf confirmed the initial interpretation.

The mockup hence juxtaposed the facades of two separate worlds, turning them into masks of two identities: the institutional office building and the personal single-family house. At first glance, these two architectures had nothing in common in terms of location, use, and architectural expression. But aside from the geographic and material differences, research in phone books, municipal newspapers, and on LinkedIn revealed an important correlation between the two: the people living in the single-family houses work for businesses such as the insurance company in question. Consequently, both buildings are habitats of the same people, of the same social class. Therefore—and this was the hypothesis—both architectures expressed shared interests and ideals—on an individual and on an institutional level.

When reading the mockup on the shore of Lake Zurich as a symbol of architectural appropriation by a particular social circle, it raises the question of spatial ownership and identity across society. This analysis led to an alternative design proposal, which served as the project for the student's master thesis. Taking inspiration from the mockup, the two architectures were mixed and brought together in one place: the city's periphery. On a formal level, this was expressed by removing parts of the office facade—then under construction—and re-installing them on the individual plot in Fehraltorf. In return, the urban space of the office building would be freed from its use by the insurance company and made accessible to all inhabitants of the city.[9]

9 Schepers, Salome: *Masquerade of Security*, accessed November 29, 2023, https://works.arch.ethz.ch/thesis/masquerade-of-security.

What Do We Learn?

The analysis of the mockup for the office building revealed an alternative perception of a sociographic narrative that affects the architecture in Zurich on a vast territorial, social, material, and architectural level. While each student chose one mockup, the studio became a collection of different narratives, allowing to cross-reference and gain an in-depth understanding for the dependencies and correlations in current building practices. The critical reading of the model could subsequently be understood as a critique of the building project as a whole. This discovery led to numerous discussions within the master thesis studio, speculating on the role of mockups in the design and building process and how points of criticism could be reintroduced in an architectural project that has been planned for years and is nearing completion.

There are two conclusions from these discussions: the investigation of mockups in this final studio formed a dense web of agendas and interdependencies shaping the construction industry of Zurich. The collection of mechanisms across the different projects and the critical observation of the status quo revealed space for improvement. As freshly graduated architects, this is crucial knowledge in order to navigate future projects in the city.

For the model itself, the use of the mockup still holds a promising prospect, in the industry as well as in the theoretical discourse. How does this type of model represent the definition of good architecture, and why, in almost all cases, is it reduced to the appearance of the facade? When did the mockup start to become a common planning tool in Swiss architectural practice, and what legal or economic framework accelerated this implementation? What are the reasons for investing these large amounts of money, labor, and material without any purpose of permanence, or, in other words, what agendas lie behind the mockup? One could formulate the hypothesis that, as an agent of specific dispositions, the mockup illustrates narratives of contemporary architecture and therefore acts as an important testimony. Tracing mechanisms of selected case studies in future research could open up a broader perspective on an economic and political legacy that regulates today's architectural landscape.

Building Density. Residential Blocks in the Old Town of Naples, 2018. [Alberto Calderoni, laboratorio A402, Laboratoriodi Progettazione Architettonica II, academic year 2018/2019, Dipartimento di Architettura, Università degli Studi di Napoli Federico II]

What We Have Learned, So Far

Physical Models as Tools for Architectural Education

Alberto Calderoni

The Model and Its Context

Studying—and teaching—architectural design is a very complex task, for two main reasons: the vagueness of the theories on which architectural design is based (a relatively new academic field compared to the hard sciences), and the lack of popular recognition of the role of architects and their expertise, especially perceived in Italy, where architectural transformations are slower due to the density of historic cities and the longing for conservation. These two realities—teachers and practitioners, theorists and professional architects—are combined and held together by very few and insufficient moments of debate. Too few to define shared values and critical categories for the growth of a scientific community that recognizes itself within these values and parameters. While on the surface this macroscopic issue seems to have nothing to do with the use of physical models and their role in design education, in reality, considering physical models as cognitive and pedagogical tools means searching for a possible common language that is useful for students and teachers, freeing them from having to immediately search for words to explain (and therefore understand) the ideas and messages contained in the forms. A possible renewal or improvement of communication, which has become necessary because of the increasing miscommunication between generations and the dissolution of common linguistic codes, may be possible through physical models.

They are a specific product of the architect's work, oscillating between being tools of representation, procedural devices, and autonomous objects.[1] Through their bodies, humans manage to measure the finiteness of the model and, by experiencing it synaesthetically, to control its image projected in their minds. Physical models persuade us that we can have direct control over the real world, an illusion that we ourselves indulge in—unconsciously—at all ages: it is the same mental operation that is enacted in child's play. Toys, as models, are always scaled-down reductions of objects from the adult world that help the child acquire awareness of external reality through comprehensible and harmless fictions.[2] The model is like a magical instrument capable of transmitting emotions to its surroundings. Models, enclosed within physical limits yet available to further modifications, reveal themselves to those who build and experience them as spaces ready to be inhabited with the use of imaginative faculties, circumscribed in the environment in which they present themselves as amplifiers of emotions.

1 Kenneth Frampton and Silvia Kolbowski, eds., *Idea as Model* (New York: Rizzoli International, 1981). Tomàs Maldonado, *Reale e virtuale* (Milano: Feltrinelli, 1994), 100.

2 Alberto Calderoni, *Il recinto di Kairòs* (Santarcangelo di Romagna: Maggioli, 2023).

Models, then, are above all an occasion for architectural design teaching. My line of research, which has unfolded over more than seven years at the Architectural Design Studio that I run at the University of Naples Federico II,[3] considers the use of the model as the fulcrum around which the entire pedagogical environment revolves.

In the design studio course, the program's pedagogical objectives determine the types of models students will create, specifying the materials and scales they should use. Typically, these models are crafted from cardboard and various colored papers of different thicknesses, and they are made at no less than a 1:100 scale. This scale is essential to capture the essence of the physical context in which the project will be situated. Within the design studio, models serve as invaluable tools for analysis, helping students focus on exploring the potential narratives inherent in domestic architecture. These narratives encompass elements such as gates, doors, windows, and balconies, which function like musical notes, defining the rhythm of a city's soundscape. Beginning from this point of departure—reading and observing the city—, students are tasked with interpreting the city's relationships by crafting models that aim to strike a balance between the focal figure (the building) and its backdrop (constructed at a 1:50 scale using colored paper). This exercise allows them to examine various methods for seamlessly extending the fabric of the ancient city. Simultaneously, students work with models at scales of 1:200 and eventually 1:100 to validate urban strategies and housing concepts. They seek typological stability and a clear schematic representation that synthesizes structural, material, and spatial considerations.

The construction of physical scale models is one of those methodological moments in the study of architecture that, perhaps more than any other, characterizes the learning path of the discipline. In recent years, there have been many interesting reflections[4] on haptic learning, its indispensability, and its deep rootedness in the human being, which are directly applicable to the teaching of architectural composition. A model is constructed in order to know, recognize, and understand the reality of a place, to study its dimensions, its scale, to analyze the relationships between things, the reasons that can generate certain conditions, material consistencies, and construction characteristics; to promote scenarios, both conceptual and material, actions and intentions, settlement principles and spatial qualities. With their construction it is possible to discretize reality, to choose what to include and what to omit, to reconfigure a third object reality that is inevitably different both from the constituted subject and from the idea preconfigured in the minds of those who imagine it. An object with its own specific physical, material, and dimensional characteristics that stands out in space, autonomous, which is what it appears to be.

A model is an allusive object that can be approached by proposing, through its physical presence, possible meanings that refer—through similarities—*to references without reference*, in which *the reference is all to be sought*. Architectural models are not cross-references to something else, that is allegories of different realities of which they are a rhetorical figure (just like doll's houses); they are not finished objects, because to call them such would be to limit the atmospheres that can emanate from the things they are; they are available objects, capable of transporting the sensations and intuitions of the observer (or of those who perceive them haptically,

3 Alberto Calderoni, ed., *Logbook 1–6*, (Napoli: Thymos Books, 2022).

4 Juhani Pallasmaa, *The Thinking Hand: Existential and Embodied Wisdom in Architecture* (Chichester: John Wiley & Sons, 2009); Richard Sennett, *The Craftsman* (New Haven & London: Yale University Press, 2008).

or also of those who produce them) into their own personal cultural structures (incessantly elaborated through experience), thanks to a process of recognition that does not consist in observing something again, but rather *in knowing something through what is already known to us*.

The construction of a physical scale model is a perfect metaphor for the most intimate purpose of teaching architectural design: to transmit a sensitivity capable of translating problems and situations from the most diverse conditions (social, political, economic, environmental, functional, performative, prescriptive, administrative, constructive, aesthetic) into form. One of the typical skills of the architect is the synthesis of volumes and living spaces, mediated precisely by an indispensable formal sensitivity that preconfigures the structure. Sitting in front of a table on which a model is placed, a play of relationships is established between the observer and the object itself, meaning that the object has the ability to convey ideas without reference to anything else outside itself and without imposing a clear cause-effect relationship. The model provokes reflection, creates sensations in space, and lets information pass without necessarily saying anything: it exists as an autonomous fact, unbound by what a linguistic narrative could cover through a story told or a written text.

Sometimes, especially for less experienced students, the models may seem silent, like mute wrappings in the face of a hasty need for answers to poorly posed questions. It is precisely thanks to their physicality, ready to generate new games of relationships, that it is possible, in a didactic environment, to revise the concept of the object through successive and renewed experiences and to draw new meanings from it. Thus it is possible to overcome the current and increasing tendency in schools to equate learning methods with production methods, opening the way to a definitive colonization of aesthetic categories by a stronger economic will, thus undermining the search for beauty and adequacy that has characterized the origin of architecture.

The physical model is the product of the use of different tools, materials, and techniques. It requires the alternation of different moments, some slow, others fast, like a musical composition. Its construction demonstrates to the student that time—just the right amount of time—is one of the indispensable factors of construction in order to obtain a result that is as close as possible to the mental image that has been formed of the product to be designed. Making a model is like learning by heart: even if the pedagogical shift of recent years against mnemonics have detached the youngest from this ritual practice that is fundamental to the training of intellectual faculties, the recursive repetition of actions and procedures seems essential to the exercise of design. Building objects, slowly acquiring an apparently technical (but in fact fundamentally intellectual) know-how by lingering over things, is a practice that makes students reflect on the extent to which the economy of speed is an empty strategy for learning architectural composition. The model of architecture is an irreplaceable pedagogical tool because, by offering itself as a support to hold on to, it stimulates thinking in the conviction that only through the formal recognition of phenomena is it possible to unveil disciplinary procedures. Amidst all these experiences, the model continues to stand out as a multifaceted object and tool, its potential still far from losing its appeal and pedagogical impact.

Model of the Halle Orphanage and adjoining buildings of the lower courtyard of the Francke Foundations, 1719/1720. [Archive of the Francke Foundations/B M 0541, photo by Klaus E. Göltz]

What Am I, Actually?

The Model of the Halle Orphanage

Holger Zaunstöck

Model and Context

The pietistic school town of the Francke Foundations (1698–1748) embodies a crucial turning point in the history of education. It represents the basic idea of compensating social disadvantage and combating societal crisis through education and strict piety, materialized in a specific purposeful building ensemble. The model of it, which was made in 1719/1720, shows the prestigious orphanage and the adjoining buildings surrounding the lower courtyard of the Francke Foundations. The only written source that mentions the model is an entry in the diary of the founder of the orphanage, August Hermann Francke, from December 30, 1719. Here he notes that the student Brunner supplied the model (the "material form") and that Christoph Semler, a priest and specialist in models, indicated in an evaluation that there were still some things to be improved.[1] The building ensemble displayed in the model was largely constructed between 1698 and 1717, although some of the structures do not correspond exactly with the buildings that existed in 1717. The orphanage building housed the institution's own pharmacy and bookstore (ground floor), the classrooms of the Latin School, which prepared middle-class boys and gifted orphan boys for university studies (1st and 2nd floors), and the dormitory for orphan boys (until 1734) in the lower section of the mansard roof. In the north wing, orphan girls and boys lived and studied; in addition, the eastern part of the wing was used for economic purposes (brewery and oast house). The south wing comprised the functional building with its large dining hall on the ground floor and the prayer and singing hall above it, extending over a height of two floors. Pupils from England as well as employees of the Foundations lived in the adjoining so-called English House.

1 Die "materielle form," accessed 2022, https://digital.francke-halle.de/mod2/content/wpage/38252.

Materiality and Functionality[2]

The model is made of cardboard, colored paper, wood (spruce, fir), and straw. It was crafted using straw marquetry technique, in which the cut and smoothed straws were glued to the base material (cardboard). The model is fixed on a wooden panel, upon which a second panel rests. The model pieces of the two rows of buildings that adjoin the orphanage at right angles are situated on tracks incorporated into the upper of the two support panels. The houses of the northern wing

2 I would like to thank Tom Gärtig and Thomas Grunewald (Halle) for their valuable contributions.

are movable and can be pulled out (possibly those of the southern wing could as well). The edge areas, as well as the non-beveled rear side, are decorated with ornamental paper. This creates an aesthetic effect that increases the value. It is possible that the paper was applied later on in the course of the model's installation in the Cabinet of Artefacts and Natural Curiosities (see below). The backs of the buildings appear unfinished, suggesting connecting parts (which have not survived).

Possibilities and Practices

No written sources have come down to us that name specific purposes for the model, but a closer examination of the material model itself gives hints about its possible use. The orphanage model can be disassembled floor by floor, revealing its inner structure and functionality in the rhythm of presentation. To deepen this effect, the model was equipped with interiors, such as the beds of the orphan boys in the dormitory, the benches and tables with hand-drawn place settings in the dining hall, or the shelves of the bookstore on the ground floor of the orphanage building. These observations indicate that the model was intended for imparting ideas, structures, and knowledge as well as for presentation—but who specifically showed it to whom and how has not been documented.

It is therefore necessary to ask about the affordances, that is, the possibilities, offers, and requests to act that emanate from the model, as well as the practices that the actors were able to employ with the model. The goal is to name plausible practices of utilization and reception.[3] This indicates six possible options for the use of the model, which likely merged or changed over time. Pedagogical practices and techniques of knowledge imparting seem to dominate.

First, in the context of the expansion of the Foundation's building ensemble, the model documents the existing buildings of 1717/1719 while also showing designs for the renovation or new construction of buildings (English House, eastern part of the north wing). This function as an architectural model is suggested through a comparison with the existent building stock and the circumstances that a colored general view from the south of the building ensemble, which is related to or corresponds with the model, has been drawn shortly before the model was made.[4] Secondly, it is part of a distinct model culture at the orphanage around 1720. In these years, four large-scale biblical models as well as two large-scale solar systems were created. Thus, the model of the orphanage was part of an innovative pedagogy with realia, in which models played a central role.[5] The miniature orphanage demonstrated the organization of everyday life as well as communicative and social processes. Its detailed interior was able to vividly depict a broad panorama of topics, from pedagogy and economics to dietetics (nutrition, hygiene, daily routines), and piety. And, thirdly, the model was part of the intensive image policy of the Foundations. The Pietists opened the orphanage to visitors, regardless of their social status, through daily tours, as well as individual visits, each accompanied by guides. It is reported that there were up to sixty visitors a day. Life in the orphanage could be depicted with the model down to the smallest ramifications of everyday schooling and care. It is an object that can be used to explain precise processes, communication relationships, and functionalities, as well as to enable viewers to intuitively and affectively experience the scope of pietistic aspirations and divine providence.[6]

3 See, e.g., Annette Cremer, "Zum Stand der Materiellen Kulturforschung in Deutschland," in *Objekte als Quellen der historischen Kulturwissenschaften*, eds. Annette C. Cremer and Martin Mulsow (Cologne, Vienna, Weimar: Böhlau, 2017), 9–31; Julia Schmidt-Funke, "Zur Sache. Materielle Kultur und Konsum in der Frühen Neuzeit," in *Materielle Kultur und Konsum in der Frühen Neuzeit*, ed. Julia Schmidt-Funke (Cologne, Vienna, Weimar: Böhlau, 2019), 11–36.

4 Thomas Eißing, "Von der Bausubstanz als Bedeutungsträger. Das Waisenhaus und das Lange Haus der Franckeschen Stiftungen – die Analyse des materiellen Bestands als Beitrag zum Verständnis von Franckes Bauintentionen," in *'Modell' Waisenhaus? Perspektiven auf die Architektur von Franckes Schulstadt*, eds. Thomas Eißing, Meinrad v. Engelberg, Sabine Heiser, Johannes Süßmann, and Holger Zaunstöck (Halle: Verlag der Franckeschen Stiftungen, 2018), 37–71, 40–46.

5 Thomas J. Müller, "Der Realienunterricht in den Schulen August Hermann Franckes," in: *Schulen machen Geschichte. 300 Jahre Erziehung in den Franckeschen Stiftungen zu Halle (Saale)* (Halle: Verlag der Franckeschen Stiftungen, 1997), 43–65; Kelly J. Whitmer, *The Halle Orphanage as Scientific Community. Observation, Eclecticism and Pietism in the Early Enlightenment* (Chicago: University of Chicago Press, 2015).

6 Holger Zaunstöck, "Museum Audiences in the Early Modern Period — Visiting the Halle Orphanage and its Collections," *Кунсткамера | Kunstkamera*, St. Petersburg, no. 4 (10) 2020: 32–48, https://journal.kunstkamera.ru/files/journal_kunstkamera/2020_04/kk_4_2020_32-48_caunshtek.pdf.

The site of the original display of the model is unknown. We only know of its transfer to the newly established Cabinet of Artefacts and Natural Curiosities (CANC) sometime between 1736 and 1741, where it was displayed on a table. Here it is integrated into a setting of natural objects, artefacts, portraits, and a variety of technical, astronomical, architectural, and biblical models. Now, fourthly, the model became a collection object, a component of a museum presentation. Thus, it was part of an interacting network of objects, images, and people.[7] The overall placement of objects in the CANC suggests the use of the model for pedagogical, demonstrative, representational, and commemorative cultural practices. It is likely that the models in the CANC were only physically handled (and in some cases removed from the cabinets) and demonstrated by teachers, tour guides, or the director. Thus, they became tangible and experienceable for visitors and students only through the mediation of others, not directly. In this way, a further, fifth dimension of impact opens up: the models in the CANC, including the orphanage model, were charged with a special aura through these practices of demonstration. They are also to be understood as attractions and objects of art.

Finally, the placement of the model in the CANC also rendered it an historical object. The model made it possible to convey the staged success story of the Foundations, and thus divine providence, on a material basis through both a rational narrative and emotional experience. The model could be utilized in a manner that fostered tradition and memory. Thus, it was part of an object-based narrative on the history of Halle Pietism.[8] A special feature here is also that the model was displayed in the very building that it represented. In this way, it showcased the iconic quality of both the orphanage and the model itself.[9]

However, which concrete impressions the visitors gained from the presentations of the model is another, open question.[10] Independent of the success story presented and the functionality of the building ensemble, the model also allowed visitors to develop their own view, an individual reflection, a direct access. In this respect, an uncontrollable moment is also inscribed in the model; it could not be completely tamed in a narrative and demonstrative way,[11] which would potentially also enable critique.

7 See, e.g., Heike Schlie, "Object Links – Objects Link," in *Object Links - Dinge in Beziehung*, ed. Institut für Realienkunde des Mittelalters und der frühen Neuzeit (Vienna: Böhlau, 2019), 9–16.

8 Thomas Müller-Bahlke, "Die Einzigartigkeit der Kunst- und Naturalienkammer in den Franckeschen Stiftungen," in *'Nützliche Künste.' Kultur- und Sozialgeschichte der Technik im 18. Jahrhundert*, ed. Ulrich Troitzsch (Münster, Munich, Berlin: Waxmann, 1999), 219–238; Stefan Laube, *Von der Reliquie zum Ding. Heiliger Ort - Wunderkammer - Museum* (Berlin: Akademie Verlag, 2011); Holger Zaunstöck, "'Seit Jahrzehnten tot und der Vergessenheit anheimgefallen'? Überlieferungsbedingungen für die Kunst- und Naturalienkammer in der Schulstadt Franckesche Stiftungen," in *Sammeln und Zerstreuen. Bedingungen historischer Überlieferung in Sachsen-Anhalt*, eds. Jan Brademann, Gerrit Deutschländer, and Matthias Meinhardt (Halle: Mitteldeutscher Verlag, 2021), 171–206.

What Am I, Actually?

The impetus for creating the model can be traced back to the founding phase of the Halle Orphanage: Georg Heinrich Neubauer, the central player in the building process, undertook a fact-finding mission to the Netherlands in 1697/1698. On this trip, he visited the Diaken Wees-Huys in Amsterdam. This had been constructed as a model made of lead before being built. The roof and the top floor of the model were removable. The model was kept at the orphanage in Amsterdam and thus was part of its representation and its culture of remembrance. In the margin of the handwritten notes from this trip is a remark that such a design model could also be made of the orphanage in Halle before its construction.[12] Therefore, it makes sense that the idea of a model-like materialization of the orphanage and its potential for imparting and pedagogical purposes was anchored in the cosmos of ideas of the Pietists in Halle from the very beginning.

The model of the Halle Orphanage is characterized by the principle of multifunctionality and a diversity of options. This can be seen in the immediate context of its creation as well as after its repositioning in the complex setting of the CANC. In both layers of time, the manifold demonstrative and pedagogical potential that was inherent in the model (and that it still possesses today) is revealed. A common thread is the practice of historicizing the history of the institution through the model. This could be told in a purposeful way, linked to the divine providence thus made visible. The model of the orphanage in Halle was a multifunctional communication tool integrated into networked mediation strategies.

9 Christina Clausen, "Eine 'lebhafte Idee' vom Glauben. Die Verwendung von Architekturmodellen für die religiöse Erziehung im frühen 18. Jahrhundert," in *Ordnen – Vernetzen – Vermitteln. Kunst und Naturalienkammern der Frühen Neuzeit als Lehr- und Lernorte*, eds. Eva Dolezel, Rainer Godel, Andreas Pečar, and Holger Zaunstöck (Stuttgart: Wissenschaftliche Verlagsgesellschaft Stuttgart, 2018), 383–414; Sabine Heiser, "Arbeit am Modell – Architekturmodelle in Kunstkammern der Frühen Neuzeit. Gebrauch, Erfreuung und Belehrung," in *'Modell' Waisenhaus? Perspektiven auf die Architektur von Franckes Schulstadt*, eds. Meinrad v. Engelberg, Thomas Eißing, Sabine Heiser, Johannes Süßmann, and Holger Zaunstöck (Halle: Verlag der Franckeschen Stiftungen, 2018), 135–167.

10 See Sebastian Fitzner, *Ein Haus für Herkules. Das fürstliche Modellhaus der Residenzstadt Kassel – Architektur und Modellpraktiken im 18. und 19. Jahrhundert* (Heidelberg: University Publishing, 2021), 138.

11 See Reinhard Wendler, *Das Modell zwischen Kunst und Wissenschaft* (Munich: Wilhelm Fink, 2013).

12 Berlin, Staatsbibliothek zu Berlin, Francke-Nachlass 28/1: 3 (subitem 53).

Fig. 1: Demonstration, Photograph, 300 × 180 cm, Jerusalem, Israel Museum, 2022. [Thomas Demand]

Are You an Ethical Agent?

On Thomas Demand's *Demonstration*

Annabel Jane Wharton

In its title, this volume reveals a commitment to understanding the model as an antonymous agent. The titles of the chapters reinforce that claim: "Who Made Me?", "Am I the Real Thing?", "What Is My Act?" The egregious state of the world now (catastrophic climate change, heinous economic disparity, reactionary repression of fundamental freedoms) suggests that there is yet another question that every model should ask: "Am I Good?" As a postscript to the collection of essays, considered here is a modified form of that question: "Are You an *Ethical* Agent?"

Thomas Demand provides the vehicle for the discussion: a monumental photograph (300 × 180 cm or about 10' × 6'), titled *Demonstration*, produced for a major exhibition of his work at the Israel Museum (fig. 1).[1] *Demonstration* invites consideration of a model's nature or ontology, as well as of its ethical status. A reader might even ask: "Where is the model here?" Is the exhibited photograph the model? Is the model the event which the photograph depicts—namely the mass demonstration in the rain in Tel Aviv in January 2023, protesting Prime Minister Benjamin Netanyahu's attempt to limit the power of the judiciary over the executive branch of the Israeli government? Is the model the media image produced by Jack Guez, published by the *Times of Israel*, which prompted Demand's work, and now owned by the Getty? Or was the model the ephemeral full-scale sculpture in cardboard, no longer extant, of the media image that Demand constructed for his camera's lens? Of course, the answer to all of these questions is "yes." Any one of those objects could be identified as a model. As Marx Wartofsky has demonstrated, "Anything [in the strongest and most unqualified sense of 'anything'] can be a model of anything else."[2] They all have model attributes. Each has a referent (material, ideal, conceptual, imaginary) to which it adverts (mimetically, symbolically, symptomatically, inferentially) but from

1 *Demonstration* was an addition to the Israel Museum's mounting of "The Stutter of History" (August 9, 2023–February 10, 2024), a traveling exhibition of Thomas Demand's work. Douglas Fogle, *Thomas Demand: The Stutter of History* (London: MACK, 2022).

2 Marx William Wartofsky, *Models: Representation and the Scientific Understanding* (Boston: Dordrecht, 1979), 3–4.

which it differs in significant ways (in its complexity, scale, material, function, way of being-in-the-world).[3] Nonetheless, *Demonstration*, the exhibition photograph, is the focal model-subject of this essay; the event, the event's media representation, and the no-longer-extant sculptural object of the camera's lens here act only as *Demonstration*'s referents. After all, as an elite artwork, *Demonstration*'s institutional setting, audience, and aesthetics introduce provocative wrinkles into the investigation of its ethical effects.

Demonstration exposes a model's agency as well as its ontology. At least for the purposes of this text, an agent is autonomous (in so far as anything in the world is autonomous), acting independently of its makers, owners, and users.[4] The agency ascribed to *Demonstration* is *not* the agency of philosophers or theologians (exclusively human and embedded in freighted concepts of morality, intentionality, and free will) but rather that ilk of agency familiar from chemistry (a chemical agent has an effect on proximate objects) and business (an agent in business acts solely on behalf of their employer). No one expects chemical agents or business agents to take responsibility for their acts. Similarly, *Demonstration* is free of any consciousness of how it acts in the world.

But how does *Demonstration* act ethically in the world? A model's truthfulness and strength may have something to do with its ethics. As philosophers of science have convincingly argued, no model represents the truth of its referent.[5] A model inevitably distorts that which it represents by changes in its complexity, scale, material, function, setting, and the like. As a consequence, the model inevitably deviates from the truth of the object it represents. Nevertheless, the best models help their observers get closer to the truth of the world by revealing aspects of their referents that had not previously been taken into account. A model may not only get nearer or farther from the truth, it may also be weak or strong. A weak model acts like a copy; as the anthropologist Clifford Geertz posits, it is a model *of*.[6] A strong model acts like an archetype; it is a Geertzian model *for*. *Demonstration* may at first appear a weak model—that is, a passive copy of the media image or the sculpture that preceded it. However, with closer attention to both the work and its context, the exhibition image reveals itself to be a strong model, acting *for* a new comprehension of the event and perhaps even *for* participation in protest. As *Demonstration* manifests, models have the peculiar capacity of oscillate between weak and strong.

A model's strength or weakness is independent of its goodness or badness. A model may be judged good or bad for innumerable reasons, most of which are qualitative: its proximity to or distance from its producers' ideas, desires, intentions, or beliefs; the aesthetics of its execution: its precision or imprecision, refinement or crudity; its persuasiveness or un-persuasiveness, its predictive capacity or incapacity, its data accuracy or inaccuracy.[7] Climate change deniers, identifying models of global warming as inaccurate, and consequently "bad," present anthropogenic climate change as a Deep State hoax.[8] Pentonville Prison, a structure built in the 19th century as a model prison, was identified as a good model: it effectively embodied its designers' intentions, represented the State monumentally, and provided the archetype for more than fifty prisons in Great Britain and its colonies within a few years of its construction.[9] *Demonstration* may also be recognized as a good model: it is an aesthetically compelling, intellectually engaging, and beautifully crafted object.[10]
Good/bad judgments are, however, distinct from ethical/unethical

3 For an elaboration and justification of these attributes, Annabel Jane Wharton, *Models and World Making: Buildings, Bodies, Black Boxes* (Charlottesville: University of Virginia Press, 2021), chapter 1.

4 Fundamental arguments for the agency of things are presented compellingly by Bruno Latour, *Reassembling the Social: An Introduction to Actor-Network-Theory* (Oxford: Oxford University Press, 2005). Other early texts contributing to thing-agency include: Ian Bogost, *Alien Phenomenology, or What It's Like to Be a Thing* (Minneapolis: University of Minnesota Press, 2012); Lorraine Daston, ed. *Things That Talk* (New York: Zone Books, 2008); Finbarr Barry Flood, "Presentation, (Re) animation, and the Enchantment of Technology," *Res*, 61/62, no. Spring/Autumn (2012); Alfred Gell, *Art and Agency: An Anthropological Theory* (Oxford: Oxford University Press, 1998); Igor Kopytoff, "The Cultural Biography of Things: Commodification as Process," in *The Social Life of Things: Commodities in Cultural Perspective*, ed. Arjun Appadurai (Cambridge, MA: Cambridge University Press, 1986); Bruno Latour, "On Actor-Network Theory: A Few Clarifications," *Soziale Welt*, 47, no. 4 (1996); Christopher D. Stone, *Should Trees Have Standing? Toward Legal Rights for Natural Objects* (Palo Alto, CA: Tioga Publishing, 1988).

5 Models as fiction is a popular subject in the philosophy of science. For an introduction, Samuel D. Taylor, "Information and Scientific Representation" (Utrecht University, 2015).

6 Clifford Geertz, "Religion as a Cultural System," in *The Interpretation of Cultures: Selected Essays* (Fontana Press, [1973] 1993), 93; Wharton, *Models and World Making*, 12–13.

7 Bad models are constructed of data that is flawed or cannot be corroborated, often for venal purposes. Henry Ergas, "For a Charter of Modelling Honesty," *Agenda*, 19, no. 2 (2012).

ones. "Ethics" for the purposes of this essay, like agency, is scrubbed of its post-Kantian individualism by distinguishing it, for the sake of clarity, from morals. Moral judgments of good and bad, like aesthetic ones, are commonly understood as personal, subjective, or even divinely ordained. Moral agents are assumed to be humans (and in the U.S.A., corporations) whose judgments involve consciousness and intention.[11] Their acts are evaluated on the basis of intent as well as effect. Murderers are moral agents who might be exonerated of a crime because of an abusive childhood or a threatening victim. In contrast, ethical evaluations are understood here as communal, historical, potentially objective, and even quantifiable. Agents, freed as they are from the murky burden of consciousness and intention, are judged to be ethical or unethical solely on the results of their acts. There is no way, statistically, to exonerate a gun or to convict the Pfizer vaccine.[12]

Ethical judgments may well be harder to make, though easier to defend, than moral ones because subjective assumptions are easier to come by than objective criteria. For example, psychiatric and sociological studies indicate that solitary confinement has irremediably destructive effects on incarcerated humans.[13] Consequently, the claim that even a good model, like Pentonville Prison, a prison that imposed solitary confinement on all its inmates, is an unethical model seems unproblematic. Similarly, modern history documents the egregious effects of autocratic power. Consequently, acts undertaken in an effort to institute autocracy (military invasion, fraudulent election claims, suppression of the judiciary) invite identification as unethical and those taken in opposition to autocracy solicit identification as ethical. It follows that Netanyahu's judiciary predations are unethical, while the demonstrations against his attempt to increase his executive power as well as any positive representations of such demonstrations are ethical. *Demonstration* is an ethical model *of* an ethical event and, particularly as it will be prominently on display in Israel's premier cultural venue, it might also act as an ethical model *for* demonstrating against the unscrupulous usurpation of a democracy's state apparatus. Not all models of ethical referents are ethical. Fox News might unethically represent an ethical demonstration. Similarly, an ethical model might have an unethical referent. Sarah Wigglesworth's model of Pentonville Prison, made for her architecture studio's "Pentonville Unlocked" community project, is utterly ethical despite the unethical nature of its archetype.[14] A model's ethical status does not necessarily depend on that of its referent.

Demonstration is a particularly powerful model-agent. It acts metaphorically in relation to its referent by provoking, through its controlled abstraction, a cognitive dissonance between it and the turbulent reality it represents.[15] The work requires its observer to rethink and react to the political event it reenacts. Reference to metaphor reveals the model's intimate relationship with other objects and to language. Texts and things enmesh *Demonstration*. There are texts and contexts to which the work is subjected (white walls, exhibition labels, catalog entries). There are also texts and contexts which the work itself generates (postcards, gestures, email chains, critical reviews, articles on the ethical agency of models). Like all models, *Demonstration* is entangled in discourse.[16] Also, like all models, *Demonstration* is political. Some models, like many scientific ones, pretend that they are not political, but they all are, if only in the micro-politics in their funding. Artworks also feign apolitical-ness, but they all are political, if only as exemplifications of power and status. Again, all models

8 Craig D. Idso, Robert M. Carter, and S. Fred Singer, *Why Scientists Disagree About Global Warming: The NIPCC Report on Scientific Consensus* (Arlington Heights, IL: The Heartland Institute, 2016). As the scientists who construct them recognize, the complexity of global warming models make them opaque. Gavin Schmidt, director of the NASA Goddard Institute for Space Studies, noted: "Today's models are flexible tools that can answer a wide range of questions, but at a price: They can be almost as difficult to analyze and understand as the real world," Gavin A. Schmidt, "The Physics of Climate Modeling," *Physics Today*, January (2007): 72.

9 For example, Joshua Jebb quotes from the Fifth Report of the Commissioners of Pentonville Prison (March 10, 1847): "There exists abundant proof of the religious and moral improvement of the prisoners, among whom a cheerful spirit of industry prevails.... We are of opinion that the adoption of Separate Confinements, as established at Pentonville Prison, promises to effect a must salutary change in the treatment of criminals, and that it is well calculated to deter, correct and reclaim the offender." Joshua Jebb, *Second Report of the Surveyor-General of Prisons* (London: W. Clowes for H.M.S.O., 1847), 34.

10 Ernest Teagarden, "A Victorian Prison Experiment," *Journal of Social History*, 2, no. 4 (1969): 364. On its export to the colonies. Joannah Clark, "Prison Reform in Nineteenth Century British-India" (University of Canterbury, 2015).

11 Peter A. French, "The Corporation as a Moral Person," *American Philosophical Quarterly*, 16, no. 3 (1979): 207–215.

are historical. *Demonstration* not only fixes a specific 21st-century moment with critical clarity, but it also documents in its digitality, scale, and site the time of its own production. If all models are political and historical, they are also all subject to ethical evaluation (fig. 2).

12 For guns in particular, Bruno Latour, *Pandora's Hope: Essays on the Reality of Science Studies* (Cambridge, MA: Harvard University Press, 1999), 176–179.

13 Christopher Wildeman and Lars H. Andersen, "Solitary Confinement Placement and Post-release Mortality Risk among Formerly Incarcerated Individuals: A Population-based Study," *Lancet Public Health*, 5, no. 2 (2020).

14 Sarah Wigglesworth, "Unlocking Pentonville: Exhibition Pamphlet," Sarah Wigglesworth Architects, 2018, accessed 2023, https://www.swarch.co.uk/wp-content/uploads/2019/04/2017_Sarah-Wigglesworth-Architects_Documenting-Unlocking-Pentonville.pdf.

15 Max Black, "Metaphor," *Proceedings of the Aristotelian Society*, 55, no. 1 (1955): 273–294.

16 Since Foucault, Hall, and Latour, discourse now, at least for humanists, involves non-textual things. Michel Foucault, *Discipline and Punish: The Birth of the Prison* (New York: Random House, [1975] 1979); Stuart Hall, *Representation: Cultural Representations and Signifying Practices* (London: Sage, 1997); Latour, "Reassembling the Social: An Introduction to Actor-Network-Theory."

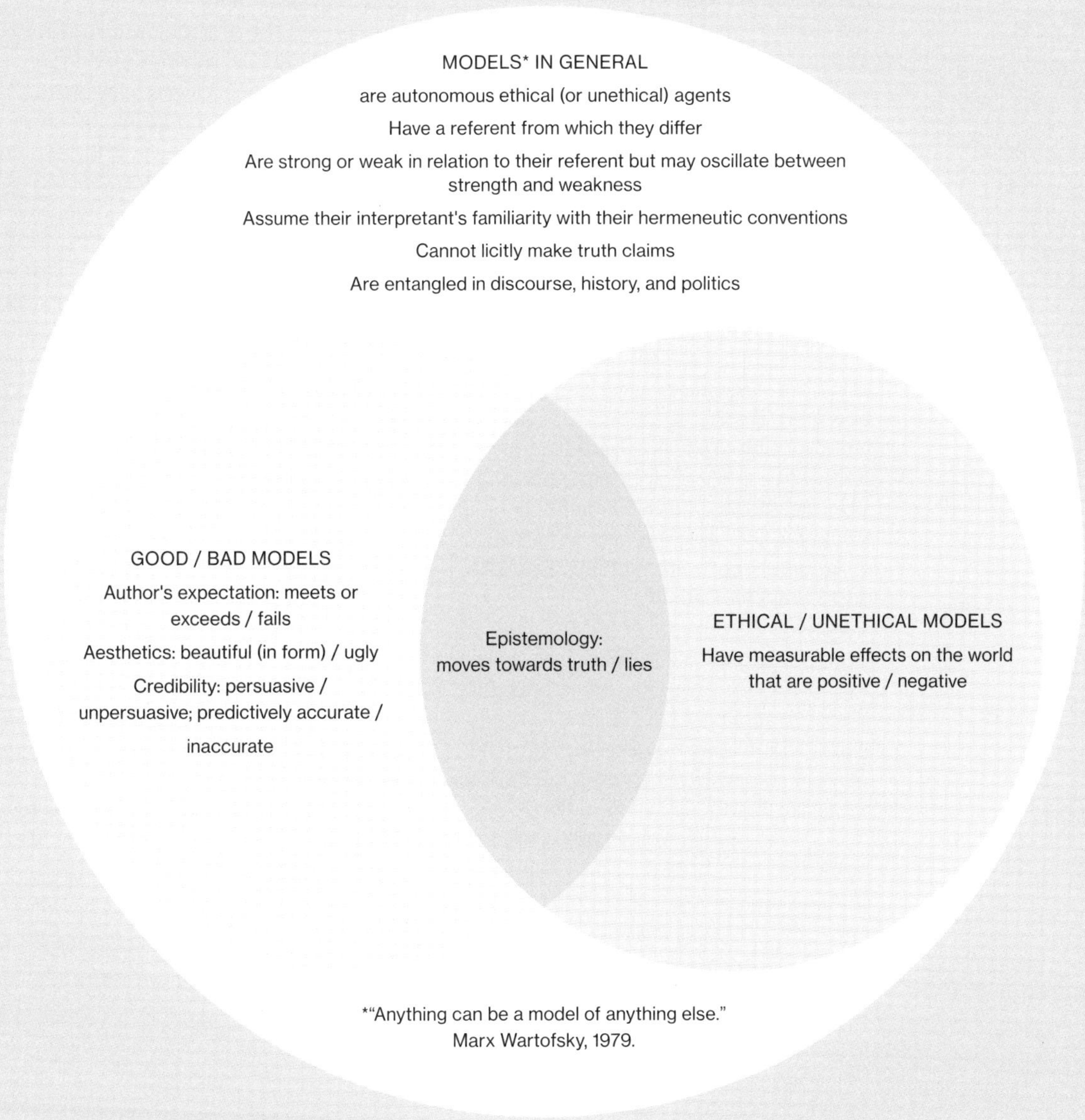

Fig. 2: Models in general. Venn diagram. (In the domain of representation, diagrams are a phylum of the kingdom of models), 2023. [Annabel Jane Wharton]

Biographical Notes

Editors

Lisa Beißwanger is a historian of art and architecture focusing on the 20th and 21st centuries. Her main topics of research include the history of performance art and its interfaces with architecture, as well as the educational architecture of the long 1960s. She is currently assistant professor at the University of Koblenz. Previously, she was a research assistant at the Department of Architecture at the Technical University of Darmstadt.

Chris Dähne researches the history and theory of architecture, media, and technology. She is a postdoctoral researcher in the LOEWE-Cluster "Architectures of Order. Practices and Discourses between Design and Knowledge" at Goethe University in Frankfurt a. M. and in the DFG project BAUdigital at TU Darmstadt. She recently published the book *Utopia Computer. The "New" in Architecture?* with Nathalie Bredella and Frederike Lausch.

Teresa Fankhänel is an associate curator at the Eli and Edythe Broad Art Museum at Michigan State University and editor-in-chief of the *Architectural Exhibition Review*. She was a curatorial assistant for the exhibition *The Architectural Model* (DAM, 2012) and has published two books on models (*The Architectural Models of Theodore Conrad*, 2021, and *An Alphabet of Architectural Models*, 2021).

Christiane Fülscher is professor for architecture history, theory, and preservation at Dortmund University of Applied Sciences and Arts. Trained as an architect and art historian, her research focuses on the cultural and socio-political objectives of architecture as well as the history of architectural education at the beginning of the 20th century. She is author of the monograph *Deutsche Botschaften. Zwischen Anpassung und Abgrenzung* (2021).

Anna-Maria Meister is an architect and historian and directs the Lise Meitner Research Group "Coded Objects" at the Kunsthistorisches Institut in Florenz – Max Planck Institute. She is also professor of architecture theory at KIT Karlsruhe, as well as co-director of the saai archive. Her work is situated between histories of architecture and histories of technology and focuses on the entanglements of processes of design and the design of processes, specifically regarding their political, social, and aesthetic consequences. She is co-curator of the international research project "Radical Pedagogies" and co-editor of the *eponymous book* (MIT Press, 2022).

Anna Luise Schubert is an architectural researcher and cultural worker. As a board member of the Centre for Documentary Architecture, she co-conceived its online archive project *documentary-architecture.org*, organized the exhibition series *The Matter of Data*, and contributed to internationally presented films such as the eight-screen video installation "Deep White" (35 min, 2019). She currently coordinates the Lise Meitner Research Group "Coded Objects" at the Kunsthistorisches Institut in Florenz – Max Planck Institute.

Authors

Giulia Amoresano is a PhD candidate in architecture at the University of California, Los Angeles, where she is completing her dissertation titled "Cultivating the Italian Empire: Architecture and the origins of the Global South (1861–1914)." In her scholarship and pedagogy, she focuses on transnational histories of architecture and the intersection of architecture to the politics of nation-state and empire building.

Deniz Avci-Hosanli is assistant professor (PhD, 2018, METU) at Izmir University of Economics in Interior Architecture and Environmental Design. She specializes in the architectural historiography and conservation of 20th-century Modern Movement architecture and its interiors in Turkey. As a committee member in "docomomo_turkey Interior Design," she is currently co-leading two grant projects: "Architecture of Convalescence: Mapping the Sanatorium Heritage of Turkey" (Turkish Architects' Association-1927) and "Between Medicine and Architecture in Mid-Century Turkey: Ankara's Atatürk (Keçiören) Sanatorium" (VEKAM Ankara Research Awards).

Yana Boeva is a postdoctoral researcher at the Institute for Social Sciences and the Cluster of Excellence "Integrative Computational Design and Construction for Architecture (IntCDC)," University of Stuttgart. Her research explores processes of algorithmization, datafication, and platformization, the transformation of skills and practice through computation and automation, and their intersection with gender, class, and sustainability. Her work has been published in *Science as Culture, Digital Creativity, Digital Culture & Society, arq: Architectural Research Quarterly*, and several edited volumes. She earned her PhD in Science & Technology Studies from York University, Toronto, and an MA in Media Studies from the Humboldt-University Berlin.

Giulia Boller is a scientific assistant and postdoctoral researcher at the Chair of the Theory of Architecture at ETH Zurich (Switzerland). She is both an engineer and an architect. Her research interests lie at the interface between history, architecture, and structural design. In 2022, Giulia completed her PhD at ETH Zurich on the role of models in the engineering practice of Heinz Isler. Before joining ETH, she gained professional experience at Renzo Piano Building Workshop. She graduated with honors in building engineering and architecture at the University of Trento (Italy) in 2015.

Stefanie Brünenberg is an architectural historian with a research focus on architecture and urban development in the GDR as well as postwar modern urban design theory. Since 2019, she has worked on various research projects at the Leibniz Institute for Research on Society and Space. In September 2023, she started her own project there on the consequences of the activities of the "Treuhandanstalt" for the architectural heritage of the GDR.

Alberto Calderoni is a researcher in architectural and urban design at the University of Naples Federico II. His research topics are mainly related to the study of the city, of the project as a tool for knowledge of reality, and of pedagogy for architectural design. Since 2021, he is editor-in-chief of the magazine *STOÀ*, a journal that aims at combining academic research and teaching practices.

Daniel Cardoso Llach is associate professor of architecture at Carnegie Mellon University and the author of publications, exhibitions, and technologies critically exploring the interplay of design and computation, including the books *Builders of the Vision: Software and the Imagination of Design* (2015) and *Designing the Computational Image, Imagining Computational Design* (2023, with Theodora Vardouli).

Wonseok Chae is an architect. His current practice is oriented towards questioning the concept of reality through the formal language of architecture. He graduated from Städelschule Architecture Class with a Master's thesis prize in 2016, and he has been teaching at Bergische Universität Wuppertal since 2018. He is currently working on his PhD thesis, designing a house, and launching a design group for art exhibitions and virtual reality based on his teaching practice.

Christina Clausen studied art history and German literature in Marburg, Padua, and Berlin. From 2014 to 2020, she was a research assistant at the Institute of Art History at the University of Hildesheim. Starting in 2020, she pursued her doctoral studies within the research project "Architectures of Order" and concluded her dissertation in 2023. Her research focused on the visual and spatial representation of medieval architecture during the 19th century. She has been a postdoctoral researcher at the Technical University of Darmstadt since January 2024.

Diana Cristobal Olave is an architect and scholar, currently pursuing a joint PhD degree in History and Theory of Architecture and the Interdisciplinary Humanities at Princeton University. She holds degrees in architecture from Columbia University and ETSA Barcelona. Her work bridges histories of science and technology with design and architecture, with a special focus on practices of computing and information visualization.

Carlotta Darò is an architectural historian, associate professor at the ENSA Paris Malaquais, and currently guest researcher at ETH Zurich. Her work explores the subject of sound media and technologies in modern architecture. She is the author of *Avant-gardes sonores en architecture* (2013), *Les murs du son : le poème électronique au Pavillon Philips* (2015) and *Paysage de lignes : esthétique et télécommunications* (2022).

Cansu Degirmencioglu is a PhD candidate in architectural history and curatorial practice at the Technical University of Munich, School of Engineering and Design. She is co-leading the project "Architecture of Convalescence: Mapping the Sanatorium Heritage of Turkey." Her research and doctoral project focus on the modernization of Turkey and the intertwined histories of medicine, welfare, and modern architecture.

Thomas Cyrillus Demand is a German sculptor and photographer. He currently lives and works in Berlin and Los Angeles and teaches at the University of Fine Arts, Hamburg.

Kai Drewes studied modern history, German literature, and media sciences at TU and HBK Braunschweig. He wrote his doctoral thesis on ennoblements of Jews in 19th-century Europe. In 2013, he became head of the Scientific Collections of the Leibniz Institute for Research on Society and Space (IRS) in Erkner near Berlin, an archive specializing in the building and planning history of the GDR.

Oliver Elser works as a curator at the Deutsches Architekturmuseum (DAM) in Frankfurt am Main and is the cofounder of the CCSA (Center for Critical Studies in Architecture). In 2016, he was the curator of *Making Heimat*, the German Pavilion at the Venice Architecture Biennale. In 2021, he was appointed guest professor for architectural theory at the KIT, Karlsruhe.

Ruth Ezra is a lecturer in art history at the University of St Andrews, where she specializes in the material and visual culture of early modern northern Europe. In 2022–2023, she was a NOMIS fellow at "eikones," University of Basel.

Erik Herrmann teaches architecture at The Ohio State University and co-directs Outpost Office. His research examines how digital technologies' biases and tendencies alter the design process, focusing on the shifting roles of architects. He is a MacDowell fellow, Walter B. Sanders fellow of the University of Michigan, and a German Chancellor's fellow of the Alexander von Humboldt Foundation.

Carolin Höfler is an art historian, architect, and professor of design theory at the TH Köln, as well as a founding member of the DFG Research Training Group "Connecting – Excluding: Cultural Dynamics Beyond Globalized Networks" at the University of Cologne. Höfler works at the intersection of cultural studies and architectural research, focusing on computational design procedures and practices with an emphasis on their specific potential for improvisation and intervention. She is co-editor of the books *Mit weit geschlossenen Augen* (2022) and *Attending [to] Futures* (2023).

Christian Janecke has been professor of art history at the University of Arts and Design in Offenbach/Main since 2006. His book publications include: *Zufall und Kunst* (1995), *Performance und Bild / Performance als Bild. FUNDUS 160*, (2004), and *Maschen der Kunst* (2011). Having published a number of essays on the stage and the stage-like, Janecke is currently working on a book outlining such approaches towards the theatrical beyond theater in visual culture.

Orkun Kasap is a senior assistant at the Chair of Construction Heritage and Preservation at ETH Zurich. He studied architecture and urbanism in Turkey, Denmark, and Switzerland and received his Master's degree in architecture from ETH Zurich in 2014. Previously, he worked at Gramazio Kohler Research and at the National Centre of Competence in Research (NCCR) Digital Fabrication.

Evangelos Kotsioris is assistant curator in Architecture & Design at The Museum of Modern Art in New York. Among other projects, he has recently co-organized the exhibitions *Architecture Now: New York, New Publics* (2023), *The Project of Independence: Architectures of Decolonization in South Asia, 1947–1985* (2022), and *Reuse, Renew, Recycle: Recent Architecture from China* (2021–2022). Trained as an architect and historian, his research focuses on the intersections of architecture with science, technology, and media. He is a co-editor of *Radical Pedagogies* (2022), which explores and documents the global history of post-World War II experiments in architectural education during the second half of the 20th century.

Silke Langenberg is full professor for construction heritage and preservation at ETH Zurich. Her professorship belongs to the Institute for Preservation and Building Research and the Institute for Technology in Architecture. She studied architecture in Dortmund and Venice. In her research, she addresses theoretical and practical challenges in the inventory and preservation of monuments as well as younger building stocks.

Sebastiaan Loosen is a lecturer and postdoctoral researcher based at ETH Zurich's Institute for the History and Theory of Architecture (gta). His postdoctoral research project aims to chart the role of architectural schools, centers, and institutes in contributing to the 1960–1980s agenda of "foreign aid" by offering "South-oriented" training programs in architecture, urbanism, and spatial planning.

Eberhard Möller studied architecture, civil engineering, and monument preservation in Munich and Madrid. He currently teaches and researches at the Faculty of Architecture and Civil Engineering at Karlsruhe University of Applied Sciences. In order to be able to deal with the challenges of our time, he conducts research into creativity and innovation processes in structural design and construction.

Christina Moushoul obtained her Master of Architecture degree from Princeton University in 2022, where she won the Suzanne Kolarik Underwood Prize and the History and Theory Prize. While at Princeton, she was an editor of *Pidgin* and a co-founder of the *Salon Series*. She is a co-founder of the design practice Office Party and the journal *Party Planner*.

Andreas Noback is a researcher working in the field of daylight simulation, archeology, and research data management at TU Darmstadt.

Ana Carolina Pellegrini is an architect (UFRGS, 1999), doctor (UFRGS, 2011), and professor at the Federal University of Rio Grande do Sul (UFRGS) in Porto Alegre, Brazil. She teaches both in undergraduate and graduate courses and researches into design as heritage, addressing architectures characterized by the coexistence of projects designed at different times—such as renovations, restorations, annexes, and reconstructions.

Eliza Pertigkiozoglou is a PhD candidate in architecture at McGill University and a Vanier Scholar. Her research examines how building design software has historically encoded and enacted architectural practices. Before pursuing her PhD, she worked at Gehry Technologies, developing custom software for complex architectural projects. She holds a Master's degree in design studies from Harvard University and a Master's degree in architecture from the National Technical University of Athens.

Andreas Pilot is an architect, research assistant at TU Darmstadt, and PhD candidate at the Chair of Digital Architectonics, ITA, ETH Zurich. He is involved in numerous BIM networks and committees, and since 2019, he has been head of the BIM Studio at TU Darmstadt, focusing on teaching and research in digital model-based and interdisciplinary methods. He is a member of the German team that won the Solar Decathlon competition in Washington D.C. in 2007, has worked as an architect on award-winning sustainability-driven and interdisciplinary projects, and is a manager and coach for collaborative BIM.

Stéphanie Quantin-Biancalani is a curator and has been head of the Contemporary Architecture Collection in the Cité de l'architecture et du patrimoine since 2016. She used to work as heritage curator in the Conservation régionale des monuments historiques – Direction des affaires culturelles de Lorraine (Heritage Division – Regional Directorate of Cultural Affairs of Lorraine) and was thereafter appointed as a fellow in the Research Department of the National Institute of Art History.

Salome Schepers is an architect and research assistant at the Chair of Construction Heritage and Preservation at ETH Zurich. She obtained her Master's degree in architecture at ETH Zurich in 2022 and subsequently co-curated the alternative diploma exhibition. In her work, she investigates the relationship between physical fragments, social narratives, and economic frameworks.

Ecaterina Stefanescu is an architectural designer, lecturer, and artist based in the UK, where she teaches architecture at the University of Central Lancashire. Her practice Estudio ESSE, co-founded in 2015, creates site installations and bespoke design work. She uses live-build, model making, and drawing in her artistic and research work to respond to places and material cultures of people.

Mara Trübenbach is an architectural designer and PhD fellow at the Oslo School of Architecture and Design, strongly interested in the intersection of craft, material, and alternative design methods in architecture such as performance and applied theater studies. In her dissertation, Mara explores the question of how material empathy contributes to the design process in architecture. She is part of the EU Horizon 2020 international training network TACK / Communities of Tacit Knowledge.

Simona Valeriani is a senior lecturer at the V&A/RCA History of Design postgraduate program. Among her recent projects are the International Research Network "Architectural Models in Context" and the resulting follow-on project culminating in the exhibition *Shaping Space-Architectural Models Revealed*, both funded by the AHRC. She has co-edited *An Alphabet of Architectural Models* (2021) and is completing a monograph on the history of building the Royal Albert Hall (2024).

Matthew Wells is a lecturer in architectural history at the University of Manchester. His research uses architecture and visual culture to examine society, institutions, and individuals in the long

19th century. Wells is the author of two monographs: *Modelling the Metropolis: The Architectural Model in Victorian London* (2023) and *Survey: Architecture Iconographies* (2021).

Baris Wenzel holds a Master's degree in architecture. He works as a computational designer mainly in infrastructure projects, where he developed a great interest in polygon meshes and their applications in architecture, civil engineering, and digital fabrication. He is a researcher and lecturer at H-KA and KIT and is completing his PhD at UIBK.

Annabel Jane Wharton, William B. Hamilton Professor of Art History, Duke University, has also taught as the Harry Porter Visiting Professor of Architectural History at the University of Virginia School of Architecture and as a Vincent Scully Visiting Professor of Architectural History at the Yale University School of Architecture. Her most recent publications include *Architectural Agents: The Delusional, Abusive, Addictive Lives of Buildings and Models* (2015) and *World Making: Bodies, Buildings, Black Boxes* (2021).

Roger Winkler is a computational designer and researcher specializing in data-driven methods and technologies. He is currently involved in the DFG-funded projects FID BAUdigital and NFDI4Ing at the University and State Library of TU Darmstadt. In his roles, he explores the peculiar connections between domain-specific digital research methods and approaches for research data management, aiming to enhance the quality, interoperability, and traceability of research outcomes utilizing web technologies and services.

Maxime Zaugg is an architect and PhD candidate at the Chair for the History and Theory of Urban Design, gta, ETH Zurich. He is also a lecturer in the History and Theory of Urban Design at the Institute Urban Landscape (IUL) at the Zurich University of Applied Sciences (ZHAW), where he teaches the history and theory of urban design. His research interests lie in the performative and participatory characteristics of physical scale models of the city, exploring how they have played a crucial role in urban planning by bridging the gap between the public and other stakeholders involved.

Holger Zaunstöck is head of the Research Centre and the Dr. Liselotte Kirchner-Fellowship Programme as well as exhibition curator at the Francke Foundations Halle. Zaunstöck studied history, social history, and economics at the Martin Luther University Halle-Wittenberg (1993 M.A.; 1998 PhD; 2008 habilitation). In 2014, he was appointed extraordinary professor. More recently, he has worked on the history of collections, public welfare and educational architecture, hygiene and medicine, youth and modernity, and Pietism.

Tamar Zinguer is an architect and architectural historian examining the pedagogy of design through history and across scales. Her book—*Architecture in Play: Intimations of Modernism in Architectural Toys* (2015)—explores how ludic models reflect their surroundings. Her present manuscript, *Sandbox: An Architectural History*, follows haptic material experiments in a ubiquitous playful space. She lives in a Bruce Goff House and teaches at the University of Oklahoma.

D

E

K

L

M

R

S

T

U

V

W

Y

Z

Italics indicate models that appear in this volume.

Every effort has been made to identify all rights holders before publication. Should any oversights or *errata* have occurred in this regard, please contact the editors.

Acquisitions editor jovis:	Felix Torkar
Project management jovis:	Charlotte Blumenthal
Copy editing and proofreading:	Bianca Murphy
Production jovis:	Susanne Rösler
Production editor:	Anna Luise Schubert
Design, setting, and cover:	Robin Weißenborn

Printed in the European Union.

Bibliographic information published by the Deutsche Nationalbibliothek. The Deutsche Nationalbibliothek lists this publication in the Deutsche Nationalbibliografie; detailed bibliographic data are available on the Internet at http://dnb.d-nb.de

jovis Verlag
Genthiner Straße 13
10785 Berlin

www.jovis.de

jovis books are available worldwide in select bookstores.
Please contact your nearest bookseller or visit www.jovis.de for information concerning your local distribution.

ISBN 978-3-98612-072-6 (Softcover)
ISBN 978-3-98612-073-3 (E-book)